THE STUDENT EDITION OF MINITAB

Limited Warranty

Addison-Wesley warrants that the Student Edition of Minitab ("the program") will substantially conform to the published specifications and to the documentation during the period of 90 days from the date of original purchase, provided that it is used on the computer hardware and with the operating system for which it was designed. Addison-Wesley also warrants that the magnetic media on which the program is distributed and the documentation are free from defects in materials and workmanship during the period of 90 days from the date of original purchase. Addison-Wesley will replace defective media or documentation or correct substantial program errors at no charge, provided you return the item with dated proof of purchase to Addison-Wesley within 90 days of the date of original purchase. If Addison-Wesley is unable to replace defective media or documentation or correct substantial program errors, your license fee will be refunded. These are your sole remedies for any breach of warranty.

Except as specifically provided above, Addison-Wesley makes no warranty or representation, either express or implied, with respect to this program, documentation or media, including their quality, performance, merchantability, or fitness for a particular purpose.

Because programs are inherently complex and may not be completely free of errors, you are advised to verify your work. **In no event will Addison-Wesley or Minitab be liable for direct, indirect, special, incidental, or consequential damages arising out of the use of or inability to use the program, documentation or media,** even if advised of the possibility of such damages. Specifically, neither Addison-Wesley nor Minitab is responsible for any costs including, but not limited to, those incurred as a result of lost profits or revenue (in any case, the program must be used only for educational purposes, as required by your license), loss of use of the computer program, loss of data, the costs of recovering such programs or data, the cost of any substitute program, claims by third parties, or for other similar costs. In no case shall the liability of Addison-Wesley or Minitab exceed the amount of the license fee.

The warranty and remedies set forth above are exclusive and in lieu of all others, oral or written, express or implied. No Addison-Wesley dealer, distributor, agent, or employee is authorized to make any modification or addition to this warranty.

Some statutes do not allow the exclusion of implied warranties; if any implied warranties are found to exist, they are hereby limited in duration to the 90-day life of the express warranties given above. Some states do not allow the exclusion or limitation of incidental or consequential damages, nor any limitation on how long implied warranties last, so these limitations may not apply to you. This warranty gives you specific legal rights and you may also have other rights which vary from state to state.

To obtain performance of this warranty, return the item with dated proof of purchase within 90 days of the purchase date to: Addison-Wesley Publishing Company, Inc., Educational Software Division, Jacob Way, Reading, MA 01867.

THE STUDENT EDITION OF MINITAB

Statistical Software . . . *adapted for education*

Robert L. Schaefer
University of Miami, Oxford, Ohio

Richard B. Anderson

Addison-Wesley Publishing Company, Inc.
Benjamin/Cummings Publishing Company, Inc.

Reading, Massachusetts • Menlo Park, California • New York
Don Mills, Ontario • Wokingham, England • Amsterdam • Bonn
Sydney • Singapore • Tokyo • Madrid • San Juan

Library of Congress Cataloging-in-Publication Data

Schaefer, Robert L.
The student edition of Minitab [computer file].

3 computer disks : col. ; $5^1/_4$ in. + 1 instructor's manual.
System requirements: IBM PC, XT, AT, or PS/2; 512K; MS-DOS 2.0 (or higher); 2 disk drives (hard disk drive optional); monochrome or color monitor; 40 or 80 column printer.
Title from manual.
Not copy protected.
Audience: College/university.
Issued also on $3^1/_2$ in. computer disk.
Summary: An interactive statistical software package for organizing, analyzing, and reporting statistical data. Statistical features include basic statistics, regression analysis, analysis of variance, and nonparametric tests, among others, with graphics to enhance the display of data.
1. Minitab (Computer system)—Software. 2. Statistics—Software. I. Anderson, Richard B. II. Title. III. Title: Minitab.
QA276.4.S35 1989 519.5′02855369 88-2306
ISBN 0-201-50533-9
ISBN 0-201-50537-1 (manual)

ABCDEFGHIJK-DO-898

0-201-50533-9 (5.25″ disk format)
0-201-50536-3 (3.5″ disk format)

▶ Preface

Welcome to the Student Edition of Minitab (release 1.1). Whether you purchased the Student Edition of Minitab as part of the required materials for a statistics course or simply to have a statistical analysis program available to you, you now have a great deal of statistical computing power at your fingertips.

Originally developed at Pennsylvania State University as a teaching aid for introductory statistics courses, Minitab is the most widely accepted statistical analysis package for college instruction, and is currently in use at over 700 schools. An established research tool as well, Minitab is installed on mainframe, mini, and microcomputers at over 2,500 sites in 51 countries worldwide, including more than half of Fortune Magazine's listing of the top 50 companies.

The Student Edition of Minitab provides you with the tools you need to analyze, display, and describe data. The interactive nature of Minitab (commands are executed immediately) allows you to view the output and make immediate changes to the analysis. Minitab's ease of use is appreciated by computer novices and experts alike. Its extensive online help is highly flexible; if a command is forgotten or if the intricacies slip your mind, the HELP function is just four keystrokes away.

Objectives

The Student Edition of Minitab allows you to analyze and describe most of the data that you will encounter in your studies. The primary objectives of this package are:

- to furnish a powerful statistical analysis tool to teachers and students

- to apply statistical concepts using computer-generated results
- to remove the drudgery of "calculation-intensive" statistical techniques so that you can focus on the results of these analyses
- to analyze real-life data that would normally be too large to analyze by hand
- to provide the means for you to use Minitab throughout your educational career

Organization of this Manual

The User's Guide for the Student Edition of Minitab is separated into four parts: Getting Started, Tutorials, Command Reference, and Appendixes.

Part One — Getting Started — covers the computer requirements for Minitab, explains installation procedures, shows you how to start and stop Minitab, and presents a sample Minitab session. The Introduction to Minitab defines the basic structure and operation of Minitab, including the worksheet, command language, and Minitab symbols.

Part Two — Tutorials — contains thirteen tutorials that provide step-by-step instructions to demontrate some of the functions and analyses that Minitab can perform. We introduce a problem or scenario, then show how the problem is addressed using Minitab. The first two tutorials provide information on data input/output and transformations, and hence should be done first. The remaining tutorials, however, need not be completed in any specific order. You can follow the order given or pick and choose whichever tutorials are relevant or pertinent to the class. Since the Student Edition of Minitab will be used in conjunction with an introductory statistics book, the order of topics selected will most likely depend upon the order of topics in your text. As is true in any text, the more advanced, and hence more difficult, topics are covered later in the manual.

Although the tutorials provide insight into how the Student Edition of Minitab can be used to analyze and describe data, not every command and option is covered. Therefore Part Three — Command Reference — explains each Minitab command in detail. This section provides in-depth information on commands and subcommands, and enables the user to readily find information on the format, options, and operation of each command.

Part Four contains a number of appendixes that cover some of the more advanced Minitab features, including formatted input and output, preparing files for transfer between PCs and mainframe computers, and a troubleshooting guide. A description of the larger data sets used in the Student Edition of Minitab is also included.

Features of the Student Edition of Minitab

Except for the size of the worksheet, virtually all of the power and flexibility of Minitab Standard release 6.1 is available in the Student Edition. Hence the you can:

- input and output both numeric and alphabetic data
- edit, manipulate, and transform the data or create new data
- describe data in both tabular and graphical format (including plots, histograms, and contingency tables)
- summarize data with descriptive statistics
- perform simple and multiple regression
- perform one- and two-way analysis of variance
- perform nonparametric analysis
- perform-time series analysis
- generate random data from any of the built-in statistical distributions
- analyze data using the most common statistical procedures

Differences Between the Student Edition and the Standard Version of Minitab

The Student Edition of Minitab worksheet is limited to 2000 data points — more than enough for most students.

The Student Edition of Minitab does not include high-resolution graphics, some regress subcommands, matrices, and some of the more advanced, exploratory data-analysis features.

In addition to the program, the disks contain over 40 data sets, including 20 new data sets, as well as the data sets in Minitab Standard.

Acknowledgments

We wish to thank all who have contributed to the Minitab Student Edition project. Such a major effort requires a diverse team, and we as authors have worked directly with only a few central figures. We'll acknowledge by name the ones we know and beg the indulgence of our unknown collaborators.

We are especially indebted to Dana Degenhardt. Her organizational skill and indispensable sense of humor have kept us communicating fruitfully across gaps of geography, background and style. Against all odds, she has kept us on a demanding schedule — and almost enjoying it.

Alan Jacobs' role as architect of the relationship between Minitab and Addison-Wesley has been largely behind the scenes, from our point of view, but we wish to recognize our debt to his able management.

We would also like to thank the many reviewers whose diligent readings and thoughtful comments strengthened this work immeasurably. These include Gwen Stimely, our key contact at Minitab, Inc.; Professor Peter W. Zehna of the Naval Postgraduate School; Mary Coffey, Addison-Wesley Software Production Supervisor; and Sharon Cogdill of Editorial Services of New England.

Sandy Beder-Miller ably supplemented our efforts by preparing the Command Reference Section of the Student Edition.

If we should have mentioned you and didn't, please chalk up the omission to our limited awareness, not to any lack of due appreciation.

▶ Contents

Part 1
Getting Started

Part II Tutorials

Part I

Getting Started

I ▶ Before You Begin

This section describes the contents of the Student Edition of Minitab, the required computer setup, and the information you will need to install, start, and stop Minitab.

Checking Your Minitab Package

The Student Edition of Minitab should contain the following items:

- Three 5 1/4-inch floppy Minitab Program diskettes, or two 3 1/2-inch Minitab Program microdiskettes
- The Student Edition of Minitab User's Manual (this book)
- A Quick Reference Card
- A Warranty Registration Card
- An Upgrade Offer, which provides a discount to students who wish to upgrade to the Standard Version of Minitab
- A License Agreement

Checking Your Computer Setup

Minitab will run in two distinct hardware environments: the IBM PC, XT, AT series (or compatibles) and the IBM Personal System/2. Minitab requires that your system run MS-DOS or IBM PC-DOS. We list two configurations: minimum and recommended. Please note that two disk drives are needed to run Minitab.

Minimum Configuration

Operating System	DOS version 2.0 or later
Memory*	320K RAM minimum
Disk Drives	Two double-sided, double-density diskette drives
Monitor	A monochrome or color video monitor (80 character width)

Recommended Configuration (for faster execution time)

Operating System	DOS version 2.0 or later
Memory*	320K RAM minimum
Disk Drives**	10 megabyte hard disk and one double-sided, double-density diskette drive
Monitor	A monochrome or color video monitor (80 character width)
Math Coprocessor	8087 for IBM-PC or -XT and for PS/2 models 25 or 30
	80287 for IBM-AT and for PS/2 models 50 or 60
	80387 for PS/2 model 80

List of Minitab Files

The Student Edition of Minitab is delivered on three 5 1/4-inch floppy diskettes or two 3 1/2-inch microdiskettes. The location and names of the files are listed below. DISK A contains the personalization/installation program (MINSTALL.EXE), Minitab executable files (MTB61_A.EXE and MTB61_A1.EXE), and the Minitab HELP system (MTB61_A.HLP). DISK 1 contains a Minitab overlay file (M61_1_A1.OVL). DISK 2 contains another overlay file (M61_2_A1.OVL), the sample data sets used in the Tutorial and Command Reference chapters and a list of known problems, including strategies to work around them (PROBLEMS.DOC).

This is the organization for 5 1/4-inch floppy diskettes:

*There must be at least 277K available after system configuration. Some memory-resident software, such as calculators or memo pads, may interfere with running Minitab. It is recommended that these be removed from memory before starting Minitab.

**The Student Edition takes approximately 1.1 Megabytes of space on a hard disk.

DISK A

```
MINITAB.BAT
MTB61_A.EXE
MTB61_A1.EXE
MTB61_A.HLP
MINSTALL.EXE
```

DISK 1

```
M61_1_A1.OVL
```

DISK 2

```
M61_2_A1.OVL
PROBLEMS.DOC
Sample Data Sets
*.MTW
*.DAT
```

The files on DISK 1 and DISK 2 are combined on DISK 1/2 in packages containing 3 1/2-inch microdiskettes.

Typographical Conventions

Minitab is controlled by keystrokes entered from the keyboard of your computer. Throughout this manual, we provide instructions for installing Minitab and examples for running Minitab. We use a special typeface to tell you what actions to perform and what keystrokes to enter.

In the sections below, the **bold** text indicates new terminology. Although we show the text you type in capitals, you do not have to type it in capitals; lower case will work just fine. For example, insert DISK A into Drive A:, then type

```
A> DIR
```

Sometimes it is necessary to use the <Ctrl> key on your keyboard. This key is operated like the <Shift> key. For example, to type <Ctrl>-Q simply hold down the <Ctrl> key while you press the Q key.

The symbol <Enter> refers to the <Enter> key. On some keyboards this key is labeled Return or ↵, but the function of the key is the same. In this guide we will use <Enter>.

Technical Support

Neither Addison-Wesley Publishing Co., Inc. nor Minitab, Inc. provides telephone assistance to students for the Student Edition of Minitab. Telephone assistance is provided to registered instructors who have adopted the Student Edition for their students.

If you encounter difficulty using the Student Edition software:

1. Read the section of this manual containing the information on the commands or procedure you are trying to execute.
2. Use the HELP screens to locate specific command information.
3. Read Appendix E, Troubleshooting, (page 336) for identifying common error messages and performing the proper corrective action.
4. Note the characteristics of the microcomputer on which you are working: brand, model, operating system version, number and type of disk drives, available memory and whether or not a math coprocessor is installed.

If you have to ask your instructor for assistance, please describe your question or problem in detail. If you have a problem, write down what you were doing (the steps or procedures you followed) that caused the problem so that you can explain to your instructor what happened. Include any error messages in exact detail.

2 ▶ Quick Installation and Starting Instructions

This section is designed for users who are very familiar with the operation of DOS and with software installation procedures and want to install and start Minitab as quickly as possible. Users who require more detailed instructions for installing Minitab should turn to the next section, Detailed Installation Instructions, on page 9.

1. Insert DISK A into drive A:.
2. Make A: the default drive by typing A:.
3. Type MINSTALL and select the menu options to do the following:
    a. Personalize Minitab
       This option must be performed first.
    b. Transfer the Minitab System
        - ▶ to a hard disk: You will be given options to specify the hard disk drive letter and subdirectory where Minitab will be copied. MINSTALL will copy the Minitab program to drive C:, subdirectory MINITAB unless you specify otherwise. The sample data sets will be copied to \MINITAB\DATA.
        - ▶ to diskettes: The transfer option will make duplicates of your original diskettes. The transfer process requires COMMAND.COM to be resident on a hard disk, otherwise MINSTALL will not be able to transfer the files automatically. In this case, use COPY A:*.* B: to make backup copies of Minitab. We recommend that you transfer the *.MTW and *.DAT files to a separate data diskette.

c. Select Screen Colors

You will be given the opportunity to choose the foreground and background colors for your Minitab screen from a color-grid menu. Your choice will be written to the file MINITAB .BAT, which has been transferred to your target diskette. If you don't make a color selection, Minitab will default to white characters on a black background.

4. Run Minitab by typing MINITAB.

- ▶ hard disk: Before typing Minitab you should create a path to the Minitab program by typing PATH = C:\MINITAB. You will then be able to run Minitab from any subdirectory on your hard disk. If you insert this command in your AUTOEXEC .BAT file in the root directory, then you will automatically have a path set to Minitab whenever you boot your system.
- ▶ dual diskette drives: Before typing MINITAB, insert DISK A into drive A:. Insert additional Minitab diskettes in drive A: as requested. You should use drive A: for the Minitab program diskettes and drive B: for your working files (data files, statistical output etc.).

5. Exit Minitab by typing STOP.

3 ▶ Detailed Installation Instructions

The Student Edition of Minitab is personalized rather than copy protected. This means that the licensee's name will be permanently written to the original DISK A and will appear in the initial Minitab screen whenever a Minitab session is begun. Since Minitab will not run until it has been personalized, you must personalize it before the program can be transferred to another set of diskettes or to a hard disk.

The process for personalizing and installing Minitab is very simple, but it is different depending on whether you are transferring Minitab files to diskettes or to a hard disk. The instructions in the following sections and a program called MINSTALL will guide you through the entire process.

When you type MINSTALL, you will see the menu that is shown in Figure INSTALL1.FIG.:

INSTALL1.FIG. ▶

```
Help
Personalize Minitab
Transfer the Minitab System
Select Screen Colors

eXit to DOS
```

Help

This section provides one screen of the basic information needed to move around in the menu. Strike <Enter> to view this screen.

Personalize Minitab

This choice will guide you through the personalization process. This must be done before any other option can be selected. The personalization process will only work once.

Transfer the Minitab System

This selection will guide you through steps needed to copy Minitab files to their proper location. If you have a hard disk, MINSTALL will automatically copy the files. Otherwise, you will be directed to the instructions described in the next section by this message:

```
COMMAND.COM cannot be found.
See your documentation for transferring Minitab to diskettes.
```

You may use this option to make additional copies of Minitab, subject to the terms of your license agreement.

Select Screen Colors

This selection will give you the opportunity to choose the foreground and background colors for your Minitab screen from a color-grid menu. If you do not make a color selection, Minitab will default to white characters on a black background. On monochrome monitors, white characters may appear as amber or green. For information on selecting screen colors, see Appendix D on page 328.

Now refer to either Installing Minitab to Diskettes or Installing Minitab to a Hard Disk, whichever is appropriate.

Installing Minitab to Diskettes

If you have have an IBM PC, XT, or AT, you will need four blank, freshly formatted, 360K floppy diskettes labeled BACKUP DISK A, BACKUP DISK 1, BACKUP DISK 2, and DATA DISK. If you have a PS/2 system, you will need three 720K microdiskettes labeled BACKUP DISK A, BACKUP DISK 1/2, and DATA DISK. Note: do not use the "/S" FORMAT option that copies system files to each diskette. There will not be sufficient room for these files.

Remember that the installation program, MINSTALL, will personalize Minitab, guide file transfer, and write your screen color selection to MINITAB.BAT. To run MINSTALL, simply insert Minitab DISK A into drive A: of your machine and type:

▶ `A> MINSTALL`

If you see the message,

▶ `COMMAND.COM cannot be found. See your documentation for transferring Minitab to diskettes.`

then MINSTALL is unable to transfer the Minitab files automatically. You will need to perform this simple step yourself, using the following instructions.

(If you are transferring files to 3 1/2 inch microdiskettes, be sure to use DISK 1/2 everywhere that we use DISK 1 or DISK 2 in the instructions.)

Insert Minitab DISK A into Drive A:

Insert your BACKUP DISK A into Drive B: and type

▶ `A> COPY A:*.* B:`

The BACKUP DISK A will now contain all the Minitab files that were on the original DISK A.

Insert Minitab DISK 1 into Drive A:

Insert your BACKUP DISK 1 into Drive B: and type

▶ `A> COPY A:*.OVL B:`

Insert Minitab DISK 2 into Drive A:

Insert your BACKUP DISK 2 into Drive B: and type

▶ `A> COPY A:*.OVL B:`

and

▶ `A> COPY A:*.DOC B:`

Leave DISK 2 in Drive A:, then

Insert your DATA DISK in Drive B: and type

```
A> COPY A:*.MTW B:
```

and

```
A> COPY A:*.DAT B:
```

When MINSTALL is complete, you will have two complete personalized copies of Minitab. One will be the original program, and the other will be a backup copy. Put write protect tabs on all of your original diskettes and store them in a safe place free of dirt, moisture, and magnetic fields. You should run Minitab from your backup diskettes or hard disk. It is also a good idea to put write protect tabs on your backup diskettes, except for the data diskette containing the .MTW and .DAT files.

Now refer to the section entitled Starting and Stopping Minitab on page 13.

Installing Minitab to a Hard Disk

To install Minitab to a hard disk, you will need at least 1.1 megabytes of available storage on the disk. MINSTALL will automatically create a directory called C:\MINITAB, where C: is the letter given to the hard drive. If you wish to use another name for the Minitab directory, MINSTALL will give you that opportunity.

Remember that the installation program, MINSTALL, will personalize Minitab, guide file transfer, and write your screen color selection to MINITAB.BAT. To run MINSTALL, simply insert Minitab DISK A into drive A: of your machine and type:

```
C>  A:
A>  MINSTALL
```

After MINSTALL is complete, put write protect tabs on your original diskettes and store them in a safe place away from dirt, moisture, and magnetic fields.

Now refer to the next section, entitled Starting and Stopping Minitab.

4 ▶ Starting and Stopping Minitab

Once you have installed Minitab to backup diskettes or to your hard disk, you can start and run Minitab as many times as you wish. Refer to either Running Minitab from Diskettes or Running Minitab from a Hard Disk, depending upon your computer setup.

Running Minitab from Diskettes

The best way to run Minitab is to use drive A: for your Minitab program diskettes and drive B: for your DATA DISK. Note: your DATA DISK is the diskette you use to store your data, worksheets, outfiles, etc.

To start Minitab, insert DISK A in drive A: and make the A: drive the default by typing:

```
A> A:
A> MINITAB
```

After a few seconds, you'll get the message:

```
* NOTE * Please insert MINITAB DISK 1.
Press <ENTER> to continue or '.' to quit Minitab ==>
```

Important note: If you are running Minitab from 3 1/2 inch microdiskettes, then always insert DISK 1/2 whenever Minitab asks for either DISK 1 or DISK 2.

Insert DISK 1 (or DISK 1/2) into drive A:. Then press:

```
<Enter>
```

and you'll soon see the initial Minitab screen. Strike any key to display the Minitab prompt:

```
MTB >
```

You can now execute Minitab commands. The section entitled A Sample Minitab Session (page 16) provides examples of common Minitab commands.

At some point during your Minitab sessions you may be prompted to insert another one of Minitab's program diskettes with a message similar to that described above. Be sure to always insert the diskette in drive A:, and strike <Enter>.

Running Minitab from a Hard Disk

If you allowed MINSTALL to create your directory structure, then it should look something like Figure INSTALL1.FIG.

INSTALL1.FIG. ▶

```
                     [THE ROOT]
                         |
      -------------------------------------
      |                                   |
Other Directories                      MINITAB
                                          |
                              ---------------------
                              |                   |
                             DATA        Minitab Program Files
                              |
                      Sample Data Sets
```

You can run Minitab from any directory, but we recommend using the DATA subdirectory. This way, all input and output files will be located in the same place. You must tell DOS where to find the Minitab program, however. This is done with the DOS PATH command, which is the second command in the following sequence. After booting your system type:

`C> PROMPT $P$G`	This will display the directory name in your prompt.
`C:\> PATH = C:\;C:\MINITAB`	Please note the use of colons and semicolons in this line.

```
C:\> CD MINITAB
C:\MINITAB> CD DATA
C:\MINITAB\DATA> MINITAB
```

This sequence of five commands can be simplified by use of a BATCH file. We discuss how to create and use this option in Appendix E, Starting Minitab with a BATCH File (page 330).

When you see the initial Minitab screen, strike any key to get the Minitab prompt:

```
▶ MTB >
```

You can now execute Minitab commands. The section entitled A Sample Minitab Session, which begins on page 16, provides examples of common Minitab commands.

Exiting Minitab

Exiting Minitab is very simple. At the MTB > prompt, type:

```
▶ MTB > STOP
```

5 ▶ A Sample Minitab Session

Sometimes the easiest way to learn a new software package is just to try it. If you would rather read more about Minitab first, read Introduction to Minitab, page 24, before proceeding.

In the sample Minitab session below, the text you type and what shows up on the screen are indicated here in a special typeface. Press <Enter> at the end of each line. If you make a mistake, Minitab will display an error message, and then you can try again.

Start Minitab from a hard disk by typing:

```
▶ C> PATH = C:\MINITAB
  C> MINITAB
```

Start Minitab from diskettes by inserting DISK A in Drive A: and your DATA DISK in Drive B:. Then set your default directory to A, and type:

```
▶ A> MINITAB
```

If you are running Minitab from diskettes, Minitab will tell you when to swap them with a message like:

```
▶ * NOTE * Please insert MINITAB DISK 1.
  Press < Enter> to continue or '.' to quit Minitab ==>
```

Enter the data in the worksheet from your keyboard.

```
MTB > READ data into C1 and C2
DATA> 68  160
DATA> 76  200
DATA> 70  175
DATA> 70  180
DATA> 69  165
DATA> 63  115
DATA> 60  100
DATA> 64  120
DATA> 62  110
DATA> 66  140
DATA> END
     10 ROWS READ
```

Name the columns. Column names must always be enclosed in single quotation marks.

```
MTB > NAME C1 'HEIGHT' C2 'WEIGHT'
```

Put the average height in constant K1

```
MTB > MEAN C1 store in K1
   MEAN     =       66.800
```

Put the average weight in constant K2. Columns used with functions in the LET command must always be enclosed in parentheses.

```
MTB > LET K2 = MEAN('WEIGHT')

MTB > PRINT K2
K2      146.500
```

Put 1's (for males) and 2's (for females) in column C3. Parentheses are used to put five 1's followed by five 2's into C3, for a total of 10 numbers.

```
MTB > SET C3
DATA> 5(1) 5(2)
DATA> END
```

Name column C3.

```
MTB > NAME C3 'SEX'
```

Look at the summary of the current worksheet.

```
MTB > INFO

COLUMN      NAME       COUNT
C1          HEIGHT        10
C2          WEIGHT        10
C3          SEX           10

CONSTANTS USED: K1     K2
```

View the data on the screen.

```
MTB > PRINT 'HEIGHT' 'WEIGHT' 'SEX' K1 K2
K1        66.8000
K2        146.500

 ROW   HEIGHT   WEIGHT    SEX

   1       68      160      1
   2       76      200      1
   3       70      175      1
   4       70      180      1
   5       69      165      1
   6       63      115      2
   7       60      100      2
   8       64      120      2
   9       62      110      2
  10       66      140      2
```

Store the data in the saved worksheet file SAMPLE.MTW

If you are running Minitab from a hard disk, type:

```
MTB > SAVE 'SAMPLE'

Worksheet saved into file: SAMPLE.MTW
```

If you are running Minitab from diskettes, type:

```
MTB > SAVE 'B:SAMPLE'

Worksheet saved into file: B:SAMPLE.MTW
```

A "snapshot" of your current worksheet is now permanently stored in the file SAMPLE.MTW and can be retrieved at any time. You may now modify the data in your curent worksheet without fear of destroying the original data.

Print descriptive statistics for height and weight separately for males and females, as in the example below. Notice that even if you type column numbers in a command (C1 and C2 in this case), column names ('HEIGHT' and 'WEIGHT') appear in the output.

```
MTB > DESCRIBE C1 and C2;
SUBC>    BY 'SEX'.

              SEX        N     MEAN   MEDIAN   TRMEAN    STDEV   SEMEAN
HEIGHT          1        5    70.60    70.00    70.60     3.13     1.40
                2        5    63.00    63.00    63.00     2.24     1.00
WEIGHT          1        5   176.00   175.00   176.00    15.57     6.96
                2        5   117.00   115.00   117.00    14.83     6.63

              SEX      MIN      MAX       Q1       Q3
HEIGHT          1    68.00    76.00    68.50    73.00
                2    60.00    66.00    61.00    65.00
WEIGHT          1   160.00   200.00   162.50   190.00
                2   100.00   140.00   105.00   130.00
```

Plot male and female heights with dots over a horizontal axis. As you would expect, the example on the following page shows that males are taller than females.

```
MTB > DOTPLOT C1;
SUBC>   BY 'SEX'.

 SEX
 1
                                 .  .  :                   .
      -+---------+---------+---------+---------+---------+----- HEIGHT
 SEX
 2
        .      .  .  .      .
      -+---------+---------+---------+---------+---------+----- HEIGHT
     60.0      63.0      66.0      69.0      72.0      75.0
```

Draw a dotplot of male weights and female weights, as in the example below.

```
MTB > DOTPLOT C2;
SUBC>   BY 'SEX'.

 SEX
 1
                                         .  .    . .      .
      ---+---------+---------+---------+---------+---------+---WEIGHT
 SEX
 2
         .    .  . .         .
      ---+---------+---------+---------+---------+---------+---WEIGHT
        100       120       140       160       180       200
```

Change the number 70 in the third row of 'HEIGHT' to 72.

```
MTB > LET 'HEIGHT'(3)=72
```

In the next example, we create a new column, C5, with height expressed in feet instead of inches and print height in inches and in feet.

```
MTB > LET C5 = 'HEIGHT'/12
MTB > PRINT 'HEIGHT' C5

 ROW  HEIGHT       C5
   1      68  5.66667
   2      76  6.33333
   3      72  6.00000
   4      70  5.83333
   5      69  5.75000
   6      63  5.25000
   7      60  5.00000
   8      64  5.33333
   9      62  5.16667
  10      66  5.50000
```

View instructions on how to use the TWOT command.

```
MTB > HELP TWOT

TWOT [K percent confidence] for data in C, subscripts in C

Subcommands: ALTERNATIVE  POOLED

Does a t-test and confidence interval for the difference of
two populations means.  TWOT is identical to the command
TWOSAMPLE, except for the form of the input data.  TWOT
expects the data for both groups to be in the first column
(the groups can be mixed together).  The second column gives
subscripts to say what group each observation belongs to.
This is the same form of input used by the command ONEWAY.

If the percent confidence is not specified, a 95 percent
confidence interval is calculated.
```

Do a 2-sample t-test on male heights versus female heights, as shown in the next example.

```
MTB > TWOT 'HEIGHT' subscripts in 'SEX'

TWOSAMPLE T FOR HEIGHT
SEX  N     MEAN     STDEV   SE MEAN
1    5    71.00      3.16       1.4
2    5    63.00      2.24       1.0

95 PCT CI FOR MU 1 - MU 2: (3.9, 12.1)

TTEST MU 1 = MU 2 (VS NE): T= 4.62  P=0.0000  DF=  7
```

Use RETRIEVE to copy the saved worksheet SAMPLE.MTW into the current worksheet. Note: Everything in the current worksheet is erased whenever you use the command RETRIEVE; be sure to save any important data before using RETRIEVE.

If you are running Minitab from a hard disk, type:

```
MTB > RETRIEVE 'SAMPLE'

WORKSHEET SAVED 3/14/1988
Worksheet retrieved from file: SAMPLE.MTW
```

If you are running Minitab from diskettes, type:

```
MTB > RETRIEVE 'B:SAMPLE'

WORKSHEET SAVED 3/14/1988
Worksheet retrieved from file: B:SAMPLE.MTW
```

The 3 lines Minitab displays after you retrieve a file have been omitted from examples in this manual to make them easier to read.

Look at a summary of the current worksheet, shown in the next example.

```
MTB > INFO
COLUMN     NAME       COUNT
C1         HEIGHT        10
C2         WEIGHT        10
C3         SEX           10

CONSTANTS USED: K1    K2
```

End your Minitab session.

```
MTB > STOP
*** Minitab Release 1.1 *** Minitab, Inc.   ***
Storage available 2000
```

6 ▶ Introduction to Minitab

Minitab is an easy-to-use, powerful tool for examining and analyzing data. Commands are used to perform statistical analyses, to display histograms, plots and tables, and to do mathematical transformations.

The Worksheet

The Minitab worksheet contains data arranged in columns (variables) and rows (observations) and in stored constants, as illustrated in Figure INTRO1.FIG. Columns can be referred to by number, such as C1, or by name, such as 'HEIGHT'. Column names must always be enclosed by single quotation marks.

INTRO1.FIG. ▶

```
                          Columns or Variables
                   ------------------------------------------
                     C1   C2   C3   C4      . . .     C50
                 1
                 2
        Rows     3
         or      4
   Observations  5
                 .
                 .
                 .
                   ------------------------------------------

                     K1 □ K2 □ K3 □ K4 □    . . .   K50 □
```

Each stored constant may contain one number. Minitab automatically assigns values to the last three constants: K48 = * (the missing value symbol), K49 = 2.718. . . (the value of "e") and K50 = 3.141. . . (the value of pi).

You may store up to 50 columns and 50 constants in the worksheet, which may contain a total of up to 2,000 numbers. That is, the number of columns used times the number of rows used cannot exceed 2,000.

The Current Worksheet

The data stored in columns and constants at any time during your Minitab session make up the current worksheet. The command:

```
MTB > INFO
```

lists the columns and constants currently in use. You can enter data into the current worksheet with the commands READ, SET, INSERT and RETRIEVE.

The current worksheet is a temporary work area, which is automatically erased when you end your Minitab session. You can store the current worksheet in a permanent file on disk in two ways: as a saved worksheet and as a data file.

Saved Worksheets

The SAVE command stores all the information in the current worksheet (columns, column names and constants) in a permanent saved-worksheet file. A saved worksheet can only be used by Minitab on another DOS microcomputer; it cannot be edited or sent to a printer. The RETRIEVE command copies a saved worksheet into the current worksheet.

Data Files

The WRITE command stores specified columns from the current worksheet in a permanent (ASCII) data file. Data files do not contain column names or stored constants; however, they can be edited, moved to different machines, sent to a printer and be read by other software packages. The commands READ, SET and INSERT are used to enter a data file into the current worksheet.

Command Language

Commands

Commands tell Minitab what to do. Each command must start on a new line and may be typed in either upper or lower case. For example, to see descriptive statistics about the numbers in column C1, you could type the command:

```
MTB > DESCRIBE C1
```

Subcommands

Many commands have optional subcommands, which provide Minitab with additional instructions. Subcommands are entered, one per line, in any order. To enter a subcommand, end the command or subcommand line preceding it with a semicolon; the last subcommand line must end with a period. For example:

```
MTB > COPY C1 C2;
SUBC> USE 1 2.
```

copies rows 1 and 2 from column C1 into column C2. To cancel a command, type the subcommand ABORT.

Arguments

Arguments, which can be columns, constants, and/or files, tell Minitab commands what to do — for example, which columns to plot, or the name of the file to read data from. Appropriate arguments for each command and subcommand are listed in the Command Reference Chapter and are available from on-line HELP.

Minitab Prompts

The prompt at the left-most side of your screen tells you what kind of information Minitab expects you to type.

MTB > is the command prompt.

SUBC> is the subcommand prompt. It appears when the previous line ends with a semicolon.

DATA> is the data prompt. It appears after the commands READ, SET and INSERT.

CONTINUE? is the paging prompt. Normally, Minitab pauses at convenient points in the output and displays this prompt. Press Enter if you want to see more output, N or No then <Enter> if you do not. To suppress this prompt, set output height to zero by typing:

```
MTB > OH Ø
```

CONT> is the continuation prompt. It appears when the previous line ends with an &, allowing you to type a command, subcommand or data row that is longer than one line.

STOR> appears after the STORE command has been issued, to accept commands for a command file or macro.

Handy Shortcuts

1. You only need to type the first four letters of any command or subcommand.
2. You can abbreviate a series of columns with a dash, for example:

```
MTB > PRINT C1-C5
```

instead of

```
MTB > PRINT C1 C2 C3 C4 C5
```

3. You can abbreviate a series of numbers with a colon, for example:

```
MTB > DELETE rows 1:5 C1
```

instead of

```
MTB > DELETE rows 1 2 3 4 5 C1
```

4. You can abbreviate numbers in many ways with SET, for example:

```
MTB > SET C1
DATA> 3(1:3)
```

instead of

```
MTB > SET C1
DATA> 1 2 3 1 2 3 1 2 3
```

Files

File Names

File names are made up of two parts: the FILENAME, which may be up to eight characters long, and the file extension, which may be up to three characters long. The two parts are separated by a period. File names used in Minitab commands must be enclosed by single quotes and may include the drive or directory location (path) of the file. You do not need to type the file extension unless it is different from the default (see File Types, below). For example:

```
MTB > RETRIEVE 'B:MYFILE'
```

retrieves the saved worksheet file named MYFILE.MTW from the disk in drive B:. If no drive or directory is specified, Minitab looks for the file in your current disk and directory.

File Types

Minitab recognizes five types of files, easily identified by the file extensions Minitab automatically gives them when they are created.

File Name	Used by the Commands	Description
FILENAME.LIS	OUTFILE NOOUTFILE	Contains Minitab output. Can be edited or sent to a printer
FILENAME.DAT	WRITE READ SET INSERT	Data file. Can be edited, printed and read by other software
FILENAME.MTW	SAVE RETRIEVE	Saved Minitab worksheet. Cannot be edited or sent to a printer.
FILENAME.MTP	SAVE; PORTABLE. RETRIEVE; PORTABLE.	Portable saved Minitab worksheet. Can be used by Minitab on non-DOS computers (e.g., a mainframe). Cannot be edited or sent to a printer.
FILENAME.MTB	STORE EXECUTE	Command file or macro which contains Minitab commands. Can be edited or sent to a printer.

STARTUP.MTB is a special command file that, if it exists in your current directory, will automatically be executed every time you start or restart Minitab. See Advanced Options in Appendix D for more information.

Minitab Symbols

*	An asterisk is the missing value symbol. It can be used in commands and subcommands and as a data value.
&	An ampersand is the continuation symbol. It enables you to continue a command, subcommand or data row onto another line.
#	The pound sign is the comment symbol. Minitab ignores all text between the # and the end of the line.
' '	Single quotation marks are used to enclose a file name or a column name.
( )	Parentheses are used in some Minitab commands to separate groups of columns.
-	The dash abbreviates a series of columns. For example C1–C5 refers to C1, C2, C3, C4 and C5.
:	The colon abbreviates a series of numbers. For example, 1:5 refers to the numbers 1, 2, 3, 4 and 5.
;	The semicolon is the last character on a line to be followed by a subcommand.
.	A period ends the last subcommand line used with a given command.

Command Notation

C	refers to a column, such as C1 or 'COST'.
K	refers to a constant, such as K10 or 2.5.
E	refers to either a column or a constant.
[ ]	enclose an optional argument.

Commands, subcommands and arguments that should be typed are shown in upper case. Lower case text is explanatory and does not have to be typed. Minitab ignores extra text in most commands and subcommands. For example:

```
▶ MTB > PRINT the data in C1-C5 to the screen
```

is equivalent to

```
▶ MTB > PRINT C1-C5
```

On-Line Help (HELP)

Minitab's HELP facility explains commands, subcommands and general topics on your screen. You may type HELP at any time during your Minitab session. To see how it works, type HELP HELP.

Limits

Important limits are usually described under individual commands in the Command Reference Chapter. In addition, two general limits apply to all Minitab commands:

1. Minitab allows any number in the range from $-1e^{18}$ to $+1e^{18}$. Any number outside this range is converted to the missing value symbol (*).
2. No command or subcommand may contain more than 50 arguments (total number of file names, columns and constants listed). For example the command:

```
▶ MTB > READ 'B:MYFILE' C1-C15
```

has 16 arguments — the file name plus 15 columns.

Part II

Tutorials

I ▶ Input/Output

Minitab can work its statistical wonders only on data that is in your computer's internal (RAM) memory. In this first tutorial, you will learn how to move data into and out of memory and how to set data up for further processing.

Objectives

When you have completed the steps of this tutorial, you will be able to:

1. enter data into Minitab from the keyboard or from an ASCII file (SET, READ, and END)
2. give a name to a column of data (NAME)
3. print the data to a screen or printer (PRINT and PAPER)
4. save a copy of the worksheet and write certain columns in ASCII format on a disk (SAVE and WRITE)
5. retrieve a previously saved worksheet and obtain information about a worksheet (RETRIEVE and INFORMATION)
6. save output to a file (OUTFILE) or to hard copy (PAPER)

Tutorials

So that you can practice the Minitab input and output operations, let's introduce an interesting data set.

A 24-item demographic questionnaire was given to all the female students in an introductory statistics class at Miami University; 197 completed it. A complete description of the resulting data set can be found in Exercise 9 at the end of this tutorial.

Minitab's **worksheet** organizes this data set into a rectangular table of 197 **rows** (cases, respondents, subjects) and 24 **columns** (variables). The whole table ($197 \times 24 = 4{,}728$ numbers) won't fit into the Student Edition worksheet, which is limited to 2,000 numbers. For our purposes, let's look at just the upper left-hand corner: Figure 1.1 displays the first five students' responses to the first seven questions.

Figure 1.1 ▶

```
2   1   5   1   1   10   2
1   1   5   2   1   6    2
1   3   3   2   1   8    2
3   3   3   2   1   5    2
1   1   3   2   1   3    2
```

Minitab doesn't care what the numbers mean, it only needs to know the column and row in which each number belongs. You provide this essential information by issuing either of two commands: **READ** or **SET**.

Data Input from the Keyboard (READ, SET)

Once you have loaded Minitab and see the Minitab prompt, "**MTB >** ", Minitab expects you to give it commands. Try the commands in Figure 1.2 to read the 35 numbers of Figure 1.1 into columns 1 through 7 of your MINITAB worksheet:

Figure 1.2 ▶

```
MTB > READ C1-C7
DATA> 2 1 5 1 1 10 2
DATA> 1,1,5,2,1,6,2
DATA> 1 3 3 &
CONT> 2 1 8 2
DATA> 3 3 3 2 1 5 2
DATA> 1 1 3 2 1 3 2
DATA> END
```

Notice that Minitab prompts you for **DATA>** after you indicate that you intend to supply seven columns of numbers. When you type in numbers, separate them with spaces (one or more) or with commas (one per separation). Tell Minitab that you are through providing data by typing END right after a DATA> prompt.

When Minitab returns with the MTB 〉 prompt, your data have been entered into the internal RAM (Random Access Memory) of the computer as you desired.

Alternatively, you could have used the SET command to provide data one column at a time. The format of SET is very similar to that of READ.

```
MTB > SET into C2
DATA> 1,1,3,3,1
DATA> END
```

Go ahead and execute these commands. Since these are the same numbers that you already provided, you won't change the worksheet.

Minitab doesn't distinguish between upper and lower case in reading commands. In our illustrations, we display in UPPER CASE the words that Minitab requires to tell it what command you're issuing. Words displayed in lower case are optional, added only to clarify what's going on; Minitab ignores them.

A few comments on Minitab features that we haven't illustrated here:

- If you need to enter two or more identical numbers or sequences of numbers with the SET command, use **parentheses**. For example, the command

  ```
  MTB > SET into C1
  DATA> 3(1 2 3)2
  ```

  puts into column C1 the following sequence of numbers:

  ```
  1 1 2 2 3 3 1 1 2 2 3 3 1 1 2 2 3 3
  ```

- In the same spirit, you can enter consecutive integers with the help of a **colon** (:). The integers 9, 10, 11, 12, and 13, for example, can be entered as follows:

  ```
  MTB > SET into C2
  DATA> 9:13
  ```

- If a number is missing from your data set, simply type an **asterisk** (*) in its place. Minitab's statistical routines will treat it as an item of missing data; various statistical routines handle missing data in various ways.

Finally, you can enter data into the worksheet through the keyboard by means of the **INSERT** command. As its name suggests, INSERT permits you to insert an omitted row (case) without having to retype everything below it in the worksheet, or to append rows to the existing columns. See the Reference Section under INSERT for details.

Checking on the Contents of the Worksheet (INFORMATION)

The **INFORMATION** command gives you a quick way to verify that the worksheet contains what you think you've put there.

```
MTB > INFO
```

If all has gone well, Figure 1.3 should match what now appears on your screen.

Figure 1.3

```
COLUMN     NAME       COUNT
C1                        5
C2                        5
C3                        5
C4                        5
C5                        5
C6                        5
C7                        5

CONSTANTS USED: NONE
```

Saving a Worksheet to Disk (SAVE)

If you leave Minitab at this point to run another program, or if your computer "goes down" because of an error or a power failure, you will lose the contents of the worksheet.

So that you won't have to retype the data each time you run Minitab, use the SAVE command to preserve a copy of your worksheet on your disk (either hard or floppy). If you haven't done so already, this is a good time to develop the habit of saving your work frequently. Try it now, supplying a filename surrounded by single quotes. Be sure to specify the drive to which you are saving by typing b: or c:, and make sure that the drive name appears within the apostrophes.

```
MTB > SAVE 'B:STUDENTS'
```

When the prompt returns, you'll have a more permanent copy of your current worksheet stored under the filename STUDENTS.MTW. Minitab automatically adds the extension ".MTW" when you save.

Loading a Worksheet from Disk (RETRIEVE)

Now that you have a worksheet saved on your disk, you can call it back (retrieve it) whenever you wish. To see how this is done, follow these steps, as displayed in Figure 1.4:

1. Start over with an empty worksheet, using the ERASE command to wipe out the contents of columns C1 through C7.
2. Check with INFO to make sure the slate is clean.
3. Retrieve the file you saved a moment ago.
4. Verify with INFO that your data have indeed returned to the worksheet.

Figure 1.4

```
MTB > ERASE C1-C7
MTB > INFO
 * ALL COLUMNS EMPTY AND UNNAMED

CONSTANTS USED: NONE

MTB > RETRIEVE 'B:STUDENTS'
 WORKSHEET SAVED 11/20/1987

Worksheet retrieved from file: B:STUDENTS.MTW
MTB > INFO

COLUMN     NAME       COUNT
C1                        5
C2                        5
C3                        5
C4                        5
C5                        5
C6                        5
C7                        5

CONSTANTS USED: NONE
```

Notice that we have specified drive B in Figure 1.4 when we retrieved the file. In all other examples in this book, the drive specification will be left out; you must specify which drive you are saving to or retrieving from. The lines printed after the RETRIEVE command in Figure 1.4 have been omitted from the other figures in this book.

RETRIEVE replaces the contents of the current worksheet with those that you previously saved, discarding whatever is there when you issued the command. If you don't want to discard the current worksheet, SAVE it first. The two lines of text that Minitab displays after you retrieve a saved worksheet are omitted from subsequent figures in this manual.

Naming Variables (NAME)

Until you give it other information, Minitab knows the seven columns (corresponding to the variables, or items on the questionnaire) only as C1, C2, and so forth through C7. Once you name a variable with the **NAME** command, you can refer to it in subsequent commands by its name enclosed in single quotes. You can still refer to columns by number, but it's a lot easier to remember what they mean when they have names. If you're reasonably clever at thinking up variable names, Minitab will put more useful labels on your statistical displays.

Name the seven columns:

▶
```
MTB > NAME C1 'Hair' C2 'Eyes' C3 'School' &
CONT> C4 'Sorority' C5 'Ohio' C6 'Birth'
MTB > NAME C7 'Religion'
```

Continuation lines work here in the same way as they do in numerical input. When naming, be sure to enclose each column name in single quotes ('). Names must consist of eight or fewer characters.

In names as in commands, Minitab doesn't care about upper and lower case: 'Hair', 'HAIR', and 'hair' are equivalent. Do not give a variable the same name as that of the saved worksheet file; see the Reference Section for more information. Check again to make sure the names went in properly.

▶
```
MTB > INFO
```

As Figure 1.5 indicates, your NAME labels are now part of the display.

Figure 1.5 ▶

```
COLUMN      NAME        COUNT
C1          Hair            5
C2          Eyes            5
C3          School          5
C4          Sorority        5
C5          Ohio            5
C6          Birth           5
C7          Religion        5

CONSTANTS USED: NONE
```

Displaying and Saving Data (PRINT, WRITE, OUTFILE, PAPER)

After you type data in by hand, you want a convenient way to review them for typos and so forth. INFORMATION, however, doesn't tell you what numbers are in the cells of the worksheet. To see the numbers themselves, you have to issue the PRINT command, as shown in Figure 1.6 and tell Minitab which variables (columns) to display. The selected columns will be displayed on your monitor screen; the result should resemble Figure 1.6.

Figure 1.6 ▶

```
MTB >  PRINT C1-C3, C7

ROW   Hair   Eyes   School  Religion

  1      2      1        5         2
  2      1      1        5         2
  3      1      3        3         2
  4      3      3        3         2
  5      1      1        3         2
```

The **WRITE** command creates a data file containing the columns you specify. For example:

```
MTB > WRITE 'table' C1-C3, C7
```

This command will send the same numbers that appear in Figure 1.6 to a file named TABLE.DAT without the column headers. Any spreadsheet or word-processing program can read and edit this ordinary ASCII file. In contrast, only Minitab can read a file created by the SAVE command.

The **OUTFILE** command also creates a disk file, storing in it all of your commands and Minitab's responses, just as they appear on your screen (as opposed to SAVE, which merely saves the data set). As with WRITE, you have to provide a filename:

```
▶ MTB > OUTFILE 'SESSION'
```

To stop recording and close this file, named SESSION.LIS, issue the NOOUTFILE command:

```
▶ MTB > NOOUTFILE
```

Similarly, you can send all or part of your Minitab session directly to a printer. To start printing, issue the command

```
▶ MTB > PAPER
```

To stop it, command

```
▶ MTB > NOPAPER
```

The OUTFILE command and the PAPER command cannot be in effect at the same time. If OUTFILE is in effect, typing PAPER will stop the OUTFILE. If PAPER is in effect, typing OUTFILE will stop the PAPER command.

Review

There are several ways to move data into Minitab and out again, each designed for different situations, but Minitab doesn't care which one you use. You should make yourself familiar with all the different methods.

List of Key Commands

Here is a list of the principal commands that you practiced in this tutorial. The comments that annotate each command clarify its application. If you find that the comments help you remember how the commands work, they can be included in the actual typed dialogue.

SET	the following data into column C
END	this is the end of the data statement and is optional
READ	the following rows of data into columns C . . . C
NAME	the data in C as 'NAME1' C as 'NAME2' . . .
PRINT	the data in C . . . C
WRITE	[to 'FILENAME'] the data in C . . . C
SAVE	a copy of the worksheet [in 'FILENAME']
RETRIEVE	the previously saved worksheet [in 'FILENAME']
INFORMATION	about the current worksheet

Practice Problems

1. Compare SET and READ for filling a column.

   a. Use the SET command to input the following numbers into column 1.

   ▶ 3 9 4 8 7 5 6 6 9 10

   b. Use the READ command to enter the same data into column C2.

   c. Which command, SET or READ, is quicker to use and takes up fewer lines in this situation?

2. Compare SET and READ for filling two columns.

   a. Use the SET command to enter the following information into columns C1 and C2. Note that the male data include one more observation than the female data. How will your SET command address this?

Males:	100.4	120.9	114.3	119.6	115.8
Females:	289.5	301.1	277.9	290.4	

   b. Use the READ command to read these data into columns C3 and C4. How will you handle the fact that the female data include one fewer observation than the male data?

   c. Which of these two input methods is quicker and easier to use?

3. Figure 1.7 below contains information on the U.S. census for each of the past 7 decades. Input these data into Minitab. Store the year information in column C4 and the population data in C1. Name the columns appropriately.

Figure 1.7 ▶

Year	US Population (in millions)
1920	106.20
1930	123.20
1940	132.16
1950	151.33
1960	179.32
1970	203.21
1980	230.49

4. The data in Figure 1.8 reflect the results of a study of Acton Lake at Hueston Woods State Park in Southwestern Ohio. The temperature of the lake was studied at three different sites (at the creek that feeds the lake, at the dam, and at the middle of the lake). The temperature was recorded at different depths at each location. Input the data into Minitab.

Figure 1.8 ▶

CREEK		DAM		MIDLAKE	
Depth (ft)	Temp (°C)	Depth (ft)	Temp (°C)	Depth (ft)	Temp (°C)
0	28	0	28	0	29
1	26	1	27	1	29
1.5	26	2	27.5	2	28
		3	27	3	27
		4	26	4	25
		5	25	5	25
		5.5	24.5	6	24
				7	23
				8	21
				9	20
				10	20

a. Input the data in Figure 1.8 into Minitab using the SET command. Put the creek data in columns 1 and 2, the dam data in columns 3 and 4, and the mid-lake data in columns 5 and 6. PRINT out the data and verify that the data have been correctly entered. NAME the columns appropriately and then SAVE the data on your Minitab disk. We will be using these data in later tutorials; if you SAVE this worksheet now, you will not have to reenter the data then.

b. Use the READ command to enter the creek data into columns 11 and 12, then use the READ command again to enter the dam data into columns 13 and 14, and finally use the READ command a third time to enter the mid-lake data into columns 15 and 16.

c. Use the READ command once to read all of the data into columns C21 to C26. (Note that, since the columns are not of equal length, you will need to use the missing value code.)

d. PRINT out the results from parts a, b, and c. Were the data stored differently in Minitab by using different data entry methods? Which method is the easiest?

5. Figure 1.9 displays the results of a study of the effect of exercise, diet, and weight on a person's blood pressure. Nine subjects were studied and the indicated items recorded.

Figure 1.9 ▶

V1=# points above normal blood pressure
V2=# kilograms overweight
V3=average # grams saturated fatty foods consumed per day
V4=average # minutes of exercise per day

Subject	1	2	3	4	5	6	7	8	9
V1	14.8	12.1	19.0	14.5	16.6	17.2	17.5	14.1	13.8
V2	7.8	6.9	9.3	6.8	11.7	8.5	12.6	7.5	8.4
V3	4.3	3.9	8.4	10.3	6.4	5.7	6.8	4.2	7.3
V4	11.5	14.3	9.4	15.2	8.8	9.8	12.2	10.9	14.7

a. Input the data using the SET or READ commands and NAME the columns appropriately.

b. Use the PRINT command to verify the data were entered correctly.

6. The results of the first hourly exam in an introductory statistics class (out of 100 possible points) are given in Figure 1.10. Put the 44 test score values in Figure 1.10 in column 5 and PRINT out the data.

Figure 1.10 ▶

71	72	49	92	85	59	66	100	93	83	69
77	70	61	82	59	53	70	94	71	93	67
54	59	77	65	67	84	74	63	69	85	90
93	85	67	84	91	70	59	68	82	62	90

7. The data in Figure 1.11 come from a study that investigated the effect of a voice training class on the quality of a person's voice. Six judges rated the quality of a subject's voice (on a scale of 1–6) before and after taking the class. The results given below are for one person who took the class. (In the actual study there were 20 subjects, ten of whom took the class and ten who did not. We will see the complete data set from this study in a later tutorial.)

Figure 1.11 ▶

Judge	Before Class	After Class
1	5	3
2	4	5
3	4	5
4	5	6
5	4	5
6	5	5

Enter the data using the SET command, NAME the two different columns for future reference, and then PRINT out the data. Enter the data using the READ command and illustrate that this is an equivalent method of entering the data. Why wouldn't we want to use the SET command to enter all 12 numbers in a single column? If you did store the data in one column, what additional information would you need to store in Minitab?

8. A zoology student investigated the effect of cadmium exposure on largemouth bass. Five fish were randomly assigned to the control group; the remaining fish were assigned to the cadmium group. The cadmium-exposed fish were housed in aquaria with a cadmium concentration of 50μg/l. The control fish were housed in aquaria containing ordinary water.

   The experiment consisted of two parts. Part I, which we will not discuss here, dealt with the behavioral changes caused by the exposure to the cadmium. Part II dealt with determining in what organ and to what degree the cadmium tended to concentrate in the fish. The organs investigated were the liver, kidney, and gill. The data are given in Figure 1.12.

Figure 1.12 ▶

Control Group				Cadmium Group			
Fish	Liver	Kidney	Gill	Fish	Liver	Kidney	Gill
1	0.051	0.032	*	6	0.093	0.775	0.259
2	0.029	0.079	0.104	7	0.441	2.130	*
3	0.025	0.034	0.121	8	0.119	0.145	0.258
4	0.034	0.175	0.082	9	0.126	0.183	0.429
5	0.020	0.317	0.055	10	0.194	0.277	0.390
				11	0.374	5.998	0.511
				12	0.207	0.725	0.256
				13	0.442	0.421	0.439
				14	0.238	1.174	0.383
				15	0.218	0.188	0.278
				16	0.167	1.873	0.256
				17	0.205	0.292	0.346

The measurements are the cadmium concentrations (in μg/g wet weight). (Note that even the control fish have measurable levels of cadmium, since cadmium is a naturally occurring element and can even be found, in small concentrations, in streams, rivers, and lakes and in ordinary tap water. The two * values represent missing values. In these two cases, the assay procedure used to measure the cadmium concentration was contaminated and the results of the assay were meaningless; therefore, we simply have no gill concentration values for fish 1 and 7.)

a. With this data set, use the READ command once to store the control-fish results in columns 1 through 4 and again to store the cadmium-fish results in columns 5 through 8.

b. Input the data using the SET command.

9. A questionnaire was given to all female students in all sections of an introductory statistics class at Miami University. The questionnaire was designed to provide demographic information about Miami University females; 197 women filled out the questionnaire. The codebook in Figure 1.13 displays the questions that were asked, the possible responses, and the manner in which the responses were coded in the computer data file.

Figure 1.13 ▶

Number	Question	Possible Responses
1	Hair color	1=Brown 2=Black 3=Blonde 4=Red
2	Eye color	1=Brown 2=Blue 3=Green
3	School	1=Applied Science 2=Arts and Sciences 3=Education 4=Fine Arts 5=Business 6=Other
4	Member of Sorority?	1=Yes 2=No
5	Ohio Resident?	1=Yes 2=No
6	Month of Birth? (1-12)	
7	Religion	1=Catholic 2=Protestant 3=Jewish 4=Other
8	Number of Brothers (0, 1, 2, . . .)	
9	Number of Sisters (0, 1, 2, . . .)	
10	Wear glasses?	1=Yes 2=No
11	Length of hair?	1=Short 2=Medium 3=Long
12	Credit hours this semester (8, 9, 10, . . . 26)	
13	Type of residence	1=Dorm 2=Apartment 3=Commute

14	Have steady boyfriend?	1=Yes 2=No
15	Drink alcohol?	1=No 2=once a Month 3=once a Week 4=more than twice a Week
16	Pierced ears?	1=No 2=Single 3=Double 4=Triple
17	Avg # hours sleep/night (4, 4.5, 5, . . . 10)	
18	Watch soap operas regularly?	1=Yes 2=No
19	Smoke cigarettes regularly?	1=Yes 2=No
20	Currently dieting?	1=Yes 2=No
21	Currently working?	1=Yes 2=No
22	Height (in inches)	
23	Weight (in pounds)	
24	Grade point average	2.0=0.00-2.00 2.5=2.01-2.50 3.0=2.51-3.00 3.5=3.01-3.50 4.0=3.51-4.00

We have provided the first 83 cases of this data set (all that will fit into the 2,000-element worksheet of the Student Edition of Minitab) on the Minitab disk. Actually, we have provided it twice: once as a worksheet saved in a file named MIAMI.MTW, and once as an ASCII text file named MIAMI.DAT. The first five lines of MIAMI.DAT are shown in Figure 1.14.

Figure 1.14▶

```
2 1 5 1 1 10 2 0 1 1 1 16 1 1 1 1 7 2 2 2 1 60  98 2.0
1 1 5 2 1 06 2 1 1 1 2 19 1 2 2 1 6 2 2 1 1 66 140 3.0
1 3 3 2 1 08 2 1 1 2 1 17 1 2 2 0 8 2 2 2 2 64 120 4.0
3 3 3 2 1 05 2 3 0 2 2 20 1 1 4 2 9 1 2 2 2 63  98 3.0
1 1 3 2 1 03 2 1 2 2 2 19 1 1 3 0 8 2 2 2 1 67 125 3.5
```

a. READ the ASCII data file MIAMI.DAT into columns C1–C24. Use INFORMATION and PRINT to verify that the data were properly loaded.

b. Clear the worksheet with RESTART and then RETRIEVE the Minitab saved file MIAMI.MTW. Use the INFORMATION command to provide you with information about the columns and names used in the file.

2 ▶ Data Manipulation, Editing, and Transformation

Objectives

In this tutorial you will learn how to correct, edit, and manipulate data that are already in your computer's memory. Minitab can "massage" your data in almost any way that you can imagine.

With Minitab's transformation commands, you can:

1. change a single number in any row or column
2. change a column of values
3. create a new column based on calculations involving the values in existing columns
4. use arithmetic operations or built-in functions to create or modify columns
5. add data to any place in a column from the keyboard or a file
6. copy any part of a column to a new column
7. delete any portion of the worksheet (rows, columns, or parts of rows or columns)
8. create one column out of several, or combine several columns into one

Tutorials

Correcting Individual Entries (LET)

Even the most skillful typist makes mistakes in entering data. To fix them, Minitab offers the LET command. Try it. First, enter the 25 quiz scores shown in Figure 2.1.

Figure 2.1 ▶

```
MTB > SET the following quiz scores in column C1
DATA> 15 13 15 15 14 14 9 14 15 13 11 10 5
DATA> 13 12 15 14 15 10 4 11 14 15 15  8
DATA> END
MTB > NAME C1 'QUIZ'
```

Suppose you discover, after entering these data, that the tenth score (13) was typed wrong and should have been a 15. To change this number, use LET:

```
▶ MTB > LET C1(10)=15
```

You have now changed the value in row 10 of column 1 to 15, discarding the previous value, 13. LET produces no output; you only have to print the data if you wish to verify that the value actually changed as you intended. Your command and Minitab's output appear in Figure 2.2.

Figure 2.2 ▶

```
MTB > PRINT C1

QUIZ
   15    13    15    15    14    14     9    14    15    15    11
   10     5    13    12    15    14    15    10     4    11    14
   15    15     8
```

Note that the 10th value is indeed 15, as you intended.

Creating New Variables or Data (LET)

With LET, you can put any number you choose into any cell (defined by a column number and a row number) of your worksheet, whether or not you had previously put data there. You could even do your initial data input with LET, one number at a time, instead of using SET or READ, although you'll seldom find it convenient to fill your worksheet in this manner.

Usually, you'll want to use LET to make new variables out of old ones. Minitab gives you a full range of mathematical tools with which to transform old variables and manufacture new ones. You wield these tools through the LET command. For example, we might want to turn the raw quiz scores in column C1 into percentages. Knowing that the quiz had fifteen items in all, we say to Minitab:

```
MTB > LET C2 = (C1/15)*100
MTB > NAME C2 'PERCNT'
```

This pair of commands creates a new variable from the data in column 1, names it 'PERCNT,' and stuffs the percentage (resulting from a simple arithmetic computation) into column 2. The available arithmetic operations are addition, subtraction, multiplication, and division (+, −, /, and *). Print the result, as shown in Figure 2.3. Note that the CONTINUE? prompt will appear when the screen is full. To save space, this prompt will not appear in the remaining figures in this manual.

Figure 2.3 ▶

```
MTB > PRINT C1-C2

 ROW   QUIZ    PERCNT

   1     15   100.000
   2     13    86.667
   3     15   100.000
   4     15   100.000
   5     14    93.333
   6     14    93.333
   7      9    60.000
   8     14    93.333
   9     15   100.000
  10     15   100.000
  11     11    73.333
  12     10    66.667
  13      5    33.333
  14     13    86.667
  15     12    80.000
  16     15   100.000
  17     14    93.333
  18     15   100.000
  19     10    66.667
  20      4    26.667
  21     11    73.333
CONTINUE? YES
  22     14    93.333
  23     15   100.000
  24     15   100.000
  25      8    53.333
```

New Data from Old: Functions

Your data-massaging tools are not limited to simple arithmetic operations. Minitab has built-in logical and mathematical **functions** that make it easy to do just about everything that people frequently want to do with data. Some of these are very simple (rounding, for example), and others are more complex. You tell Minitab to apply one of its functions by building the name of the function into a LET command. The function's **argument** follows the function name, enclosed in parentheses. For example:

```
MTB > LET C3 = ROUND(C2)
```

Try this command and PRINT the result to see how a simple Minitab function works.

The Reference Section of this manual discusses the available functions; they include:

ABSOLUTE	gives the absolute value of the argument
SQRT	gives the square root of the argument
LOGTEN	gives the log to the base 10 of the argument
LOGE	gives the log to the base e of the argument
EXPO	calculates e to the power of the argument
ANTILOG	calculates 10 to the power of the argument
ROUND	rounds the argument to the nearest integer
SIN	computes the sine of the argument, which must be in radians
COS	computes the cosine of the argument, which must be in radians
TAN	computes the tangent of the argument, which must be in radians
ASIN	computes the inverse or arc sine of the argument and outputs the result in radians
ACOS	computes the inverse or arc cosine and outputs the result in radians
ATAN	computes the inverse tangent and outputs the result in radians
SIGNS	outputs +1 for a positive argument, −1 for a negative argument, and 0 for a zero value
NSCORES	computes normal scores for the data — normal scores are transformations of the data into standard normal distribution values and are useful in determining whether a set of numbers is approximately normally distributed
PARSUMS	calculates partial or cumulative sum — the sum of the argument column thus far.
PARPRODUCTS	calculates partial or cumulative products — the product of the argument column thus far.

You can use functions and operators singly or in combination, and the result of one function can serve as an argument for another function. For example:

```
MTB > LET C4 = SIN(C1*3.14159/(90*2))
```

This command calculates the sine of the angles (measured in degrees) stored in C1 after first transforming the degrees to radians. The results don't mean much here, since C1 contains quiz scores, not angles — Minitab processes the numbers, and you supply the meanings.

Note that the usual rules of the order of arithmetic operations hold:

1. Functions are evaluated first.
2. Expressions in parentheses are evaluated next.
3. Exponentiation (**) is performed before multiplication and division (* and /), which are performed before addition and subtraction (+ and −).
4. Operators with the same priority (* and /, or + and −) are performed in order from left to right.

Here's another example:

```
▶ MTB > LET C19 = SQRT(C1+1)
```

This transformation adds 1 to each value in column 1, takes the square root, and stores the result in column 19. You will encounter this transformation in your study of statistics.

```
▶ MTB > LET C4 = LOGE(ABSOLUTE(C4-5))
```

This command subtracts 5 from each value in column 4, computes the absolute value of the difference, calculates the logarithm to the base e of the absolute value, and stores the result back in column 4. Note that this operation discards the original values in column 4.

Here's another example that uses the LET command to create new data from data already stored in more than one column. Clear the worksheet, and then use SET and NAME to load columns 1 and 2 with the first two exam scores for a small statistics class, as shown in Figure 2.4.

Figure 2.4 ▶

```
MTB > ERASE C1-C50
MTB > SET the first exam scores into C1
DATA> 89 56 78 88 94 87 96 72
DATA> END
MTB > SET the second exam scores into C2
DATA> 83 77 91 87 99 80 85 75
DATA> END
MTB > NAME C1 'EXAM 1' C2 'EXAM 2'
```

The instructor, wondering how each student is doing thus far, wants to compute the average of the first two scores. One way to do this would be to add up the values in the first two columns and divide by two. Try it:

▶
```
MTB > LET C3 = (C1 + C2)/2
MTB > NAME C3 'AVERAGE'
MTB > PRINT C1-C3
```

Figure 2.5 displays the result:

Figure 2.5 ▶

ROW	EXAM 1	EXAM 2	AVERAGE
1	89	83	86.0
2	56	77	66.5
3	78	91	84.5
4	88	87	87.5
5	94	99	96.5
6	87	80	83.5
7	96	85	90.5
8	72	75	73.5

Row-Manipulation Commands

People who work with data often want to calculate the average (mean) of several variables (columns) for the same person (row). Minitab has set up the command RMEAN to make this operation easier. Here's how it works:

▶
```
MTB > RMEAN of C1-C2 store in C4
MTB > NAME C4 'RMEAN'
MTB > PRINT C1-C4
```

Figure 2.6 shows the result. Columns 3 (AVERAGE) and 4 (RMEAN) contain identical numbers, of course.

Figure 2.6 ▶

ROW	EXAM 1	EXAM 2	AVERAGE	RMEAN
1	89	83	86.0	86.0
2	56	77	66.5	66.5
3	78	91	84.5	84.5
4	88	87	87.5	87.5
5	94	99	96.5	96.5
6	87	80	83.5	83.5
7	96	85	90.5	90.5
8	72	75	73.5	73.5

Commands that manipulate the data row by row include:

RCOUNT	counts the number of values in the specified columns, both missing and nonmissing
RN	counts the number of nonmissing values in the specified columns
RNMISS	counts the number of missing values (asterisks) in the specified columns
RSUM	sums all nonmissing values in the specified columns
RMEAN	computes the mean of the nonmissing values
RSTDEV	computes the standard deviation of the nonmissing values
RMEDIAN	computes the median of the nonmissing values
RMINIMUM	finds the smallest nonmissing value in the row
RMAXIMUM	finds the largest nonmissing value in the row
RSSQ	computes the uncorrected sum of the squares of the nonmissing values in a row

In each case, the resulting value for each row is stored in the corresponding row of the column you designate.

Summarizing the Data in Columns

Similar commands make it easy to massage whole columns of data. For example, using the quiz score data in Figure 2.1, we could obtain the average for the first exam by using the column mean function:

```
MTB > MEAN of 'EXAM 1'
MEAN = 82.500
```

When you issue the MEAN command, Minitab immediately computes the desired mean and outputs it, labelled, to the current output device (monitor screen and/or printer). If you want to save the mean for use in future computations, just tell Minitab into which constant you wish to put it, as in Figure 2.7.

Figure 2.7

```
MTB > MEAN of 'EXAM 1' store in K1
    MEAN    =      82.500
MTB > PRINT K1
    K1      =      82.500
```

All the column-manipulation commands work in the same way. They include:

COUNT	counts the number of both missing and nonmissing values in the specified column
N	counts the number of nonmissing values in the column
NMISS	counts the number of missing values in the column
SUM	sums all nonmissing values in the column
MEAN	computes the mean of the nonmissing values in the column
STDEV	computes the standard deviation of the nonmissing values in the column
MEDIAN	computes the median of the nonmissing values in the column
MINIMUM	finds the smallest nonmissing value in the column
MAXIMUM	finds the largest nonmissing value in the column
SSQ	computes the uncorrected sum of the squares of the nonmissing values in the column

Note that the column-manipulation commands operate on entire columns; you can't pick and choose rows (except by deleteing them from the worksheet; we'll discuss that later).

Also remember that each column operation yields only one value, whereas its corresponding row operation yields a column of values, one value for each row. You can use column functions in LET commands; for example, these two commands are equivalent:

```
▶ MTB > LET K1 = SUM(C1)/N(C1)
  MTB > LET K1 = MEAN(C1)
```

Removing Data from the Worksheet (ERASE, DELETE)

Minitab also allows the user the option of deleting data from a worksheet. You can erase complete columns, complete rows, or any rectangular segment from the worksheet. You may have a very large data set but need only part of it for a particular analysis. By deleting the unneeded data you free up memory that Minitab can use for temporary storage and calculations.

For example, the original Miami University female data set has been reduced so that it just fits in the Student Edition of Minitab's worksheet. In order to make room in memory for calculations or new variables, you should eliminate unneeded columns. Suppose we are only interested in the physical characteristics of the Miami University females; these are stored in columns C1, C2, C10, C11, C16, C22, and C23, as you may wish to verify. To erase the other columns:

```
▶ MTB > RETRIEVE 'MIAMI'
  MTB > ERASE C3-C9 C12-C15 C17-C21 C24
```

The resulting worksheet includes only those columns that contain physical characteristics. The ERASE command erases complete columns of data.

You may often encounter a situation in which you want to drop an entire respondent or group of respondents, particularly if their eligibility to take part in your study or the credibility of their responses becomes compromised in some irreparable way.

The DELETE command lets you remove specified rows or respondents from specified columns. The contents of later rows then move up to fill in the gaps. Here's how it works. You'll delete rows 3 and 6 through 9 from columns C1 through C2, C10 through C11, C16, and C22 through C23.

```
MTB > DELETE rows 3, 6:9 of C1-C2, C10-C11, C16, C22-C23
```

Data rows are deleted *only* in those columns specified. Other columns remain untouched. Notice that you can use a **colon** to indicate an inclusive series of rows and a **hyphen** to indicate a series of columns.

A note of caution about the ERASE and DELETE commands is in order. When you ERASE a column or DELETE a row or segment, the data that were there flutter off to the land of Entropy, never to return. Minitab offers no undo command to bring removed data back. If you might need certain columns or contents in the future, then make sure that you store them in a file before erasing or deleting them.

Copying Selected Data from One Part of Your Worksheet to Another (COPY)

It is sometimes useful to duplicate a column in a data set, putting the copy in a more convenient place than the original occupies. The COPY command does this very conveniently. We input a small data set and copy column 2 to column 5. The results are in Figure 2.8.

Figure 2.8

```
MTB > COPY the data in column C3 to C5
MTB > PRINT C2-C5

 ROW     C2      C3     C4       C5

   1      9    0.45            0.45
   2     11    0.89            0.89
   3     10    0.77            0.77
   4     12    0.62            0.62
   5     10    0.83            0.83
   6      9    0.99            0.99
   7     11    0.76            0.76
   8      8    0.55            0.55
   9      7    0.80            0.80
  10     14    1.22            1.22
```

More frequently, though, your reason for copying a column will be to create a modified version of it, including cases (row entries) or leaving them out according to some rule. COPY gives you this power through its USE and OMIT subcommands. Try the dialogue in Figure 2.9.

Figure 2.9 ▶

```
MTB > COPY C3 C8 to C4 C5;
SUBC> USE ONLY C2=8:11.
MTB > PRINT C2-C5 C8-C9

 ROW    C2     C3     C4     C5     C8    C9

   1     9   0.45   0.45    5.3    5.3     1
   2    11   0.89   0.89    5.2    5.2     2
   3    10   0.77   0.77    6.4    6.4     3
   4    12   0.62   0.83    4.3    9.8     4
   5    10   0.83   0.99    5.2    4.3     5
   6     9   0.99   0.76    9.9    5.2     6
   7    11   0.76   0.55    8.4    9.9     7
   8     8   0.55                  8.4
   9     7   0.80                  9.8
  10    14   1.22                 11.6
```

Minitab has copied column 3 to column 4, and column 8 to column 5, as you instructed, *only* when the entry in column 2 lies within the range from 8 through 11 (8:11). Note that the copied data are no longer in the same rows they were copied from: when Minitab follows your orders and skips an entry, it doesn't leave a blank space.

The OMIT subcommand operates in a similar fashion.

Notice that you use a **semicolon** (;) to signal to Minitab that you wish to elaborate on the COPY command with a **subcommand**. Minitab responds with the prompt SUBC>. The **period** (.) denotes the end of the compound command; appearances notwithstanding, it's not a decimal point.

Summarizing Ranges of Data with Codes (CODE)

We often collect data in more detail than we want to display, so it makes sense to collapse a variable with many possible values into a few meaningful distinctions. You might wish, for example, to label ages 0 to 3 as "infancy," 4 to 12 as "childhood," 13 to 17 as "adolescence," and so forth. Letter grades, as another example, can be codes that reflect ranges of achievement. Practice by following the dialogue in Figure 2.10.

Figure 2.10 ▶

```
MTB > RETRIEVE 'STA368'
MTB > CODE (14:15) 1, (12:13) 2, (9:11) 3, (7:8) 4 (0:6) 5 &
CONT> IN 'QUIZ' store in C10
MTB > NAME C10 'GRADE Q1'
MTB > PRINT C1 C10

 ROW    QUIZ  GRADE Q1

   1      15         1
   2      13         2
   3      15         1
   4      15         1
   5      14         1
   6      14         1
   7       9         3
   8      14         1
   9      15         1
  10      15         1
  11      11         3
  12      10         3
  13       5         5
  14      13         2
  15      12         2
  16      15         1
  17      14         1
  18      15         1
  19      10         3
  20       4         5
  21      11         3
  22      14         1
  23      15         1
  24      15         1
  25       8         4
```

Concatenating Columns of Data (STACK)

Sometimes you have organized data into several columns for one purpose, but find that you need to treat them as a single column for another purpose. The STACK command makes it easy to put several columns or constants on top of one another to form a new column of data.

As an example, let's retrieve the 'EXAM' worksheet. It stored two exam scores for a graduate statistics class as columns 1 and 2. You've already seen how to use MEAN to compute the average for each test separately, as shown in Figure 2.11.

Figure 2.11 ▶

```
MTB > MEAN of 'EXAM 1'
   MEAN     =        82.500
MTB > MEAN of 'EXAM 2'
   MEAN     =        84.625
```

Suppose now that you want to find the average exam score for both tests combined. You need to STACK column 1 ('EXAM 1') and column 2 ('EXAM 2') together in a single column. Now the MEAN command will yield the average of both exam scores combined; follow the dialogue in Figure 2.12.

Figure 2.12 ▶

```
MTB > STACK 'EXAM 1' on 'EXAM 2' store in C5
MTB > NAME C5 'BOTH'
MTB > PRINT C1 C2 C5

 ROW  EXAM 1  EXAM 2   BOTH

   1      89      83     89
   2      56      77     56
   3      78      91     78
   4      88      87     88
   5      94      99     94
   6      87      80     87
   7      96      85     96
   8      72      75     72
   9                     83
  10                     77
  11                     91
  12                     87
  13                     99
  14                     80
  15                     85
  16                     75

MTB > MEAN C5
   MEAN     =        83.562
```

Breaking Down a Composite Column (UNSTACK)

As you might suspect, the UNSTACK command works just as STACK does, only backwards. It takes a column of data and breaks it into shorter columns. You tell it where to put the new columns by listing them in the command itself. You indicate which items belong in each new column by specifying a column in the SUBSCRIPTS subcommand: entries with the same subscript wind up in the same column.

If you leave out the subscripts subcommand, Minitab will create a new column (with one entry), or a new constant, for each row of the specified column.

To show how UNSTACK works, let's retrieve the quiz score worksheet again. As you will recall, the last time we saw this data set you had used the CODE command to summarize the quiz scores into five letter-grade groups. Now let's put the As in one column, the Bs in another, and so forth. Follow Figure 2.13.

Figure 2.13 ▶

```
MTB > UNSTACK (C1) into (C11) (C12) (C13) (C14) (C15);
SUBC> SUBSCRIPT in C10.
MTB > NAME C11 'A' C12 'B' C13 'C' C14 'D' C15 'F'
MTB > PRINT C1 C10 C11-C15

 ROW  QUIZ 1  GRADE Q1    A    B    C   D   F

   1      15         1   15   13    9   8   5
   2      13         2   15   13   11       4
   3      15         1   15   12   10
   4      15         1   14        10
   5      14         1   14        11
   6      14         1   14
   7       9         3   15
   8      14         1   15
   9      15         1   15
  10      15         1   14
  11      11         3   15
  12      10         3   14
  13       5         5   15
  14      13         2   15
  15      12         2
  16      15         1
  17      14         1
  18      15         1
  19      10         3
  20       4         5
  21      11         3
  22      14         1
  23      15         1
  24      15         1
  25       8         4
```

If you wanted to, you could now use the COUNT command on columns 11 to 15 to obtain the frequency of each grade. But there are easier ways to get frequencies, as you'll discover later.

Review

In this tutorial you have learned how to edit, manipulate, and transform data in Minitab. You can change a single number anywhere in the worksheet; create a whole new column from scratch or from data contained in other columns; insert data anywhere you want in a column or a group of columns; collapse data into fewer categories; copy any portion of a column to a new column; delete any portion of the worksheet; turn several columns into one, or one column into several.

List of Key Commands

LET	E = expression
ERASE	columns or constants E . . . E
DELETE	rows K thru K of C . . . C

COPY the data in columns C . . . C to columns C . . . C

Subcommands:

USE	rows K . . . K
USE	rows where C = K . . . K
OMIT	rows K . . . K
OMIT	rows where C = K . . . K

COPY	the contents of column C into constants K . . . K
COPY	the constants K . . . K into column C
CODE	values (K . . . K) to K, . . . (K . . . K) to K, for C . . . C, put in C . . . C

STACK the data in (E . . . E) . . . on (E . . . E), put in C . . . C

Subcommand:

SUBSCRIPTS stored in C

UNSTACK the data in (C . . . C), put unstacked data in (E . . . E) . . . (E . . . E)

Subcommand:

SUBSCRIPTS to unstack can be found in C

Practice Problems

1. The following temperatures (degrees Fahrenheit) were recorded at a meteorological observation station:

```
56 90 34 88 59 92 98 27 67 71 85 10 38 62 99
```

   a. Enter the temperatures into column C1 using the SET command.

   b. Change the 14th value from 62 to 26.

   c. Create a new column (C2) in which the temperatures have been changed to degrees Celsius. In case you've forgotten, Celsius = 5/9 (Fahrenheit − 32).

   d. Create a new column (C3) in which the temperatures (in °F) are coded as 1 for less than freezing (<32°F) or 2 for freezing or above.

   e. Obtain the median temperature and store the result as constant K5.

   f. Copy to C4 the temperatures you coded 2 in part d.

   g. Using the results of part d, put the below freezing temperatures in C5 and the freezing or higher temperatures in column C6.

2. The following are 12 measurements made by a Geology graduate student. He was studying the amount of deflection of certain iron-ore formations from true north. The measurements are recorded in degrees.

```
78   81   99   80   86  72   75   94   89   82   96  79
```

   a. Enter these data into Minitab in column C1.

   b. Change each angle from degrees to radians.

   c. Create a new column, C2, and fill each of its entries with the tangent of the angle in the corresponding row of C1.

3. On the Minitab disk we have saved quiz and test results from an introductory statistics class. The file name is STA261.MTW. The data given are the 11 quiz scores (out of 15 possible points), the 3 hourly exam scores (out of 100 possible points), and the final exam score (out of 100 possible points).

    a. Retrieve the grade data. In what columns were the data stored and what name has been given to each column?

    b. Obtain and save the quiz averages for each student and change the average to a percentage.

    c. Obtain and save the hourly test averages. Why don't we need to convert these averages to percentages?

    d. Obtain and save the course average for each student based on the quiz, test, and final exam results.

    e. Round the course averages to the nearest integer and save the results.

    f. Create a new column in which the rounded course averages are changed so that 90% or above is an A, 80 to 89% is a B, 70 to 79% is a C, 60 to 69% is a D, and below 59% is an F.

    g. What is the average class quiz score? That is, the average of all 11 quizzes for all 44 students?

4. Retrieve CD1.MTW, the data set about cadmium levels in fish. We've saved it for you on the Minitab disk. Use it to answer the questions below.

    a. Print out the data to refresh your memory as to how they are stored.

    b. Obtain the average cadmium concentration for each fish in the control and cadmium groups separately.

    c. Obtain the average cadmium concentration for each organ of the control and cadmium groups separately.

    d. Obtain the average cadmium concentration for each organ for the combined control and cadmium groups.

    e. Using the fish number and the CODE command, create a new column containing a code which distinguishes the control group (fish 1 to 5) from the cadmium group (fish 6 to 17).

3 ▶ Displaying Data

Objectives

In this tutorial you will learn how to display or summarize a set of data using a pictorial display. You will learn how to:

1. produce a histogram
2. produce a dotplot (a horizontal version of a histogram)
3. produce a stem-and-leaf diagram
4. produce a boxplot
5. plot one variable against another
6. plot several pairs of variables against one another on the same graph
7. plot one column against another, getting the plot character from a third column
8. produce a plot of a time series

Later we will make a broad distinction between summarizing the information in one column and summarizing the relationships among several columns.

Tutorials

Minitab provides a way to display a variety of pictorial summaries. To illustrate the Minitab commands that produce these summaries, we return to the data about the fish exposed to cadmium. These data are stored in two different formats in two different worksheet files: CD1.MTW and CD2.MTW. The two formats reflect the requirements of different descriptive commands, as you will see.

In file CD1.MTW, the control fish data are stored in columns C1 to C4 and the cadmium exposed fish data in columns C5 to C8. Columns 1 and 5 respectively contain individual fish-identification numbers for the two groups and the remaining columns in each group contain the cadmium concentrations in liver, kidney, and gill.

In CD2.MTW the same data have been stacked into columns C1 to C4, and C5 contains a group identifier: 1 for control and 2 for cadmium exposed. We will use these data to illustrate how to summarize single columns of data (variables) and relationships among variables.

Pictorial Displays of One Column of Data (HISTOGRAM, DOTPLOT, STEM-AND-LEAF, BOXPLOT)

Four Minitab commands create pictorial displays from the data in a single column: HISTOGRAM, DOTPLOT, STEM-AND-LEAF, and BOXPLOT. Each highlights different characteristics of the data; you choose one or more depending on the point you're trying to make.

First, retrieve the CD1 data set, and follow the dialogue in Figure 3.1.

Figure 3.1 ▶

```
MTB > RETRIEVE 'CD1'

MTB > HISTOGRAM C8

Histogram of CD GILL   N = 11   N* = 1

Midpoint   Count
    0.24       4  ****
    0.28       1  *
    0.32       0
    0.36       1  *
    0.40       2  **
    0.44       2  **
    0.48       0
    0.52       1  *
```

The HISTOGRAM command breaks the data range down into a reasonable set of intervals and assigns each datum to the midpoint of the interval within which it falls.

DOTPLOT generates a horizontal display similar to a histogram. Figure 3.2 shows how it works.

Figure 3.2 ▶

```
MTB > DOTPLOT C8

1 POINTS MISSING OR OUT OF RANGE

     ::   .               .         ..        . .              .
  -+---------+---------+---------+---------+---------+-----CD GILL
0.250     0.300     0.350     0.400     0.450     0.500
```

The dotplot's "bars" are vertical, arrayed across what looks like a continuous range, although the dotplot is broken down into intervals, just as the histogram is.

The STEM-AND-LEAF display, shown in Figure 3.3, is somewhat more complex, showing a number of the important characteristics of the data set at a glance.

Figure 3.3 ▶

```
MTB > STEM-AND-LEAF 'CD GILL'

Stem-and-leaf of CD GILL    N  = 11
Leaf Unit = 0.010           N* =  1

    5    2 55557
   (1)   3 4
    5    3 89
    3    4 23
    1    4
    1    5 1
```

The middle column of the STEM-AND-LEAF diagram contains its **stems**. The variable-length rows to the right of the stems are the **leaves**; there is one leaf for each observation.

The leftmost column shows the distribution of the data around their median. Each leaf's entry shows the number of observations that fall in that leaf or closer to the near end of the distribution. Parentheses highlight the number of entries in the leaf that contains the median.

In the example, CD1 contains 11 nonmissing gill concentration values for the cadmium-exposed fish. Five of these values fall above 0.346, the value for fish 17, and five below. So, the median value is 0.346. The legend above the diagram (Leaf Unit = 0.010) indicates the placement of the decimal point: read the first observation (2 5) in the stem-and-leaf diagram as 25*0.010 or 0.25.

Now try the **boxplot**. Figure 3.4 shows how it works.

Figure 3.4 ▶

```
MTB > BOXPLOT C8
           -------------------------------
          -I                 +            I--------------------
           -------------------------------
      --+---------+---------+---------+---------+---------+----CD GILL
    0.250     0.300     0.350     0.400     0.450     0.500
```

The median is indicated by a plus sign (+). The box covers the range of the middle half of the data, ending at the left and right hinges.

Note that Minitab has chosen the scales (of the displays, not of the fish) in these examples. If you prefer to choose the scales yourself, suitable subcommands offer you that control. Check in the reference section for details.

The HISTOGRAM, DOTPLOT, and STEM commands can also operate on more than one column at a time. If you name more than one column in issuing one of these commands, Minitab will generate a separate summary for each variable you specify.

The SAME subcommand forces Minitab to use the same scales on all the columns you specify in a single command. Try this command in Figure 3.5.

Figure 3.5 ▶

```
MTB > DOTPLOT C6-C8;
SUBC> SAME.

       .
      ::
      ::.:
    +---------+---------+---------+---------+---------+-------CD LIV
       :
      .: . :   .     . .                              .
    +---------+---------+---------+---------+---------+-------CD KIDN
    1 POINTS MISSING OR OUT OF RANGE
       .
       :..
       :::
    +---------+---------+---------+---------+---------+-------CD GILL
  0.0       1.2       2.4       3.6       4.8       6.0
```

You can see plainly that the cadmium concentrations are more spread out in the kidney than in the gill or liver in the cadmium-exposed fish. Also, the cadmium concentrations in the kidney tend to be almost 3 to 4 times greater than the concentrations in the gill and liver.

If you store the data in one column and put a sample identifier in another, then any of the four pictorial display commands (HISTOGRAM, DOTPLOT, STEM-AND-LEAF, and BOXPLOT) issued with the BY subcommand, will yield a set of parallel displays, one for each value of the sample identifier. If you also issue the SAME subcommand, then all the displays in the set will have the same scale. The SAME command only works with DOTPLOT and HISTOGRAM. When the BY subcommand with BOXPLOT, the same scales are automatically used.

Displaying a Relationship Between Two Variables (PLOT)

Suppose that we want to know whether high concentrations of cadmium in one part of a fish tend to be associated with high concentrations elsewhere. A plot can address this question.

First, let's ignore the distinction between the control and the cadmium-exposed fish and look at the numbers for all the fish pooled together. The file named CD2.MTW contains the data organized in this manner, with the organ concentrations stored in columns C2 to C4 for both kinds of fish.

First, plot the liver concentrations against the kidney concentrations. Figure 3.6 displays the dialogue that you will have with your computer:

Figure 3.6 ▶

```
MTB > RETRIEVE 'CD2'

MTB > PLOT C2 C3

          -
     0.45+     *              *
          -
LIVER     -
          -                                 *
          -
     0.30+
          -
          -          *
          -  2   *
          -  *         *
     0.15+
          - **
          -      *
          - *
          - *2 *
     0.00+
           +---------+---------+---------+---------+---------+------KIDNEY
          0.0       1.2       2.4       3.6       4.8       6.0
```

Each asterisk (*) in the plot represents a fish. If two or more observations fall at the same point, the number of coinciding observations appears instead.

Overlaying One Plot on Another (MPLOT, LPLOT)

Have we confused the issue by mixing the control and exposed fish? Perhaps the relationship might be different within each group.

We could plot the liver and kidney concentrations separately for the two groups (PLOT C2 vs C3, then PLOT C6 vs C7, using the data stored in CD1.MTW); that's easy, but it doesn't illustrate anything new. It would take some fiddling, moreover, to make the two sets of axes comparable. Instead, let's try out Minitab's ability to distinguish two related plots while plotting them on the same set of axes.

To accomplish this feat, tell Minitab to plot (MPLOT) two pairs of columns against one another on the same set of axes; this amounts to overlaying two separate plots on one graph. Figure 3.7 shows the Minitab commands needed to produce such a plot using the data in CD1.MTW and the output that would result.

Figure 3.7 ▶

```
MTB > RETRIEVE 'CD1'

MTB > MPLOT C2 versus C3 and C6 versus C7

        -
    0.45+     B             B
        -
        -
        -                                                   B
        -
    0.30+
        -
        -           B
        -   2   B
        -   B             B
    0.15+
        -  BB
        -       B
        - A
        - A2 A
    0.00+
          +---------+---------+---------+---------+---------+------
        0.0       1.2       2.4       3.6       4.8       6.0

         A = CTL LIV vs. CTL KIDN  B = CD LIV vs. CD KIDN
```

As expected, the control fish (indicated by A in the plot) tend to have lower levels of cadmium in their bodies, whether in their liver or kidney, than the exposed fish (indicated by B). The range of concentration in the control fish is really too narrow (and the number of control fish is too small) to draw any important conclusions about liver-kidney relationships for them. The A entries clearly don't interfere substantially with the pattern apparent in the more numerous and variable Bs, so nothing was lost by pooling the two groups for this comparison.

The LPLOT command offers a way to get exactly the same plot by a slightly different logical route. With LPLOT, you tell Minitab to plot one column against another, taking the plot character from a third column. The approach you choose will depend on the organization of your data.

Retrieve the file CD2.MTW, and use LPLOT to plot the liver and kidney concentrations, using the grouping variable in column C5 as the plot character. The results are in Figure 3.8.

Figure 3.8 ▶

```
MTB > LPLOT C2*C3 by C5

          -
     0.45+      B             B
          -
  LIVER   -
          -                                  B
          -
     0.30+
          -
          -           B
          -   2   B
          -   B              B
     0.15+
          -  BB
          -       B
          - A
          - A2 A
     0.00+
           +---------+---------+---------+---------+---------+------KIDNEY
          0.0       1.2       2.4       3.6       4.8       6.0
```

The same plot is produced in Figures 3.7 and 3.8 from two different files and two different sets of commands. Each control fish shows as an A and each exposed fish as a B.

In general, the LPLOT command determines the plot character from the value in the third column. The third column must contain integer values and the values are plotted using the following rule:

```
▶  . . .  -1   0   1   2   3  . . .  24   25   26   27  . . .
   . . .   Y   Z   A   B   C  . . .   X    Y    Z    A  . . .
```

It is typical of Minitab that you can get the same results from rather different-looking operations. This feature gives you flexibility to operate on data bases organized in various ways with a minimum of preprocessing. As we go along, we will frequently point out alternative methods of producing the same output.

Plotting Time Series (TSPLOT)

Sometimes your data take the form of a **time series**. You can do both simple and sophisticated statistics with time series.

A simple time series plot can give you a feel for the way that observations change over time. For example, let's consult a series of data recorded by a local real estate company. Over a period of four years, starting in January 1984, the company noted the number of homes sold each month. The file named HOMESALE.MTW on the Minitab disk contains the resulting time-series data set. It consists of a single column of data, labeled 'SOLD'. Retrieve the file and use TSPLOT to plot the data; Figure 3.9 shows the commands and the resulting time-series plot.

Figure 3.9 ▶

```
MTB > RETRIEVE 'HOMESALE'

MTB > TSPLOT period = 12 C1


SOLD      -
          -                  7                       7
          -
     12.00+                              78        5
          -       8                    5              8
          -
          -    5 7
          -                5  8      3
      8.00+     6                       6        3
          -         0       6   0A          0           0
          -
          - 2            34                9 A    4    9 A
          -  34                   B   4       B
      4.00+        9           9    2               6
          -          AB1                       12
          -
          - 1            2          1
          +-----------+-----------+-----------+-----------+
          0          12          24          36          48
```

Minitab displays its time-series plots in much the same format as its other plots. At first glance, there's not an obvious difference between the two, except that the time-series plot has a larger number of distinct plot characters.

By its nature, a time-series plot won't have two observations that hit the same spot, so the numbers don't indicate the number of piled-up entries. If you look more closely, you will note that there are only twelve plot characters: 1234567890AB. Reading from left to right, the first entry is 1, the second 2, and so forth, and when the sequence of twelve runs out, it starts over again.

The twelve characters correspond to the months of the year. You told Minitab that it was processing a monthly time series by inserting the optional PERIOD = 12 specification into the TSPLOT command. Other PERIOD values can set up daily data over a period of several weeks (PERIOD = 7), for example, or quarterly data over a period of years (PERIOD = 4).

Now that the plot's meaning is clear, note that peak sales tend to occur in the summer months (5, 6, and 7 correspond to May, June, and July). Similarly, the slowest sales periods are in December, January, and February (B, 1, and 2). The Time-Series Tutorial will deal in greater detail with the periodicity of time-series data.

You can change the size of a plot with the WIDTH and HEIGHT commands. WIDTH controls the width of BOXPLOT, DOTPLOT, LPLOT, MPLOT, PLOT, and TPLOT (but not TSPLOT). HEIGHT controls the height of PLOT, MPLOT, LPLOT, TPLOT, and TSPLOT. It does not affect the height of HISTOGRAM, DOTPLOT, STEM, or BOXPLOT.

Review

In this tutorial you have learned some basic techniques of displaying data. Various simple diagrams and plots make it easy to describe the distribution of the values of a single variable or the relationships among variables. Your purposes in addressing a data base and the nature of your data will determine the descriptive techniques you choose.

List of Key Commands

Here is a list of the commands used in this tutorial. The list does not include all the plot commands that Minitab offers. (Refer to the reference section for information on the commands not used in this tutorial: TPLOT, WIDTH, and HEIGHT.)

HISTOGRAM	the data in C . . . C
DOTPLOT	the data in C . . . C

HISTOGRAM and DOTPLOT have the subcommands:

INCREMENT	= K
START	at K [end at K]
BY	C
SAME	scales on all output

STEM-AND-LEAF diagrams of the data in C . . . C
Subcommands:

TRIM	outliers
INCREMENT	= K
BY	C

BOXPLOT for the data in C
Subcommands:

START	at K [end at K]
INCREMENT	= K
BY	C
LINES	= K
NOTCH	[K percent confidence] sign confidence interval
LEVELS	K . . . K [for C]

PLOT the data in C on the y-axis against the data in C on the x axis

Subcommand:

SYMBOL	= 'symbol'

MPLOT	C vs C, and C vs C, and . . . C vs C
LPLOT	C against C using the labels in C
TPLOT	C vs C vs C

PLOT, MPLOT, LPLOT, and TPLOT have the subcommands:

YINCREMENT	= K
YSTART	at K [end at K]
XINCREMENT	= K
XSTART	at K [end at K]

Practice Problems

1. Twenty male heart-transplant recipients were studied. The age of each at the time of his first heart transplant is recorded on the Minitab disk as data set HEART.MTW. Display the HISTOGRAM, DOTPLOT, STEM-AND LEAF, and BOXPLOT for this set of age data. What characteristics are apparent from your summaries? Are these characteristics apparent in all four summaries? Use subcommands to change the scales in each of your summaries to display the ages by decades: 0 to 9, 10 to 19, 20 to 29, etc.

2. An experiment investigated the effects of varying levels of acidity/alkalinity (pH) in the ambient water upon the parental care behavior of 40 pairs (one male and one female) of fish. Ten pairs were housed in each of four tanks containing water at four pH levels: 7.0, 6.5, 6.0, and 5.5. The investigator monitored the percentage of time that each member of each pair spent in guarding their nest site over the course of ten days, recording the fraction for each fish on each day. The average for each of the ten days over fish is stored on the Minitab disk in the file named GUARD.MTW. Column C1 contains the guarding percentages for the fish exposed to the water with a pH of 7.0 (neutral); C2, pH 6.5, etc.

    a. Obtain the four pictorial summaries for this data. Which of the four displays is more informative?

    b. The first 10 observations in the data set are the guarding times for the male fish and the next 10 are the guarding times for the female fish. Create a new variable for the sex of the fish, then obtain the DOTPLOT for each sex separately. Is the comparison of the sexes clearer?

3. STA261.MTW contains data on grades achieved by students in an introductory statistics class. Use them to answer the following questions.

    a. Summarize the scores on the first exam (C12, named 'T1') with HISTOGRAM, DOTPLOT, and STEM-AND-LEAF. Which of the summaries is most informative? From which of the summaries could you obtain the original exam scores?

    b. Plot the results of exam 1 against the second exam result (C13). Is there a relationship between the scores on the two exams?

c. Average the quiz scores (C1 through C11), and save the result. Then average the three exam scores (C12 through C14), and save the result. Create a new variable that is the average of the quiz average, the exam average, and the final exam score. Then apply a grading system that assigns letter grades as follows: 100 to 90 = A, 89 to 80 = B, 79 to 70 = C, etc., to create a new variable which represents the students' final grades. Use A = 1, B = 2, C = 3, etc. Finally, plot the first and second exam scores using the final grade as the plot character. What can you say about the students' performance on the first two exams and their final course grades?

4. Consumption of electricity (in KWH) and of water (in gallons) was collected for a one-family home over the course of several years. The resulting data are stored on the Minitab disk in the file UTILITY. MTW.

   a. Retrieve the data set and use the INFO command to determine what data have been stored in the file.

   b. Plot the electrical and water usage as time series. What should the period be?

   c. Plot the electrical usage against the water usage. Is there a relationship? Would you expect one?

5. Use the Miami (MIAMI.MTW) data set to answer the questions that follow.

   a. DOTPLOT the diet variable. Is the plot very useful? DOTPLOT the number-of-brothers variable. Is this plot very informative? Finally, DOTPLOT the height variable. Does this plot provide any information? (Our point is that the four pictorial summaries are most useful with numeric data. For categorical data, especially with just a few distinct values, Minitab has more efficient and informative descriptive tools, as we will see in Tutorial 4.)

   b. Plot the number of brothers against the number of sisters. Is there a relationship?

   c. Plot the number of brothers against the number of sisters, with religion supplying the plot character. Does religion have an effect on the relationship?

6. The heights and weights of 73 first graders are stored on the Minitab disk in the file 1STGRADE.MTW. Plot weight against height. Are the variables related?

7. In a geological study of the earth, the percentage of mud was determined every ten feet in a core sample. The resulting data are stored in the file COREDATA.MTW. Plot the percentage of mud against the depth. What kind of relationship exists between the two variables?

4 ▶ Numerical Summaries

Objectives

In this tutorial you will learn how to obtain numerical descriptions of data sets. You will learn how to:

1. obtain various numerical summaries of the characteristics of the data in a single Minitab column
2. obtain a frequency summary for the data in a single column
3. obtain a numerical summary of the relationship between a pair of variables

Tutorials

To illustrate the Minitab commands that compute useful numerical summaries, we return to the cadmium and Miami data sets introduced in Tutorial 1.

Basic Descriptive Statistics (DESCRIBE)

Retrieve the saved worksheet file CD2.MTW. It contains, as you will recall, the cadmium-concentration data for exposed and control fish stacked together in columns C1 to C4, with the group identifier in C5.

With one command, DESCRIBE, you can compute eleven common numerical summaries of the data contained in one or several columns. Figure 4.1 displays your dialogue with Minitab.

Figure 4.1 ▶

```
MTB > RETR 'CD2'

MTB > DESCRIBE the data in C2 C3 C4

                N        N*      MEAN    MEDIAN    TRMEAN     STDEV    SEMEAN
LIVER          17         0    0.1755    0.1670    0.1681    0.1381    0.0335
KIDNEY         17         0     0.872     0.292     0.586     1.462     0.354
GILL           15         2    0.2778    0.2590    0.2770    0.1404    0.0363

              MIN       MAX        Q1        Q3
LIVER      0.0200    0.4420    0.0425    0.2280
KIDNEY      0.032     5.998     0.160     0.975
GILL       0.0550    0.5110    0.1210    0.3900
```

With DESCRIBE, you get the total number of observations, the number of missing observations (N*), the mean, the median, the 5% trimmed mean (found by deleting the largest 5% and the smallest 5% of the nonmissing values and averaging the remaining 90% of the data), the standard deviation, the standard deviation of the mean, the minimum and maximum values, and the first and third quartiles.

These summary statistics can help you clean your data, especially when you have made mistakes that make some data (outliers) much larger or smaller than others in their neighborhood. If the mean and the trimmed mean differ notably, then it pays to look for outliers. Similarly, the minimum and maximum values provide a useful check.

Simple Breakdown Tables (DESCRIBE; BY)

Sometimes you gather experimental data with the idea that the experiment will make a difference. That is, you expect the numbers to come out differently for one group (experimentals) than for another group (controls). With the help of the BY subcommand, DESCRIBE can give you displays of this sort.

You simply tell Minitab which group each case belongs to by filling an extra column with group identifiers, and you'll get a separate set of DESCRIBE output for each group. Not by accident, the CD2.MTW data set, which you have already loaded into Minitab, is organized in exactly this way: the data for control and cadmium-exposed fish are stacked on top of one another, and column C5 contains a suitable group identifier.

Apply the BY subcommand, as shown in Figure 4.2.

Figure 4.2▶

```
MTB > DESCRIBE C2 C3 C4;
SUBC> BY C5.

          GROUP        N      N*      MEAN    MEDIAN    TRMEAN
LIVER         1        5       0   0.03180   0.02900   0.03180
              2       12       0    0.2353    0.2060    0.2289
KIDNEY        1        5       0    0.1274    0.0790    0.1274
              2       12       0     1.182     0.573     0.804
GILL          1        4       1    0.0905    0.0930    0.0905
              2       11       1    0.3459    0.3460    0.3376

          GROUP    STDEV  SEMEAN       MIN       MAX        Q1        Q3
LIVER         1  0.01190  0.00532  0.02000   0.05100   0.02250   0.04250
              2   0.1200   0.0346   0.0930    0.4420    0.1363    0.3400
KIDNEY        1   0.1208   0.0540   0.0320    0.3170    0.0330    0.2460
              2    1.657    0.478    0.145     5.998     0.210     1.698
GILL          1   0.0285   0.0143   0.0550    0.1210    0.0618    0.1168
              2   0.0907   0.0273   0.2560    0.5110    0.2580    0.4290
```

You get the same DESCRIBE output, but it is broken down to display the control and experimental groups separately. The two groups are indeed different: the cadmium-exposed group had over seven times as much cadmium in the liver as did the control group. The other contrasts are less striking — a fact which in itself suggests directions for further research and interpretation.

Other Descriptive Statistics in Minitab

Statisticians use other descriptive statistics beyond those that DESCRIBE provides. Even when you can't call them up by a simple command, Minitab gives you the flexibility to compute these measures for yourself. Take skewness, for example, a measure of the tendency of a distribution to pile up on one side or the other, rather than being symmetrical. One common skewness measure is the ratio of the third sample moment to the second sample moment, raised to the 3/2 power.

With the MEAN and LET commands, the moments can be computed and stored. For example, the following commands will compute and print the skewness measure as defined above.

```
MTB > LET K1 = MEAN ((C3 - MEAN(C3))**2) # the 2nd sample moment
MTB > LET K2 = MEAN ((C3 - MEAN(C3))**3) # the 3rd sample moment
MTB > LET K3 = K2/(K1**1.5) # the skewness
MTB > PRINT K3
```

Using Minitab, almost any descriptive measure can be computed. As you have probably noticed, we have introduced another feature of Minitab in the above commands. Using the # sign, you can annotate your commands as much as you like. When Minitab encounters a # sign on a command, it ignores everything that comes after it. Hence you can put in comments and notes on any Minitab command or subcommand.

Simple Frequency Counts (TALLY)

You'll find the TALLY command useful for summarizing categorical variables (those which include only a relatively small number of discrete integers). A continuous variable containing numbers with decimal digits cannot be used with TALLY. While DESCRIBE provides useful information for continuous variables, TALLY provides useful information for categorical data.

To illustrate the operation of the DESCRIBE and TALLY commands on categorical data, return to the Miami data set. After retrieving the saved worksheet file, use DESCRIBE and TALLY on the hair color, eye color, and school data (found in columns C1, C2, and C3 respectively). The results are in Figure 4.3.

Figure 4.3 ▶

```
MTB > RETRIEVE 'MIAMI'

MTB > DESCRIBE C1 C2 C3

                N      MEAN    MEDIAN    TRMEAN     STDEV    SEMEAN
HAIR           83     1.590     1.000     1.493     0.976     0.107
EYE            83    1.9277    2.0000    1.9200    0.7930    0.0870
SCHOOL         83     2.964     3.000     2.960     1.254     0.138

              MIN       MAX        Q1        Q3
HAIR        1.000     4.000     1.000     3.000
EYE        1.0000    3.0000    1.0000    3.0000
SCHOOL      1.000     5.000     2.000     3.000

MTB > TALLY C1-C3

    HAIR  COUNT             EYE  COUNT       SCHOOL  COUNT
       1     59               1     29            1      9
       2      3               2     31            2     22
       3     17               3     23            3     32
       4      4              N=     83            4      3
      N=     83                                   5     17
                                                 N=     83
```

As expected, the DESCRIBE output is not very informative. It tells us nothing about the relative frequency with which each hair or eye color occurs, and it says nothing about how the subjects are distributed among the various schools in the university. It does confirm that the data in these three columns fall within the boundaries of possible responses.

The TALLY output, on the other hand, not only provides this information but also indicates the relative frequency of occurrence of each category. It shows that eye colors are fairly uniformly distributed among the three categories, whereas almost three-fourths of the girls have brown hair.

The TALLY command has five subcommands, COUNT, PERCENTS, CUMCOUNTS, CUMPERCENTS, and ALL, with which you can choose what you want to see displayed.

A Summary Index of the Relationship Between Two Variables (CORRELATION)

Statisticians have devised numerical measures that indicate the strength of some common types of relationships. The most familiar of these is ρ, the Pearson correlation coefficient. With Minitab's CORRELATION command you can obtain a numeric measure of the linear aspect of the relationship between two variables. Returning to the cadmium data (CD2.MTW), for example, correlate the liver and kidney concentrations as shown in Figure 4.4.

Figure 4.4▶

```
MTB > RETRIEVE 'CD2'
MTB > CORRELATE the data in C2 with the data in C3

Correlation of LIVER and KIDNEY = 0.556
```

The output of the CORRELATION command is the Pearson correlation between the variables in the two columns specified. The observed correlation of 0.556 indicates a moderate positive relationship between the liver and kidney concentrations.

If you specify more than two columns in the CORRELATION command, Minitab will compute the correlation for each pair of columns and summarize the results in a matrix. For example, try ordering the pairwise correlations among the concentrations in all three organs. The results appear in Figure 4.5.

Figure 4.5▶

```
MTB > CORRELATE C2 C3 C4

           LIVER   KIDNEY
KIDNEY     0.556
GILL       0.840    0.496
```

As before, the liver-kidney correlation is 0.556, the liver-gill correlation is 0.840, and the kidney-gill correlation is 0.496. It would appear that the strongest relationship exists between the liver and gill concentrations.

Review

In this tutorial you have learned some of the ways Minitab summarizes data. Some of these summaries work particularly well for relatively small bodies of data; these numerical summaries become more powerful with larger data bases. Some of these summaries work particularly well with categorical data and others particularly well with continuous variables. You will want to keep a variety of summarizing devices in your bag of tools and suit their application to the nature of your data and to the point you are trying to make. In many instances, a combination of a picture and a number will give you what you want.

List of Key Commands

We have used three Minitab commands in this tutorial.

DESCRIBE the data in columns C . . . C

Subcommand:

BY C

TALLY the data in columns C . . . C

Subcommands:

COUNTS

PERCENTS

CUMCOUNTS outputs the cumulative counts

CUMPERCENTS outputs the cumulative percents

ALL outputs all four values

CORRELATE the data in C . . . C, in a pairwise manner

Practice Problems

1. Retrieve the exam data from the EXAM.MTW saved worksheet.

   a. Describe the two sets of exam scores, and compare the students' performance on the two exams.

   b. Using the same data, correlate the two exam results. Are the exam scores related?

2. Retrieve data about the number of home sales in Oxford, Ohio, from the file HOMESALE.MTW.

    a. Describe the data with the DESCRIBE command.

    b. Would the mean or median be a good indicator of the average number of homes sold per month?

    c. What about the standard deviation? Is it large or small? Would this affect your answer to Part a?

    d. Recall that we plotted the home-sales data in Tutorial 3 using the time-series plot command. Does the periodicity we discovered explain somewhat your answers to Parts b and c?

3. In problem 5 of Tutorial 1, we described a study involving exercise, diet, weight, and blood pressure. This data set is stored on the Minitab disk in the file BPRES.MTW. Obtain the correlations among the four variables. Which variable has the strongest relationship to blood pressure?

4. Retrieve the data set stored in REALEST.MTW, and answer the questions that follow.

    a. Characterize the typical home that was sold in Oxford in 1987.

    b. How much less do sellers typically get for their home than their asking price?

    c. Are the asking price and selling price related? To what degree?

    d. What is the average number of baths and bedrooms in the typical Oxford home?

    e. How many baths and bedrooms is the typical home most likely to have? (Note that the baths variable is not in integer format, but can easily be transformed into integer values using the LET or CODE commands.) Is your answer the same as in Part d? Should it be?

    f. What percentage of the homes sold had two or more baths? What percentage had basements? What percentage had garages?

5. Obtain the correlation between the depth and the percentage of mud of the core sample data that has been stored in COREDATA.MTW. Are the results puzzling? Plot the percentage of mud against the depth. Are your results still puzzling? Why?

5 ▶ One-Sample Inference

Tutorials 1 and 2 introduced you to the purely mechanical housekeeping functions of Minitab: moving data into worksheets, moving them around and cleaning them up, and getting them out again. Tutorials 3 and 4 gave you some practice in **descriptive statistics** — the art of boiling down a lot of numbers to a few numbers or a simple picture, in order to find patterns in the data. In this tutorial, we enter into the realm of **inferential statistics**, through which we can speak with confidence and authority, not only about the data we have before us, but also about much larger bodies of data that we haven't even measured.

Objectives

Minitab includes many tools with which you can perform various kinds of statistical inference. In fact, most of the remaining tutorials will deal with inferential procedures of one kind or another.

In this tutorial you will learn how to:

1. obtain an interval estimate or confidence interval for a single population mean, assuming the population variance is known
2. obtain an interval estimate or confidence interval for a single population mean, assuming the population variance is unknown
3. test a hypothesis concerning a single population mean, assuming the population variance is known
4. test a hypothesis concerning a single population mean, assuming the population variance is unknown

Tutorials

In the tutorials that follow we present the Minitab commands that will be used in statistical inferences about a single population mean. We will use several data sets to illustrate these commands to give you some exposure to the various questions that can be asked and the various scenarios that arise in statistical inference.

Testing a Sample Mean Against a Population Mean When σ^2 is Known (ZTEST)

In the first tutorial we introduced a set of quiz scores from an introductory statistics course. These quiz scores have been saved in the file STA368.MTW on the Minitab disk. When a class takes a quiz, the instructor may want to know how the results compare to past results, and hence, how this class compares to past classes.

Suppose that we were to tell you that the quiz that was administered was one of a set of standard quizzes that had been administered the past seven years to a total of 35 different sections of this course. Over the seven years, the average (mean) score was 11.35 with a variance of $\sigma^2 = 8$. The population standard-deviation is therefore $\sigma = 2.83$ (the square root of 8.00). Armed with this information, we ask Minitab to tell us how this year's scores on this quiz compare to past years' results.

Figure 5.1 ▶

```
MTB > RETRIEVE 'STA368'

MTB > ZTEST of mu=11.35 assuming sigma=2.83 using the data in C1

TEST OF MU = 11.350 VS MU N.E. 11.350
THE ASSUMED SIGMA = 2.83

              N       MEAN     STDEV    SE MEAN         Z     P VALUE
QUIZ         25     12.440     3.203      0.566      1.93       0.054
```

In Figure 5.1 we first test with the ZTEST command whether the quiz results in C1 differ significantly from past results, using the null hypothesis: this year's quiz grades aren't different from past years' grades.

Since the previous results give us a large number of observations from the population, we accept their variance as the population variance (that is, $\sigma^2 = 8$). Note that you have to supply the population standard-deviation value just before specifying the column or columns where the new data reside.

Since you asked for a ZTEST on one variable (column), Minitab supplies a single line of output. It indicates that the 25 quiz scores in column C1 have a mean of 12.440 and a standard deviation of 3.203. The difference of 1.09 points between the population and sample means amounts to z = 1.93 standard errors of the mean, which corresponds to a p-value of 0.054.

This doesn't quite reach the conventional cutoff level of 95% confidence, though it's quite close. And there is nothing sacred about 95%.

Since you didn't instruct it to do otherwise, Minitab automatically performed a two-sided or **two-tailed test**. You indicated, by default, that you didn't care whether the current class fell above or below the long-term score level: you were interested in whether there was any difference in either direction. This is called a **nondirectional alternative hypothesis**.

Had you wished to provide a more specific, directional hypothesis, you could have done so with the ALTERNATIVE subcommand, in one of three forms:

ALTERNATIVE = +1	Test an upper-tailed alternative hypothesis (that this year's scores are *higher* than usual)
ALTERNATIVE = 0	Test a two-tailed alternative hypothesis (the default: that this year's scores are *different* from the usual level)
ALTERNATIVE = −1	Test a lower-tailed alternative hypothesis (that this year's scores are *lower* than usual)

Figure 5.2 presents the output from ZTEST under the one-tailed (upper) hypothesis.

Figure 5.2 ▶

```
MTB > ZTEST of mu=11.35 assuming sigma=2.83 using the data in C1;
SUBC> ALTERNATIVE = +1.

TEST OF MU = 11.350 VS MU G.T. 11.350
THE ASSUMED SIGMA = 2.83

               N      MEAN    STDEV   SE MEAN         Z   P VALUE
QUIZ          25    12.440    3.203     0.566      1.93     0.027
```

Note that Minitab displays the two hypotheses in the output: the **null hypothesis** is equality:

▶ `'' . . . MU = 11.350 . . . ''`

and the alternative hypothesis is directional, as you specified:

▶ `'' . . . MU GT 11.350''`

The output in Figure 5.2 contains the same kinds of information as in the two-tailed test. Since the alternative hypothesis was changed, the p-value changed to reflect the more restrictive hypothesis.

Computing a Confidence Interval for a Population Mean When σ^2 is Known (ZINTERVAL)

The sample mean gives you an approximation of the true population mean. A **confidence interval** tells you how close an approximation it is.

When you know the population variance in advance, you can get a confidence interval with the ZINTERVAL command. Like ZTEST, ZINTERVAL requires you to supply the population standard-deviation value immediately before specifying the columns whose means are to be tested. The command and output appear in Figure 5.3.

Figure 5.3 ▶

```
MTB > ZINTERVAL assuming sigma=2.83 using the data in C1

THE ASSUMED SIGMA =2.83

               N      MEAN    STDEV  SE MEAN    95.0 PERCENT C.I.
QUIZ          25    12.440    3.203    0.566  (11.329,   13.551)
```

This output indicates that you can be 95% confident that the true population mean of this year's scores lies between 11.329 and 13.551 points.

Minitab assumes, as always, that the 25 scores in column C1 are a simple random sample of the population. You can specify the confidence level to be any value you wish. If you don't specify a value, Minitab defaults to 95%.

Testing a Sample Mean Against a Population Mean When σ^2 is Unknown (TTEST)

When you don't know the population variance in advance, use TTEST and TINTERVAL instead of ZTEST and ZINTERVAL. They have the same format and subcommands as their z-test counterparts except that you do not supply a population standard deviation (sigma).

To illustrate the TTEST command we use the real estate data in file REALEST.MTW. We ask whether the average price of a home in Oxford, Ohio, is less than the average price of a home in the U.S. (currently about $84,000). We don't know the population variance, so we use the TTEST command. The dialogue appears in Figure 5.4.

Figure 5.4 ▶

```
MTB > RETRIEVE 'REALEST'

MTB > LET C1=C1/1000    # transform selling price to $1,000.00
MTB > TTEST of mu=84 using the data in C1;
SUBC> ALTERNATIVE is lower tailed = -1.

TEST OF MU = 84.000 VS MU L.T. 84.000

              N      MEAN     STDEV   SE MEAN         T     P VALUE
SELL $       51    57.578    20.696     2.898     -9.12      0.0000

MTB > TINTERVAL of selling price in C1

              N      MEAN     STDEV  SE MEAN    95.0 PERCENT C.I.
SELL $       51     57.58     20.70     2.90  (    51.76,    63.40)
```

This TTEST output looks very much like what you got from ZTEST. The test statistic is called T rather than Z, but otherwise the two displays contain the same information, including the lower-tailed p-value (since you requested a lower-tailed test). The only difference lies in the way in which the test statistic is computed.

Computing a Confidence Interval for a Population Mean When σ^2 is Unknown (TINTERVAL)

Figure 5.4 also includes the confidence interval output for the selling price of a home. Since you don't know the population variance, you use the TINTERVAL command. Since we did not specify the confidence level, Minitab defaults to 95%. With this degree of confidence we conclude that the average selling price of a home in Oxford lies between \$51,750 and \$63,400.

Note that you can apply any of these four commands (ZTEST, ZINTERVAL, TTEST, and TINTERVAL) to several columns of data at once. For example,

```
MTB > TTEST C1-C4
```

would generate tests for the data contained in the first four columns.

Review

In this tutorial you have learned how to use Minitab to make inferences about a single population mean. These inferences take two forms: tests of hypotheses and tests of confidence intervals. You can test one-tailed or two-tailed hypotheses, and the one-tailed tests can go in either the upward or the downward direction. You can specify any null value or level of confidence you choose. If you know the population variance (or standard deviation) in advance, Minitab can also make use of this information to strengthen your tests.

List of Key Commands

The Minitab commands used in this tutorial are:

ZTEST [of mu = K], assuming sigma = K for the data in C . . . C
Subcommand:

  ALTERNATIVE = K

ZINTERVAL [with K confidence] for the data in C . . . C

TTEST [of mu = K] for the data in C . . . C
Subcommand:

  ALTERNATIVE = K

TINTERVAL [with K confidence] for the data in C . . . C

Practice Problems

1. Retrieve the mean height and weight of first graders stored in 1STGRADE.MTW.
   a. Obtain 99% confidence intervals for each variable.
   b. The U.S. government says that first graders (i.e., 6 year olds) weigh on the average 53 pounds and are 49 inches tall. Test to determine whether our data are representative of the U.S. population of 6 year olds.
2. Previous studies have shown that the variability in the percentage of mud in core samples is 9.8.
   a. Obtain a 98% confidence interval for the mean percentage of mud in the core sample data stored in COREDATA.MTW.
   b. Test whether the mean percentage of mud is greater than 10.
   c. Suppose we did not know that the variability of the percentage of mud in core samples was 9.8. Redo the test in part b using the t-test. Are your results the same? Would you expect them to be? If they are different, explain why.
3. Obtain the 95% confidence interval for the average age of first heart transplant using the data in HEART.MTW.
4. Retrieve the fish parental behavior data from file GUARD.MTW.
   a. Create a column containing a sex index (the first 10 observations are of male fish and the others are of female fish).
   b. Unstack the pH 7.0 data into two columns, one corresponding to males, and the other to females.
   c. Obtain the 95% confidence intervals for the average percentages of time that the male and female fish spent guarding their nest. What do you conclude?
5. The study of cadmium-exposed fish asked whether cadmium affected the aggressive behavior of the fish exposed to it. Five fish were randomly assigned to the control group, and five to the cadmium-exposed group. The ten fish were monitored for a week, and the average number of aggressive behaviors towards the other four fish was recorded each day. The control group was then exposed to tap water for a week and the experimental group was exposed to a high level of cadmium for a week. The fish were then

monitored for another week, and the average number of aggressive behaviors per day was recorded. The resulting data are stored on the Minitab disk in the file AGGRESS.MTW. Retrieve the data set and use the INFORMATION command to learn how the data were stored. Then obtain 95% confidence intervals for the average number of aggressive encounters per day for each group both before and after exposure.

6. Retrieve the data on usage of electricity and water from UTILITY. MTW, then obtain the 99% confidence intervals for the average amount of water used per month and the average cost per month. Why is the standard deviation of the cost per month so large? (Hint: A plot of the data over time might help.) What would be a better way to determine the average cost per month?

6 ▶ Two-Sample Inference

Objectives

In this tutorial you will learn how to compare two population means. Specifically, you will learn how to test the equality of two population means and to compute a confidence interval for the difference between two means. You will practice:

1. testing the means of two populations for equality using independent samples
2. testing the means of two populations for equality using dependent samples
3. computing a confidence interval for the difference between two population means using independent samples
4. computing a confidence interval for the difference between two population means using dependent samples

Tutorials

As you seek to answer more complex questions with statistics, you have to pay attention to some new issues in order to choose the proper statistical test. The answers to three questions determine which procedure (and hence, which Minitab command) you use to compare two population means:

1. Are the samples dependent or independent?
2. Are the population variances equal or unequal?
3. How are the data stored in the Minitab worksheet?

The following exercises address each question in turn and illustrate the Minitab command appropriate to each case.

Our familiar data base about cadmium in fish illustrates

- independent and dependent samples
- two common formats for data of this kind (in files CD1.MTW and CD2.MTW)

The Minitab commands that compare means handle these formats appropriately and differently. Minitab is a very flexible system; it can accommodate almost any data format, as you will see.

Two Independent Samples in Separate Columns (TWOSAMPLE)

First, retrieve the CD1.MTW data set, in which the control and experimental data are stored in separate groups of columns. The investigator wanted to learn how exposure to high levels of cadmium would affect the cadmium concentrations in the various organs. One question might be a comparison of the means: in each organ, is the mean cadmium concentration the same for the control and experimental fish?

To choose the proper procedure, let's address the three issues, one at a time.

Independence

We have no reason to suppose that the measurements on the five control fish might have affected those on the twelve exposed fish. They were separate fish, held in separate tanks. So, we can reasonably consider the two samples to be independent. If we had been comparing measurements on the same fish at different times, on the other hand, we would have to choose a procedure for dependent samples. TWOSAMPLE and TWOT are Minitab's independent sample procedures.

Variability

We'll have to look at the two samples to decide whether one is more variable than the other. When the two samples have equal variability, you should tell Minitab to pool the two samples into one when it makes its estimate of the (common) population variance. POOLED is a subcommand of each two sample mean-comparison command.

Organization

The two files contain the data organized in the two ways that Minitab is set up to handle:

1. CD1.MTW has the samples in separate columns; the TWOSAMPLE command accepts data in this form.
2. CD2.MTW has them stacked in a single column, with another column containing an index that tells in which sample each datum belongs. TWOT accepts data in this form.

Retrieve CD1.MTW, and tell Minitab to describe the data in each column from C2 through C4, and C6 through C8. Then order dotplots for the two liver concentrations (C2 and C6) on the same scale, and similarly for the kidney (C3 and C7) and gill (C4 and C8) concentrations. The resulting output is too extensive to reproduce here; when you get it, though, you will conclude that one would be hard put to look at the two LIVER dotplots and call their variabilities (or anything else about them) equal. The numerical summaries put the standard deviations of the control and experimental livers at 0.0119 and 0.12, respectively: different by a factor of 10. Since variance is the square of standard deviation, the corresponding variances differ by a factor of 100. The KIDNEY variances are even more discrepant, while the GILL variances are somewhat more similar. In order to illustrate the POOLED subcommand, we shall assume later on that the gill variances are equal.

Figure 6.1 ▶

```
MTB > TWOSAMPLE t 99% confidence  using the data in C2 and C6;
SUBC> ALTERNATIVE = -1.

TWOSAMPLE T FOR CTL LIV VS CD LIV
          N      MEAN     STDEV   SE MEAN
CTL LIV   5    0.0318    0.0119    0.0053
CD LIV   12     0.235     0.120     0.035

99 PCT CI FOR MU CTL LIV - MU CD LIV: (-0.3124, -0.095)

TTEST MU CTL LIV = MU CD LIV (VS LT): T= -5.81  P=0.0000  DF=  11
```

Figure 6.1 shows Minitab commands and output for testing the equality of mean cadmium concentrations in the livers of the control and experimental populations. With the data stored in two columns named 'CTL LIV' and 'CD LIV', we use the TWOSAMPLE command. By naming 'CTL LIV' (or C2) first, we tell Minitab to test the difference defined by

the mean of the control group liver concentrations
minus
the mean of the experimental group liver concentrations

or, in Minitab shorthand,

MU CTL LIV − MU CD LIV.

We expect this difference to be *negative*, corresponding to higher cadmium concentrations in the experimental group of fish.

The subcommand ALTERNATIVE K specifies the form of the alternative hypothesis, as in the ZTEST and TTEST commands. Remember that K = −1 for a lower-tailed test (difference less than zero), K = 0 for a two-tailed test (difference greater than zero), and K = +1 for an upper-tailed test (difference zero or greater). We ask for lower-tailed tests, since we don't expect (and wouldn't be particularly interested in) a finding that cadmium exposure reduced concentration in the bodies of our fish.

After the column summary data, the 99% confidence interval (CI) for the first TWOSAMPLE result appears, labelled with the formula for the difference under test: "MU CTL LIV − MU CD LIV." Then Minitab prints the null hypothesis (and the alternative in parentheses) together with the test statistic, its p-value, and its degrees of freedom.

Run TWOSAMPLE for the kidney concentrations (C3 and C7) in the same way for practice. The results don't illustrate anything new about Minitab, so we haven't reproduced the results here.

Figure 6.2 ▶

```
MTB > TWOSAMPLE t 99% confidence  using the data in C4 and C8;
SUBC> ALTERNATIVE = -1;
SUBC> POOLED.

TWOSAMPLE T FOR CTL GILL VS CD GILL
            N      MEAN      STDEV   SE MEAN
CTL GILL    4    0.0905     0.0285     0.014
CD GILL    11    0.3459     0.0907     0.027

99 PCT CI FOR MU CTL GILL - MU CD GILL: (-0.397, -0.113)

TTEST MU CTL GILL = MU CD GILL (VS LT): T= -5.42  P=0.0000  DF=  13

POOLED STDEV =      0.0807
```

Figure 6.2 shows the TWOSAMPLE dialogue for comparing the gill concentrations (C4 and C8). It illustrates the POOLED subcommand, which we invoke here because, as we mentioned earlier, the variances seemed similar enough to justify the assumption of equal variance. With POOLED in effect, Minitab adds the pooled standard deviation to the output.

We conclude that the cadmium concentrations are significantly different in the two groups in all three organs. The p-values for each test are well below the alpha cutoff value of 0.05. The confidence intervals provide an idea of the size of each difference. These 99% confidence intervals don't correspond, by the way, to the alpha value of 0.05 that was used in the tests.

Two Independent Samples Stacked in a Single Column (TWOT)

It is often convenient to store data on independent samples (separate groups of individuals) in stacked format. Dependent samples usually come from parallel measurements of the same individuals and so are commonly stored in separate columns.

Minitab compares the means of stacked independent samples with the TWOT command. TWOT works the same way as TWOSAMPLE, except that you have to specify two columns: the one with the data, and the one containing the group-membership information. The group-identifier values can be any integer values between −10,000 and +10,000, and there can be only two distinct values in the group membership column. The data don't need to appear in any special order, as long as the identifier variable splits them unambiguously between the two groups. The POOLED and ALTERNATIVE subcommands work here, as before.

Figure 6.3

```
MTB > RETRIEVE 'CD2'

MTB > TWOT t test 99% confidence  data in C2 groups in C5;
SUBC> ALTERNATIVE -1.

TWOSAMPLE T FOR LIVER

GROUP    N       MEAN      STDEV   SE MEAN
1        5     0.0318     0.0119    0.0053
2       12      0.235      0.120     0.035

99 PCT CI FOR MU 1 - MU 2: (-0.3124, -0.095)

TTEST MU 1 = MU 2 (VS LT): T= -5.81  P=0.0000  DF=  11
```

Figure 6.3 illustrates the same analysis as Figure 6.1, with the data coming from CD2.MTW, where the two groups are stacked for each organ (liver in C2, kidney in C3, and gill in C4). Column C5 distinguishes the two groups.

As you can see, the TWOT output is identical to the TWOSAMPLE output, apart from slight labelling changes that reflect the role of the group variable. The group identifier also defines the order of computation of the difference under test; it is

the mean of the group identified by the smaller number
minus
the mean of the other group.

In Figure 6.3 the difference is therefore group 1 (control) mean minus group 2 (experimental), as the labels indicate.

Run TWOT again for the kidney (C3) and gill (C4) samples, in the same manner. For the gill concentrations, apply the POOLED subcommand, as before.

Two Dependent Samples (TTEST, TINTERVAL)

TWOSAMPLE and TWOT assume that the samples are independent. When the data are paired or otherwise dependent, you have to perform a **paired t-test**.

Using as an example once again our unfortunate cadmium-soaked fish, we note that the data set includes several measurements (liver, kidney, and gill concentrations) for each of the 17 fish. We may legitimately wonder whether the cadmium concentrations differ significantly from one organ to another for the fish within each group. We will address this question for the control fish in this tutorial. For practice, you might compare the same concentrations for the experimental fish.

The paired t-procedure requires no commands other than those you have already encountered. After you preprocess the paired data a bit, you'll need only the TTEST and TINTERVAL commands introduced in Tutorial 5. Here's how it works.

First, compute the difference between the two measurements. Then investigate the resulting sample of differences with a one-sample t-test to determine whether its mean is different from zero.

To compute the pairs, you will need the data organized as in the CD1.MTW data set, with the measurements arrayed in parallel columns. We will compare the liver concentration to the kidney concentration, the liver concentration to the gill concentration, and the kidney concentration to the gill concentration. Figure 6.4 shows the required Minitab commands and output.

Figure 6.4▶

```
MTB > RETRIEVE 'CD1'

MTB > LET C10=C2-C3      # computes the liver and kidney differences
MTB > LET C11=C2-C4      # computes the liver and gill differences
MTB > LET C12=C3-C4      # computes the kidney and gill differences
MTB > NAME C10 'LIV-KID' C11 'LIV-GILL' C12 'KID-GILL'
MTB > TTEST of the differences in C10-C12

TEST OF MU = 0.0000 VS MU N.E. 0.0000

              N      MEAN     STDEV   SE MEAN        T    P VALUE
LIV-KID       5   -0.0956    0.1278    0.0572    -1.67       0.17
LIV-GILL      4   -0.0635    0.0273    0.0137    -4.65      0.019
KID-GILL      4    0.0608    0.1535    0.0768     0.79       0.49

MTB > TINTERVAL 99% confidence using the differences in C10 C11 C12

              N      MEAN     STDEV  SE MEAN   99.0 PERCENT C.I.
LIV-KID       5   -0.0956    0.1278   0.0572  ( -0.3587  0.1675)
LIV-GILL      4   -0.0635    0.0273   0.0137  ( -0.1433  0.0163)
KID-GILL      4    0.0608    0.1535   0.0768  ( -0.3877  0.5092)
```

Note that suitable labels for the three differences clarify the output substantially. In the control fish, it appears that cadmium tends to concentrate more in the gill than in the liver. This was the only one of the three test results that showed a t-statistic significant at the 0.05 level. At the 99% confidence level, all three confidence intervals include zero — not surprising given the very small samples.

Review

In this tutorial you have learned how Minitab compares two population means. The TWOSAMPLE and TWOT commands compare independent samples, and TTEST and TINTERVAL handle comparisons for paired data. In each case, you can set the degree of confidence for the confidence intervals at will. There are also options for testing one- and two-tailed alternatives and for pooling or not pooling the sample variances.

List of Key Commands

Only two new MINITAB commands were introduced in this tutorial:

TWOSAMPLE	t test [K % confidence] using the data in C and C
TWOT	t test [K % confidence] using the data in C and identifier in C

Both TWOSAMPLE and TWOT have the following subcommands:

ALTERNATIVE	hypothesis code K
POOLED	sample variances

Practice Problems

1. Retrieve the Miami data set MIAMI.MTW and test whether females with jobs carry significantly fewer credit hours than females without jobs. Also, obtain a 98% confidence interval for this difference.
2. Use the statistics exam score data in EXAM.MTW to determine whether class performance was significantly different on the two exams. (Note that the data were entered in random sequence: the scores in a given row don't necessarily correspond to the same person.)
3. Retrieve the real estate data set (REALEST.MTW) and test whether the average selling price of a home in Oxford is less than the average asking price. Obtain a confidence interval for the difference in the means; use 97% confidence. Should you pair these data or not? What are the consequences of pairing?
4. Retrieve the fish-guarding data in GUARD.MTW and answer the questions that follow.
    a. For the pH 7.0 group, test whether the average time spent guarding the nest is the same for males and females. (You will have to create the sex variable. Refer to problem 2b in Tutorial 3.)
    b. Obtain an interval estimate of the difference between the average times that female and male fish spent guarding.
    c. For the male fish, test whether the pH level affects the mean time spent guarding the nest. Note that you will have to compare each pair of pH values to answer this question. You will

also have to manipulate the data to isolate the data on male fish in a separate column.

5. From the voice-training data (VOICE.MTW), determine whether the voice class helped the first person. The data for the first person are stored in columns 1 and 2. Why should you pair in this case?
6. Retrieve the fish aggression data from AGGRESS.MTW, and test whether the control fish differ significantly from the experimental fish in the average number of aggressive encounters per day. Note that the data on the five fish within each group are dependent, or paired. However, we want to determine if there are differences between the groups. How can you eliminate the dependency between the before and after scores and use this information to test the hypothesis?
7. Retrieve the introductory statistics course data in STA261.MTW and obtain a 95% confidence interval for the difference between the average exam score and the final exam score.

7 ▶ Analysis of Variance

Objectives

In this tutorial you will learn how to compare the means of several populations. The general technique is called analysis of variance, or ANOVA for short. You will learn how to use Minitab to:

1. compare the means of several populations in a one-way ANOVA
2. assess the effect of two factors on a mean response in a two-way ANOVA
3. check the assumptions of an ANOVA
4. output the information necessary to perform multiple comparisons of the means

Tutorials

Since you are probably getting tired of cadmium-laden fish, quiz scores, and female students in Miami, we'll try a couple of new data sets to illustrate the ANOVA techniques. The first data set has to do with different methods of controlling the speed of cars along a highway, and the second deals with determining the residual levels of the pesticide DDT in falcons.

Comparing the Means of Several Populations (AOVONEWAY, ONEWAY)

A traffic engineer wants to find the most effective way to control the speed of cars on a certain highway. The highway in question has a speed limit of 55 mph, and the engineer would like to investigate how well four speed-control methods work. In each case the speed limit is prominently displayed. The four methods are:

Method I	Only the speed limit signs are posted
Method II	"Speed Limit Strictly Enforced" signs are also posted
Method III	"Speed Radar Controlled" signs are posted
Method IV	An empty highway patrol car is parked on the side of the road

Radar speed measurements were taken on four randomly chosen Wednesdays. Only cars with out-of-state license plates were monitored: local drivers who are familiar with the route and speed limit might respond to their knowledge rather than to the experimental stimulus. The speeds of the out-of-state cars are given in Figure 7.1.

Figure 7.1 ▶

```
              METHOD
I          II          III          IV
--------------------------------------
72         61          60           55
55         60          55           52
63         54          62           62
61         55          53           54
74         69          49           55
52         58          66           50
56         66          62           58
67         73          55           55
68         68          53           48
68         53          59           62
71                     61           58
66
```

What method should the engineer recommend to the highway department to control the speed on this highway?

The first question of interest in this example takes the classic one-way ANOVA form: do the different speed-control methods result in different average speeds for cars on the highway? The engineer would like to implement the method that keeps the average speed closest to the posted speed.

These data have been stored on the Minitab disk in the file CARSPEED.MTW. Each column contains speed data gathered under one of the four traffic-control methods. We use the one-way ANOVA technique to determine whether the mean speeds differ significantly for the four methods.

Figure 7.2 displays a one-way ANOVA of the car speed data.

Figure 7.2 ▶

```
MTB > RETRIEVE 'CARSPEED'
MTB > AOVONEWAY of the car speed data in C1-C4

ANALYSIS OF VARIANCE
SOURCE      DF        SS        MS        F        p
FACTOR       3     555.4     185.1     5.12    0.004
ERROR       40    1447.7      36.2
TOTAL       43    2003.2
                                   INDIVIDUAL 95 PCT CI'S FOR MEAN
                                     BASED ON POOLED STDEV
LEVEL        N      MEAN     STDEV   -------+---------+---------+---------
METHOD 1    12    64.417     7.103                     (------*------)
METHOD 2    10    61.700     6.961               (------*-------)
METHOD 3    11    57.727     5.081        (------*-------)
METHOD 4    11    55.364     4.456   (-------*------)
                                     -------+---------+---------+---------
POOLED STDEV =     6.016                   55.0      60.0      65.0
```

The output from AOVONEWAY comes in four parts:

1. an ANOVA table, which includes the ANOVA F-test and its p-value
2. a descriptive summary (sample size, sample mean, and sample standard deviation) of each column identified on the AOVONEWAY command
3. a diagram of the 95% confidence interval for the mean of each column, based on the pooled standard deviation. The * shows the sample mean, and the ( ) represent the 95% confidence limits
4. the pooled standard deviation

The four speed-control methods do yield different average speeds, as the small ANOVA F-test p-value indicates. As a follow-up, we could apply any one of several multiple comparison methods to determine which means were different from one another. Although Minitab does not have any multiple comparison procedures programmed, the descriptive summary portion of the AOVONEWAY output does provide most of the information that you need to do the calculations by hand.

Although we do not present the results here, we used DOTPLOT to plot the four samples to check the assumptions of the ANOVA. The spread was roughly equal in the four plots, so we concluded that the assumption of homogeneity of variance is not seriously violated in these data. With such small samples, we could not say much about the assumption of normality.

If our CARSPEED data had been stored in stacked format, the appropriate Minitab command would have been ONEWAY. To illustrate, we now STACK the data and request that the subscripts be saved. We then use the ONEWAY command, with the results that appear in Figure 7.3.

Figure 7.3 ▶

```
MTB > RETRIEVE 'CARSPEED'

MTB > STACK the car speed data in C1 C2 C3 C4, store in C5;
SUBC> SUBSCRIPTS put into C6.
MTB > NAME C5 'SPEED' C6 'METHOD'
MTB > ONEWAY car speeds in C5 methods in C6 store resids in C7 fits in C8

ANALYSIS OF VARIANCE ON SPEED
SOURCE      DF       SS       MS        F        p
METHOD       3    555.4    185.1     5.12    0.004
ERROR       40   1447.7     36.2
TOTAL       43   2003.2
                                 INDIVIDUAL 95 PCT CI'S FOR MEAN
                                 BASED ON POOLED STDEV
LEVEL        N     MEAN    STDEV  -------+---------+---------+---------
    1       12   64.417    7.103                    (------*------)
    2       10   61.700    6.961               (------*-------)
    3       11   57.727    5.081         (------*-------)
    4       11   55.364    4.456  (-------*------)
                                  -------+---------+---------+---------
POOLED STDEV =     6.016                55.0      60.0      65.0
```

The ONEWAY output is identical to the AOVONEWAY output with the exception of two slight labelling differences. The source of variation label for the factor is the name of the subscript column and the summary levels are the values of the subscript column.

Unlike AOVONEWAY, ONEWAY gives you the option of computing and storing **fitted** and **residual values**.

Note that, to save the residuals, we had to specify an extra column in the ONEWAY command; the fitted values required yet another column. If you want to save the fitted values, you must also save the residuals.

The fitted values, in this context, are simply the means of the samples; the residual of each observation is computed by subtracting the corresponding fitted value (group mean) from the observation itself.

The residuals give us a way of testing the normality of the individual or pooled sample distributions. As Figure 7.4 illustrates, we first apply the NSCORE function to compute the normal scores of the residuals and then plot these normal scores against the residuals. For a numerical summary of the relationship, compute the correlation of the normal scores with the residuals.

Figure 7.4 ▶

```
MTB > NSCORES of resids in C7 store in C9
MTB > NAME C7 'RESIDS' C8 'FITS' C9 'NSCORES'
MTB > PLOT resids in C7 against the normal scores in C9

RESIDS  -
        -                                                        *
        -                                                   *
     8.0+                                                **   *
        -                                           ** 2
        -                                        2 *
        -                                   *2* 2
        -                                 *2
     0.0+                              * 3
        -                            ***
        -                        ***2
        -                    * 2
        -                   *
    -8.0+         *  ** **
        -       *
        -
        -  *
          --------+---------+---------+---------+---------+--------NSCORES
             -1.60     -0.80      0.00      0.80      1.60

MTB > CORR C7 and C9

Correlation of RESIDS and NSCORES = 0.993
```

If, as in Figure 7.4, the resulting graph is approximately a straight line, then the sample is approximately normally distributed. Likewise, if the correlation between the normal scores and the residuals is large, the data are approximately normal. (Critical values for the correlation can be found in the Minitab Reference Manual, release 6.1.)

The residuals also provide a convenient way to check the assumption that there are similar distributions in the four samples, ignoring the mean differences for which we are testing. Simply plot the residuals against the population identifier, as in Figure 7.5. The distributions of the four samples appear with their means aligned along the horizontal axis, and you can see clearly any substantial differences in variability or in general distribution shape. Analogous plots will be even more useful when we get to the two-way ANOVA.

Figure 7.5▶

```
MTB > PLOT the resids in C7 against the population identifier in C6

RESIDS   -
         -                   *
         -    *
      8.0+    *              *                *
         -    *              *                                 2
         -                   *                2
         -    3                               *                2
         -    *                               2
      0.0+                   *                                 3
         -    *              *                                 *
         -    *              *                2                *
         -                                    2                *
         -                   *
     -8.0+    *              2                *                *
         -    *
         -
         -    *
          ------+---------+---------+---------+---------+---------+METHOD
             1.20      1.80      2.40      3.00      3.60      4.20
```

Assessing the Effects of Two Factors on a Response (TWOWAY)

The pesticide DDT was used quite extensively in the United States during the 1950s and 1960s. Because of adverse environmental effects, it was banned here and in Canada in the 1970s, but is still being used in other countries. DDT is now showing up in measurable and unhealthy quantities in penguins in the Arctic region (and in the environment in general) since many Third World countries are still using it.

Peregrine falcons, which once ranged throughout North America, have been reduced in numbers by DDT. Many years after the banning of DDT, a zoologist wished to determine

1. whether DDT was still around, causing residual effects
2. whether DDT was particularly a problem in the Arctic region

He captured falcons and classified them with respect to their age (young, middle aged, or old). He hoped to find that the ban on DDT had resulted in lower concentrations of DDT in younger birds than in older ones.

He was also interested in learning the effect of different countries' pesticide policies on residual DDT concentrations, so he gathered data from three nesting areas: the United States, Canada, and the Arctic region.

The investigator captured three falcons from each age group within each nesting area, and measured the DDT concentration in parts per million (ppm) in the body of each of the 27 birds. This is a two-factor (3 x 3) study. Figure 7.6 displays his results.

Figure 7.6 ▶

```
            |              Site              |
            ----------------------------------
   Age      |    US    |  Canada  |  Arctic  |
----------------------------------------------
   Young    |  19  16  |  16  16  |  74  72  |
            |    17    |    13    |    69    |
----------------------------------------------
Middle Aged |  25  24  |  28  24  |  82   80 |
            |    29    |    26    |    80    |
----------------------------------------------
   Old      |  34  37  |  36  39  |  91  88  |
            |    36    |    37    |    90    |
----------------------------------------------
```

Is the average DDT concentration in the falcons different for the different sites and/or the different ages of birds?

Figure 7.7 presents the commands and output for an application of TWOWAY to the falcon data, which is stored in the file FALCON.MTW. The DDT concentrations measured in the 27 falcons are stored in column C1, the nesting site information in C2, and the age in C3.

Figure 7.7 ▶

```
MTB > RETRIEVE 'FALCON'

MTB> TWOWAY analysis of ddt levels in C1 and factors in C2 and C3 &
CONT > resids C4 fits C5;
SUBC> MEANS  of factor in C2 and factor in C3.

ANALYSIS OF VARIANCE  DDT

SOURCE         DF        SS        MS
SITE            2  17785.41   8892.70
AGE             2   1721.19    860.59
INTERACTION     4     17.70      4.43
ERROR          18     62.00      3.44
TOTAL          26  19586.30

                       Individual 95% CI
    SITE        Mean   ----+---------+---------+---------+-------
       1       26.33    (*
       2       26.11    *)
       3       80.67                                       (*)
                       ----+---------+---------+---------+-------
                       30.00     45.00     60.00     75.00

                       Individual 95% CI
     AGE        Mean   -----+---------+---------+---------+------
       1       34.67    (-*-)
       2       44.22                   (-*-)
       3       54.22                                  (-*--)
                       -----+---------+---------+---------+------
                        36.00     42.00     48.00     54.00
```

To invoke the TWOWAY command, you must specify the column in which the response data are stored, and the columns in which the factor values are stored.

If you want to store the residuals and fitted values, tell Minitab where to put them by specifying another column for each.

TWOWAY has two subcommands: MEANS and ADDITIVE.

- ▶ The MEANS subcommand tells Minitab to compute and display marginal (row and column) means and individual 95% confidence intervals for each factor whose column you specify in the subcommand.

- ▶ The ADDITIVE subcommand instructs Minitab to fit an additive, or no interaction, model.

TWOWAY requires balanced data. With three birds for each of the nine cells, the FALCON data set satisfies this requirement. If you try to apply TWOWAY to unbalanced data, Minitab will return an error message and will not perform the analysis.

TWOWAY does not compute F-test statistics and their corresponding p-values automatically, but it gives you all the information you need to compute the F statistics with LET and then look up the p-values with the CDF command, as illustrated in Figure 7.8. CDF provides cumulative probabilities for various distributions, and you can compute p-values from these. Tutorial 12 and the Command Reference section discuss CDF in more detail.

Figure 7.8 ▶

```
MTB > NAME C4 'RESIDS' C5 'FITS'
MTB > #
MTB > #  compute the appropriate F statistics and corresponding
MTB > #  p-values
MTB > #
MTB > LET K1=4.43/3.44       #  compute the interaction F statistic
MTB > CDF K1 K2;             #  compute the interaction p-value
SUBC>     F 4 18.
MTB > LET K2=1-K2
MTB > PRINT K1 K2            #  print interaction F and p-value
K1        1.28779
K2        0.311732
MTB > LET K3=8892.70/3.44    #  compute the site F statistic
MTB > CDF K3 K4;             #  compute the site p-value
SUBC>     F 2 18.
MTB > LET K4=1-K4
MTB > PRINT K3 K4            #  print site F and p-value
K3        2585.09
K4        0
MTB > LET K5=860.59/3.44     #  compute the age F statistic
MTB > CDF K5 K6;             #  compute the age p-value
SUBC>     F 2 18.
MTB > LET K6=1-K6
MTB > PRINT K5 K6            #  print the age F and p-value
K5        250.172
K6        0
```

We conclude that there is no significant interaction between the two factors, but that both factors are significant. The results of the MEANS subcommand indicates that the falcons of the Arctic region have DDT levels much higher than those of their cousins in the U. S. and Canada. In all three sites, moreover, older birds clearly have more DDT in their bodies than younger ones. These data don't tell us whether this is because DDT accumulates in a falcon's body throughout its life, or because DDT pollution has decreased in the environment over the lifetime of the birds now living, so that older falcons encountered more DDT in their youth.

We're now interested to know which of the group means in the study are significantly different from each other. The confidence interval display in Figure 7.7 makes the answer quite obvious, in a qualitative sense.

If you want to run quantitative comparisons, the TABLE command displays the statistics you will need. As illustrated, it tabulates a variety of descriptive statistics for each combination of values of the row and column variables that you specify. In Figure 7.9, we define the rows and columns by the values of the two factors, C2 and C3 respectively.

Figure 7.9 ▶

```
MTB > #
MTB > #  obtain summary information on the DDT values for each
MTB > #  site - age combination
MTB > #
MTB > TABLE of rows in C2 by columns in C3;
SUBC> STATS of ddt levels in C1.

 ROWS: SITE     COLUMNS: AGE

            1         2         3       ALL

  1         3         3         3         9
       17.333    26.000    35.667    26.333
        1.528     2.646     1.528     8.124

  2         3         3         3         9
       15.000    26.000    37.333    26.111
        1.732     2.000     1.528     9.791

  3         3         3         3         9
       71.667    80.667    89.667    80.667
        2.517     1.155     1.528     7.953

  ALL       9         9         9        27
       34.667    44.222    54.222    44.370
       27.821    27.390    26.626    27.447

  CELL CONTENTS --
                DDT:N
                    MEAN
                    STD DEV
```

You issue subcommands to specify what you want in the cells: MEANS, MEDIANS, SUMS, STDEV, N, NMISS (more are available. For a complete list of the available statistics, please consult the Command Reference section). We asked for STATS in Figure 7.9, which generated sample size, mean, and standard deviation for each cell of the table. You need these to apply any standard multiple-comparison technique to your data.

We have also saved the residuals and fitted values in columns C4 and C5, respectively. We haven't used them to check the assumptions of the ANOVA model as in the ONEWAY example, but we could have done so very easily. You may wish to extend the example for practice.

Since we're convinced that the two factors do not interact, we can gain some power in the ANOVA by leaving out the hypothesis that they do. This is the job of the ADDITIVE subcommand. The results appear in Figure 7.10.

Figure 7.10 ▶

```
MTB > TWOWAY of ddt in C1 factors in C2 C3;
SUBC> ADDITIVE.

ANALYSIS OF VARIANCE  DDT

SOURCE        DF         SS         MS
SITE           2   17785.41    8892.70
AGE            2    1721.19     860.59
ERROR         22      79.70       3.62
TOTAL         26   19586.30
```

The only difference in the output is that the "interaction" source of variation in the ANOVA table has been deleted. You'll also get different residuals and fitted values under the additive model. Verify this by printing and comparing the residuals and fitted values from the two models.

Review

In this tutorial you have learned how to do the calculations for an analysis of variance with one or two factors. Minitab does one-way ANOVA on data that is either stacked and labeled or stored as separate variables. Minitab can also fit a balanced two-way ANOVA model, including or excluding the interaction term at your option.

List of Key Commands

The following commands were introduced in this tutorial:

AOVONEWAY	of the data in C . . . C
ONEWAY	of data in C, factors in C, [store resids in C [fits in C]]

TWOWAY	of data in C, factors in C and C [store resids in C [fits in C]]

Subcommands:

MEANS	of factor C [and C]
ADDITIVE	model

TABLE	the data C . . . C

Subcommands:

MEAN	of the data in C for each cell
STDEV	of the data in C for each cell
N	of the data in C for each cell
STATS	for the data in C for each cell

See the reference section for a complete list of subcommands available with TABLE.

Practice Problems

1. Retrieve the real estate data from REALEST.MTW.
   a. Determine whether the average selling price differs for homes with different numbers of bedrooms.
   b. Redo part a, determining whether the price depends on the number of baths. (Hint: use LET to transform C3.)
2. Use the Miami data set to determine if the average number of sibs (brothers *and* sisters) differs for the different religions.
3. Use the fish-guarding time data (GUARD.MTW) to answer the questions that follow.
   a. Compare the four pH levels and determine if the pH of the water affects the average time spent guarding.
   b. Determine whether sex and pH affect the average time spent guarding.
   c. Look only at the pH 7.0 data and determine whether the day and sex affect the average time spent guarding. Recall that the first 10 observations in the pH 7.0 column are the male fish averages on day 1 through day 10. The last 10 observations are the female data for those 10 days.

4. Retrieve the STA261.MTW data.

   a. Test whether the students performed differently on the three exams. For this question and part b, assume that the samples are independent, even though the same student took the quizzes, exams, and final, and hence, the data are really paired in nature.

   b. Compute each student's average quiz score as a percentage. Determine whether the students performed differently on the quizzes, the three exams, and the final.

8 ▶ Regression

Objectives

In this tutorial you will learn to use Minitab's regression features to investigate relationships among variables, particularly those relationships that enable you to predict a variable from one or more others. You will

1. apply simple linear regression to investigate the form of a linear relationship between two variables
2. apply multiple regression to investigate the form of the linear relationship between one variable and several other variables
3. perform stepwise regression to explore the relative importance of predictor variables

Tutorials

To illustrate the regression techniques that are available with Minitab, we will apply them to the exam (EXAM.MTW) and real estate (REALEST.MTW) data sets.

Fitting a Straight Line to Data: Simple Linear Regression (REGRESS)

Suppose that we want to know whether the results of the two exam grades in EXAM.MTW are linearly related. Back in Tutorial 4 (Practice Problem 1.b), we asked you and Minitab to compute the correlation between the two exam results. If you collaborated effectively, you obtained a value of 0.586, which represents a moderate degree of positive linear relation between the two exam scores. We now investigate the form of the linear relationship between the two variables with simple linear regression.

The Minitab command to perform a simple linear regression (or a multiple regression, for that matter) is called REGRESS. To invoke the REGRESS command, you must give Minitab three pieces of information, in exactly the following sequence:

1. where the dependent variable is stored
2. how many independent variables there are
3. in which columns the independent variables are stored

Figure 8.1 shows you the REGRESS command format and its default output. You don't have to receive all this output, if you don't want it; later on, we'll illustrate the BRIEF command.

Figure 8.1 ▶

```
MTB > RETRIEVE 'EXAM'

MTB > REGRESS 'EXAM 2' on 1 predictor in 'EXAM 1'

The regression equation is
EXAM 2 = 56.2 + 0.344 EXAM 1

Predictor        Coef        Stdev     t-ratio        p
Constant        56.25        16.22        3.47    0.013
EXAM 1         0.3440       0.1944        1.77    0.127

s = 6.846       R-sq = 34.3%       R-sq(adj) = 23.3%

Analysis of Variance

SOURCE        DF          SS          MS         F        p
Regression     1      146.70      146.70      3.13    0.127
Error          6      281.18       46.86
Total          7      427.87
```

Minitab first presents the estimated regression equation. If you substitute a student's EXAM 1 score into this regression equation, the result is a prediction of that student's score on EXAM 2. It is also an estimate of the mean of the EXAM 2 score for all students having that EXAM 1 score.

The table following the estimated regression equation contains the estimate for each of the regression coefficients, their estimated standard deviations, and the t-statistics and p-values for testing whether the coefficient is different from zero. We conclude that the second exam score does not depend on the first exam.

The next line of statistics includes:

- the estimated standard deviation of the regression line
- the R-squared value, or coefficient of determination
- the adjusted R-squared

Finally, Minitab presents the significance test for the regression in an ANOVA form, with an F-statistic and p-value as before.

The simple linear regression analysis speaks only to the possibility of a linear relationship. Of course, the two exam results might be related in some nonlinear manner.

You could investigate this possibility by plotting the data (always a wise idea whenever performing a regression).

Figure 8.2

```
MTB > BRIEF output level 3
MTB > REGRESS 'EXAM 2' on 1 predictor in 'EXAM 1'

The regression equation is
EXAM 2 = 56.2 + 0.344 EXAM 1

Predictor        Coef        Stdev     t-ratio        p
Constant        56.25        16.22        3.47    0.013
EXAM 1         0.3440       0.1944        1.77    0.127

s = 6.846        R-sq = 34.3%      R-sq(adj) = 23.3%

Analysis of Variance

SOURCE        DF          SS          MS         F        p
Regression     1      146.70      146.70      3.13    0.127
Error          6      281.18       46.86
Total          7      427.87

Obs.  EXAM 1     EXAM 2       Fit  Stdev.Fit  Residual    St.Resid
  1     89.0      83.00     86.86       2.73     -3.86       -0.61
  2     56.0      77.00     75.51       5.69      1.49        0.39
  3     78.0      91.00     83.08       2.57      7.92        1.25
  4     88.0      87.00     86.52       2.65      0.48        0.08
  5     94.0      99.00     88.58       3.29     10.42        1.74
  6     87.0      80.00     86.17       2.57     -6.17       -0.97
  7     96.0      85.00     89.27       3.57     -4.27       -0.73
  8     72.0      75.00     81.01       3.17     -6.01       -0.99
```

Figure 8.2 illustrates additional output you can get by issuing the BRIEF level 3 command in conjunction with the REGRESS command. Minitab offers three levels of brevity:

Level 1 provides the smallest amount of output
Level 2 is the default value, illustrated in Figure 8.1
Level 3 generates the most complete report, as in Figure 8.2

Note that once you have issued the BRIEF command, the level of output remains in effect until you STOP, RESTART, or issue a different BRIEF command.

In addition, BRIEF 3 provides, for each case in the data base:

- the independent (predictor) value — here, the EXAM 1 score
- the observed dependent (response) score — here, the EXAM 2 score
- the fitted or predicted value, that is, the estimated mean value of EXAM 2 calculated from the EXAM 1 score and the regression equation
- the standard error of the fitted value
- the residual
- the standardized residual

As in ANOVA, you can store the residuals and fitted values for further analysis and display. When issuing the REGRESS command, simply specify one extra column for the standardized residuals and another (optionally) for the fitted or predicted values. If you want to save the fitted values, you must save the standardized residuals as well, but you can save the residuals alone.

You can use the standardized residuals and fitted values to check the assumptions of the regression analysis, much as in the analysis of variance in the previous tutorial. If you have saved the fitted values, then you can use MPLOT to plot the observed and fitted data on the same graph to see how well the line fits the data.

Multiple Regression (REGRESS)

To illustrate Minitab's multiple regression features, we will apply REGRESS to the real estate data in REALEST.MTW and try to determine which of the variables in the data set predict the selling price of a home.

To run a multiple regression, simply specify several predictors when issuing your REGRESS command. Before you indicate the columns in which the predictors are stored, you must tell Minitab how many of them to expect. Figure 8.3 presents some of the commands and output for the multiple regression analysis of the real estate data. We will only investigate the continuous independent variables in this data set.

Figure 8.3 ▶

```
MTB > RETRIEVE 'REALEST'

MTB > BRIEF output level 2
MTB > LET C1=C1/1000
MTB > LET C2=C2/1000
MTB > REGRESS 'SELL $' on 5 independent variables in C2 C3 C4 C5 C7

The regression equation is
SELL $ = 6.36 + 0.712 ASK $ + 2.79 BATHS + 0.22 BEDROOMS - 0.111 AGE
           + 3.37 CARS

43 cases used 8 cases contain missing values

Predictor         Coef        Stdev    t-ratio        p
Constant         6.364        3.269       1.95    0.059
ASK $          0.71242      0.03433      20.75    0.000
BATHS            2.786        1.774       1.57    0.125
BEDROOMS         0.217        1.068       0.20    0.840
AGE           -0.11065      0.02948      -3.75    0.001
CARS            3.3746       0.8318       4.06    0.000

s = 4.045        R-sq = 96.5%     R-sq(adj) = 96.0%

Analysis of Variance

SOURCE       DF          SS          MS         F         p
Regression    5     16694.1      3338.8    204.09     0.000
Error        37       605.3        16.4
Total        42     17299.4

SOURCE       DF      SEQ SS
ASK $         1     15901.3
BATHS         1       369.0
BEDROOMS      1         7.3
AGE           1       147.3
CARS          1       269.2

Unusual Observations
Obs.    ASK $     SELL $        Fit Stdev.Fit   Residual    St.Resid
  1        60     55.500     45.837     1.542      9.663       2.58R
 22        50     33.500     42.033     1.279     -8.533      -2.22R
 43       170    125.000    132.565     3.330     -7.565      -3.30RX
 46        98     95.000     91.556     2.828      3.444       1.19 X

R denotes an obs. with a large st. resid.
X denotes an obs. whose X value gives it large influence.
```

In preparation for the multiple regression exercise, we set the BRIEF level to 2 (the default). We also scaled the asking and selling prices (C1 and C2) from dollars ($) to thousands of dollars ($K) to avoid introducing unnecessary roundoff errors into the analysis.

Multiple regression output from REGRESS is somewhat similar to its simple regression counterpart. The output includes:

- the estimated regression equation, with a summary of missing data (REGRESS ignores cases (rows) with missing values.)
- the coefficient table, which displays each predictor's coefficient estimate, standard deviation, t-test, and p-value
- summary information on the standard deviation about the regression surface, R-squared, and adjusted R-squared values
- the ANOVA table
- the sequential sum of squares table

  Each 'SEQ SS' represents the reduction in the sum of squared error (SSE) that results from adding an independent variable to the regression equation, which already includes all predictors above the current one in the table.

  The independent variables enter the sequential list in the order that you listed them in the REGRESS command. If you are interested in the contributions of the predictors taken in a particular order, follow that order in issuing the REGRESS command.
- a table of unusual observations in the data set (An observation can be unusual in either or both of two ways: as an outlier, or as an influence point.)

These are interesting results. First, we note that the five predictors account for 96% of the variance in the selling price. It's not surprising, for example, that asking price is a good indicator of selling price. Even with that taken into account, though, some of the remaining variables make a contribution.

The results seem to indicate that the selling price can be predicted from the asking price, the age of the house, and the size of the garage (CARS). Given these variables, the number of bedrooms and baths appear not to add to our ability to predict the selling price of a home. Several subcommands are associated with the REGRESS command; the Reference Section discusses them in operational detail.

- NOCONSTANT causes Minitab to delete the intercept from the regression equation, forcing the regression line through the origin.
- COEFFICIENTS C requests that the estimated coefficients be stored in the column C.
- RESIDUALS C stores the residuals in the column C.
- DW requests that the Durbin-Watson statistic for checking serial correlation in the data be output.
- PREDICT orders up predicted values and 95% confidence and prediction intervals for a given set of independent variable values. You can issue a PREDICT subcommand for each set of Xs for which you wish to predict, up to ten within any REGRESS operation, or you can include X values in one or several columns.

Variable Selection in Regression (STEPWISE)

With its STEPWISE command, Minitab offers several related variable-selection procedures. All have the same goal: to select from a large set of candidates the independent variables that, taken together, best predict the dependent variable.

By specifying different subcommands in association with the STEPWISE command you can do

1. a general stepwise selection, in which predictors can be removed or added at each step
2. a forward variable selection, in which independent variables can only be added to the equation
3. backward elimination, in which independent variables can only be removed from the equation

As you know, Minitab is an interactive program. That is, you get your results right after typing the command. However, STEPWISE is even more interactive in that you can modify the regression equation by adding or deleting independent variables during the execution of the command.

STEPWISE will stop and ask you if you want to change the current regression equation after it goes through the current default number of steps. The default depends on width of the output device and will be a number around 7. If you want control after each step, use the STEP = 1 subcommand, and you will be able to enter or remove variables after each step.

STEPWISE has many subcommands, more than we have space to detail here. We will illustrate the most important ones; when you have mastered them, you will be able to do forward and backward selection.

First, however, we will illustrate the stepwise variable selection method itself by applying it to the real estate data. Figure 8.4 displays Minitab commands and output to perform a stepwise regression.

Figure 8.4 ▶

```
MTB > STEPWISE y var in C1, the x vars in C2 C3 C4 C5 C7

STEPWISE REGRESSION OF  SELL $  ON  5 PREDICTORS, WITH N =   43
 N(CASES WITH MISSING OBS.) =    8 N(ALL CASES) =    51

    STEP         1        2        3        4        5
CONSTANT    6.4188   0.6128  -0.5208   6.6762   9.3907

ASK $        0.819    0.736    0.744    0.715    0.737
T-RATIO      21.59    18.66    20.29    22.32    24.61

BATHS                   7.1      5.3      2.9
T-RATIO                3.79     2.88     1.70

CARS                             2.57     3.39     3.95
T-RATIO                          2.76     4.14     5.15

AGE                                     -0.108   -0.125
T-RATIO                                  -4.00    -4.84

S             5.84     5.07     4.70     3.99     4.09
R-SQ         91.92    94.05    95.02    96.50    96.23

MORE? (YES,  NO,  SUBCOMMAND,  OR HELP)
SUBC> NO
```

The STEPWISE output is not quite as extensive as the REGRESS output, but it is not meant to provide as much detail. We are focusing here on determining which variables are important. Once we have determined which independent variables to concentrate on, we can run a full regression to get more detail.

The five numbered columns of Figure 8.4 describe five **steps**. At each step, STEPWISE adds or deletes a predictor.

Step 1

Minitab adds the asking price variable to the prediction equation.* With only this variable and the intercept in the equation, the constant term is 6.4188 and the regression coefficient is 0.819, with a (huge) t-value of 21.59. If you were to stop here, you could translate the prediction equation as, "I predict that the selling price of a house in this market will be $6,418.80 plus 81.9% of the asking price." At the bottom of the column appear summary statistics of the fit of the regression equation (the estimated standard deviation of the regression line and the R-square value, 5.84 and 91.92%, respectively).

Step 2

The variable BATHS enters the model. R-squared goes up, as it must, and s goes down a little, indicating that the new variable does indeed improve prediction. The equation is now

SELL $ = 0.6128 + (0.736 * ASK $) + (7.1 * BATHS)

Step 3

CARS (size of garage). The R-squared value goes up and S goes down; our equation is now

SELL $ = −0.5208 + (0.744 * ASK $) + (5.3 * BATHS) + (2.57 * CARS)

Step 4

AGE enters as a negative factor: the older your house, other things being equal, the less you'll get for it.

Step 5

BATHS has now become nonsignificant, and so at Step 5 it is deleted from the equation.

At this point STEPWISE pauses to ask you whether you want to do any more to the equation. You can now

*Unless you issue the NOCONSTANT command before STEPWISE, the equation will always contain a constant term for the intercept. While NOCONSTANT is in effect, all REGRESS and STEPWISE operations will not include an intercept term. The R-square value will also not be printed on any output, since its interpretation is difficult when the regression line is forced to pass through the origin.

- add a variable with the ENTER subcommand
- take one out with the REMOVE subcommand
- respond YES to ask STEPWISE to continue where it left off
- respond NO to end the STEPWISE procedure

The stepwise output indicates that, after the asking price, the size of the garage, and the age have been included in the equation, the other variables do not add much to it.

Figure 8.5

```
MTB > STEPWISE y var in C1, the x vars in C2 C3 C4 C5 C7;
SUBC> FREMOVE = 0.

 STEPWISE REGRESSION OF  SELL $  ON  5 PREDICTORS, WITH N =   43
 N(CASES WITH MISSING OBS.) =   8 N(ALL CASES) =   51

    STEP        1        2        3        4
CONSTANT   6.4188   0.6128  -0.5208   6.6762

ASK $       0.819    0.736    0.744    0.715
T-RATIO     21.59    18.66    20.29    22.32

BATHS                  7.1      5.3      2.9
T-RATIO               3.79     2.88     1.70

CARS                           2.57     3.39
T-RATIO                        2.76     4.14

AGE                                   -0.108
T-RATIO                                -4.00

S            5.84     5.07     4.70     3.99
R-SQ        91.92    94.05    95.02    96.50

MORE? (YES,  NO,  SUBCOMMAND,  OR HELP)
SUBC> NO
```

In Figure 8.5, we use the real estate data to show how STEPWISE can be used to perform a forward variable selection. In forward mode, STEPWISE will not remove any predictor: once it is in the equation, it is there to stay. At each step, therefore, a variable can only be added to the equation.

To have STEPWISE perform a forward selection we simply set an unachievable criterion for predictor deletion. The FREMOVE subcommand tells Minitab not to delete a predictor until its F-value drops below zero. Since an F-ratio is the ratio of two sums of squares, this won't happen.

The results are the same as those in Figure 8.4 except that there is no step 5.

Finally, Figure 8.6 illustrates the backward selection procedure. The idea here is to start with all potential independent variables in the equation and then to drop, one at a time, those variables that are not significant. We also want to prevent any deleted variable from reentering the equation.

Figure 8.6 ▶

```
MTB > STEPWISE y var in C1, the x vars in C2 C3 C4 C5 C7;
SUBC> FENTER = 100000;
SUBC> ENTER C2 C3 C4 C5 C7.

 STEPWISE REGRESSION OF  SELL $  ON  5 PREDICTORS, WITH N =   43
 N(CASES WITH MISSING OBS.) =    8 N(ALL CASES) =   51

    STEP         1        2        3
CONSTANT     6.364    6.676    9.391

ASK $        0.712    0.715    0.737
T-RATIO      20.75    22.32    24.61

BATHS          2.8      2.9
T-RATIO       1.57     1.70

BEDROOMS       0.2
T-RATIO       0.20

AGE         -0.111   -0.108   -0.125
T-RATIO      -3.75    -4.00    -4.84

CARS          3.37     3.39     3.95
T-RATIO       4.06     4.14     5.15

S             4.04     3.99     4.09
R-SQ         96.50    96.50    96.23
MORE? (YES,  NO,  SUBCOMMAND,  OR HELP)
SUBC> NO
```

The ENTER and FENTER subcommands control the operation. With ENTER, we put all the independent variables into the equation at step 1. We then set the FENTER value impossibly high (FENTER 100000), so that no previously deleted variable will re-enter the equation.

Figure 8.6 shows the result. Note that the order of subcommands is not important.

All variables are in the equation at step 1. Then at each subsequent step the least significant variable is dropped until all the remaining variables are significant. At step 2, the least significant variable, BEDROOMS, is dropped. At step 3, the least significant variable of those remaining is dropped, in this case BATHS. After dropping BATHS all of the remaining variables are judged to be significant and the process ends.

Review

In this tutorial, you have seen Minitab's regression commands. The REGRESS command is used to obtain detailed information on the form of the regression equation, whether it is a simple linear regression or a more complex multiple regression. You have also seen how the STEPWISE command can be used to perform a stepwise, forward selection stepwise, or backward elimination stepwise regression.

List of Key Commands

The commands used in this tutorial are:

REGRESS the y variable in C on the K predictors in C . . . C [store the standardized residuals in C [store the fitted or predicted values in C]]

Subcommands:

NOCONSTANT	(use no intercept for this regression only)
COEFFICIENTS	store in C
PREDICT	using E . . . E
RESIDUALS	store in C
DW	statistic

STEPWISE	regression y in C, predictors in C . . . C
Subcommands:	
FENTER	f value to enter predictor is K (default 4)
FREMOVE	f value to remove predictor is K (default 4)
FORCE	predictors C . . . C into the equation
ENTER	predictors C . . . C into the equation
REMOVE	predictors C . . .C from the equation
BEST	K alternative predictors (default is 0)
STEPS	between user interaction is K (default depends on output width)
NOCONSTANT	use no intercept in any following regression or stepwise commands
CONSTANT	use intercept in all following regression and stepwise commands
BRIEF	output level is K (default is 2)

Practice Problems

1. In the Miami data set (MIAMI.MTW), investigate more fully, using regression, the relationship between Miami females' height and weight. (Which of the two variables should you use as the dependent variable?)

2. Use the first grader data (1STGRADE.MTW) to estimate the relationship between the heights and weights of first graders. Which is the dependent variable? How strong is the relationship? Is the relationship significant? What other variables might also affect the dependent variable?

3. Use the fish nest-guarding time data in GUARD.MTW to investigate how the guarding times changed over the 10-day period. Remember that the first 10 observations are the averages for the male fish on days 1 through 10, and that the second 10 observations in the column are the averages for the female fish. Use only the guarding data for the third group — the pH 6.0 group — in column C3.

    a. Create a new variable for the day, coded 1 through 10. Use the SET command and either type in the 20 values or use the parentheses ( ) and colon : options of the SET command. Plot the guarding times against the day and regress the guarding times on the day. What do you conclude?

b. Create a variable corresponding to sex and use LPLOT to plot the guarding times against the day separately for each sex. Is the relationship between the time spent guarding and day the same for both sexes? Are the slopes the same for both sexes?

4. Regress the percentage of mud values in the file COREDATA.MTW against the depth values. Is there anything of interest? Now plot the data. Can you explain what happened? What kind of relation exists?

5. Regress the home sales data in HOMESALE.MTW against month. (You will have to create the month variable.) What do you conclude? Plot the data and connect the points on the graph using a pen. What kind of relationship do we have here?

6. Use the STA261 data set and multiple regression to determine which of the quiz and exam scores are related to the final exam score.

7. Use the three stepwise procedures from the tutorial to rework problem 6. Do the three procedures yield the same results? Would you expect them to?

8. Recall the blood pressure data from Tutorial 1. Use these data, stored in BPRES.MTW, to determine which of the three variables most affects blood pressure. Use stepwise selection to determine the best equation. Use forward selection and backward selection on the data. Are your equations the same?

9 ▶ Categorical Data Analysis

Objectives

In this tutorial you will learn how Minitab analyzes categorical or nonnumeric data. You will learn how to use Minitab to:

1. perform a chi-square goodness-of-fit test
2. perform a chi-square test of independence between categorical variables in a contingency table supplied by the user
3. perform a chi-square test of independence between categorical variables using raw data

Tutorials

In the tutorials that follow, we will examine the MIAMI.MTW data set, which offers several categorical variables.

Comparing an Observed Distribution to an Expected Distribution

In Tutorial 4 we used the TALLY command to obtain the observed distribution of hair colors in our sample of female students in Miami. We observed that, out of the 83 females, 59 had brown hair, 3 had black hair, 17 were blonde, and 4 were redheads. What can we infer from these data about the distribution of hair color in that population? Specifically, how likely is it that the observed data were drawn from a population in which the four hair colors occur uniformly?

If the distribution of hair color among Miami females were uniform, then we would expect about 83/4 or approximately 21 of each hair color in our sample. Minitab does not have a specific program to perform the chi-square goodness-of-fit test, but you have already encountered all the commands you will need to put it together. Figure 9.1 illustrates the process.

Figure 9.1 ▶

```
MTB > SET the hair color distribution into C1 # input cell observed frequencies
DATA> 59 3 17 4
DATA> END
MTB > SET the expected frequencies into C2 # input cell expected frequencies
DATA> 20.75 20.75 20.75 20.75
DATA> END
MTB > LET C3=(C1-C2)**2/C2  # compute cell chi square values
MTB > NAME C1 'OBS' C2 'EXPCTED' C3 'CHISQR'
MTB > SUM the values in C3 and store in K1 # compute chi square GOF statistic
   SUM     =       99.892
MTB > CDF of K1 store in K2;
SUBC>      CHISQUARE with 3 df.
MTB > LET K2=1-K2    # compute the p-value
MTB > PRINT C1-C3 K1 K2
K1        99.8916
K2        0

 ROW   OBS  EXPCTED    CHISQR

   1    59    20.75   70.5090
   2     3    20.75   15.1837
   3    17    20.75    0.6777
   4     4    20.75   13.5211
```

To perform the calculations of the chi-square goodness-of-fit test, as Figure 9.1 illustrates:

- SET the observed frequencies in one column and the expected frequencies in another. We could have Minitab compute the expected frequencies (assuming a **uniform** distribution) with the commands

▶
```
MTB > LET K1 = SUM(C1)/4
MTB > PRINT K1
```

- LET Minitab compute each cell's contribution to the chi-square statistic. As you can see, this contribution is the squared difference between the observed and expected values, divided by the expected value.
- SUM the four cell values, storing the total chi-square value, and finally
- Invoke CDF to look up the test statistic in a table and determine its p-value. The chi-square value of 99.8916 is highly significant, with

three degrees of freedom. We would conclude that it is unlikely that the observed hair-color distribution came from a uniform distribution.

Testing for a Relationship Between Two Categorical Variables in a Contingency Table (CHISQUARE)

Let's extend the idea in the previous tutorial one step and ask the question "Are hair and eye colors related in some manner?" Are blondes, for example, more likely to have blue eyes, or doesn't it matter?

We now ask whether two categorical variables are related; to answer the question we rely upon the chi-square test of independence.

For the MIAMI.MTW data, the observed frequencies are as shown in Figure 9.2.

Figure 9.2 ▶

```
Hair     |           Eye Color
Color    | Brown        Blue        Green
---------|----------------------------
Brown    |  23          21           15
Black    |   3           0            0
Blonde   |   1           9            7
Red      |   2           1            1
```

We could either SET this table into columns C1, C2, and C3 or READ the 4 rows into 3 columns C1 to C3 (as in Figure 9.3). Either way, once the table of observed frequencies is stored in this fashion, Minitab is ready to apply the CHISQUARE command.

Figure 9.3 ▶

```
MTB > READ C1-C3
DATA> 23 21 15
DATA> 3 0 0
DATA> 1 9 7
DATA> 2 1 1
DATA> END
      4 ROWS READ
MTB > CHISQUARE of the table stored in C1-C3

Expected counts are printed below observed counts

            C1        C2        C3    Total
    1       23        21        15       59
         20.61     22.04     16.35

    2        3         0         0        3
          1.05      1.12      0.83

    3        1         9         7       17
          5.94      6.35      4.71

    4        2         1         1        4
          1.40      1.49      1.11

Total       29        31        23       83

ChiSq =  0.276 +  0.049 +  0.111 +
         3.634 +  1.120 +  0.831 +
         4.108 +  1.107 +  1.112 +
         0.260 +  0.163 +  0.011 = 12.783
df = 6
* WARNING * 1 cells with expected counts less than 1.0
          * Chisquare approximation probably invalid
7 cells with expected counts less than 5.0

MTB > CDF 12.78 store in K1;
SUBC> CHISQUARE with 6 df.
MTB > LET K1=1-K1
MTB > PRINT K1
K1        0.0465848
```

The output from CHISQUARE is fairly self explanatory. It includes:

- the table of observed and expected frequencies, with the expected frequency displayed below the observed in each cell
- row and column totals

- the table of cell chi-square values and the total chi-square statistic, with its degrees of freedom. Minitab also issues a standard warning that some expected cell frequencies are small.

To get the p-value, we resort once more to the CDF table look-up routine. The p-value of 0.046 is too marginal to resolve for all time the question of whether hair and eye color are related.

If we were eager to pursue the question further, we could either beef up the overall sample or collapse categories in the table so that the expected cell frequencies are adequate. If we were to collapse hair color into two groups, brown and other, the expected frequencies would probably be sufficient. We leave this for the reader as an exercise.

Testing for a Relationship Between Two Categorical Variables Using Raw Data (TABLE)

You don't have to give Minitab the contingency table through the keyboard in order to carry out a chi-square test of independence. You can just tell Minitab where the raw data are stored, and Minitab will count up the observed frequencies and compile the table from the raw data.

In the MIAMI.MTW data set, the data for hair and eye color are stored in columns C1 and C2. Each column includes 83 values. To collapse these data into the required table of observed frequencies and to compute the chi-square test, we call on the TABLE command (introduced in Tutorial 7), and invoke the CHISQUARE subcommand; the results appear in Figure 9.4.

Figure 9.4 ▶

```
MTB > RETRIEVE 'MIAMI'

MTB > TABLE the data in C1 and C2;
SUBC> CHISQUARE output code 3.

 ROWS: HAIR      COLUMNS: EYE

              1         2         3       ALL

  1          23        21        15        59
          20.61     22.04     16.35     59.00
           0.53     -0.22     -0.33        --

  2           3         0         0         3
           1.05      1.12      0.83      3.00
           1.91     -1.06     -0.91        --

  3           1         9         7        17
           5.94      6.35      4.71     17.00
          -2.03      1.05      1.05        --

  4           2         1         1         4
           1.40      1.49      1.11      4.00
           0.51     -0.40     -0.10        --

 ALL         29        31        23        83
          29.00     31.00     23.00     83.00
             --        --        --        --

CHI-SQUARE =     12.783    WITH D.F. =    6

  CELL CONTENTS --
                  COUNT
                  EXP FREQ
                  STD RES

MTB > CDF 12.783 store in K1;
SUBC> CHISQUARE with 6 df.
MTB > LET K1=1-K1
MTB > PRINT K1
K1        0.0465335
```

The chi-square statistic is of course the same as the one we got from CHISQUARE, and our conclusions remain unchanged.

The format of the output is slightly different.

- The table of observed and expected frequencies includes the cell residual, defined as

$$\text{cell residual} = \frac{(\text{observed} - \text{expected})}{\sqrt{\text{expected}}}$$

  which is the square root of the cell chi-square, with the appropriate sign attached.
- As before, the total chi-square statistic and degrees of freedom appears, but not the p-value. Again we can easily get that from the CDF command.
- Note also that the TABLE command with the CHISQUARE subcommand does not issue the warning about small expected frequencies that we got from the CHISQUARE command. This does not mean that the problem has gone away, only that the warning is not a feature of TABLE.

With the CHISQUARE subcommand, we specified output level 3 to get the most output. Output level 1 (the default value) displays only the observed frequencies, the total chi-square statistic, and the degrees of freedom. Output level 2 adds the expected frequencies under the assumption that the two variables are independent. Level 3, as we see above, adds the cell residuals.

The TABLE command can handle more than two columns of categorical variables. If you specify more than two columns, Minitab forms the table from the first two columns and then performs a separate chi-square test of independence for each distinct combination of values in the remaining columns, called "control" columns.

Review

In this tutorial you have seen two major approaches to the analysis of categorical data: the chi-square goodness-of-fit test and the chi-square test of independence. For the chi-square goodness-of-fit test, you had to combine several Minitab commands to do the calculations and look up the p-value of the final test statistic. Minitab has specific commands for the chi-square test of independence.

It's useful to remember that Minitab's many convenient "canned" routines are there to make life easy for you, not to limit your freedom of movement. When you want to go beyond the limits of REGRESS,

CHISQUARE or ONEWAY, Minitab's basic data-manipulation features usually offer at least one way to do it in an interactive fashion. Think of Minitab as a programming language, similar to BASIC or FORTRAN.

List of Key Commands

The commands used in this tutorial were:

CHISQUARE	analysis of the table in C . . . C
TABLE	the data in C . . . C

Subcommands:

CHISQUARE	output level K

Practice Problems

1. Redo the chi-square test of independence in Figure 9.2 after collapsing the hair color data into two categories: brown and other.
2. Redo the chi-square test of independence in Figure 9.3 after coding the hair color data into two categories: brown and other.
3. In the MIAMI.MTW data, determine whether birth months are uniformly distributed among the twelve months.
4. Use the Miami data (MIAMI.MTW) to determine if females in a sorority are more likely than others to have a boyfriend.
5. Are Miami females who smoke more likely to drink also?
6. Redo Problem 5 and control for sorority membership.
7. The following data set looked at approximately 1,400 college freshmen who averaged at least a C in high school. Their high school and first-year college averages were recorded as a grade. The results are summarized in Figure 9.5.

Figure 9.5 ▶

```
High School  |      College Grade
Grade        |    A       B       C
-----------------------------------
A            |  219     273      79
B            |  149     161     184
C            |   41     103     179
```

Are high school and college freshman performances related?

8. In the real estate data set (REALEST.MTW), determine whether the number of baths was related to the number of bedrooms for homes sold in Oxford.

10 ▶ Nonparametric Analysis

Objectives

In this tutorial you will be exposed to several of the nonparametric statistical methods that Minitab offers. Specifically, you will learn how to

1. test whether a sample was drawn at random
2. analyze the central tendency of one population with the sign and Wilcoxon signed-rank procedures
3. compare the medians of two populations for equality with the Mann-Whitney procedure
4. compare the medians of k populations with the Kruskal-Wallis test
5. sort and rank columns of data

Tutorials

Minitab offers several nonparametric procedures. We will document only a few here, selecting the ones that parallel closely the parametric procedures we have already illustrated. For details on the others, which include some very elegant and advanced applications, please consult the Command Reference section.

Checking a Sample for Randomness with the Runs Test (RUNS)

With the RUNS test, you can check a sample to see whether its pattern of "runs" (groups of consecutive numbers either greater than, less than, or equal to a given number) is consistent with the assertion that it is a random sequence. We'll apply it to the number of homes sold by a local real estate company over the past several years. The monthly data are stored in HOMESALE.MTW on the Minitab disk.

There's nothing random about the way these data were gathered, of course; we plotted them as a time series in Tutorial 3 and observed that the plot had many peaks and valleys, as a random sequence might, but that it displayed something like an annual cycle — a very nonrandom feature.

Figure 10.1 ▶

```
MTB > RETRIEVE 'HOMESALE'

MTB > RUNS test using the data in 'SOLD'

    SOLD

    K =      6.8085


    THE OBSERVED NO. OF RUNS =  23
    THE EXPECTED NO. OF RUNS =  24.4043
    22 OBSERVATIONS ABOVE K   25 BELOW
              THE TEST IS SIGNIFICANT AT  0.6776
              CANNOT REJECT AT ALPHA = 0.05
```

In Figure 10.1 we retrieve the HOMESALE.MTW data set and exercise the RUNS command. Unless you specify a different value, Minitab checks runs above and below the mean of the data. Minitab assumes that the data were entered in the order in which they were collected. The issue is whether the sequence of collection can pass as random.

The home-sale series includes 23 runs, as you can verify from Figure 3.7 in Tutorial 3. Draw in the horizontal line corresponding to the mean, 6.8085, and count the runs. In a random sample of 47 observations, Minitab says one would expect 24 runs: not significantly different (p-value = 0.6776) from what we observe. Based on the runs test, we cannot prove that it is not a random series.

Comparing One Sample's Median to a Constant with the Sign or Wilcoxon Signed-Rank Procedures (STEST, SINTERVAL, WTEST, WINTERVAL)

The four Minitab commands that we illustrate in this tutorial are very similar to the parametric one-sample inference commands that we saw in Tutorial 5.

- Just as ZTEST and TTEST test the location of a mean, STEST and WTEST test the location of a median.
- Just as ZINTERVAL and TINTERVAL construct a confidence interval for the mean of a sampled population, SINTERVAL and WINTERVAL construct a confidence interval for its median.

STEST and SINTERVAL apply the sign procedure, and WTEST and WINTERVAL the Wilcoxon signed-rank procedure. We will illustrate only the sign procedure in this tutorial. The command and output formats for the Wilcoxon operations closely resemble those for the sign test, and we will leave them as an exercise for the reader.

In an earlier tutorial, we introduced the data on blood pressure, stored in BPRES.MTW. The first variable is the number of points above normal blood pressure for each individual. If a patient's blood pressure is more than 10 points above normal, then he is considered to be in a high-risk group.

We will apply the sign test to the BPRES data to determine whether the median score of the population is significantly greater than 10; if so, we would judge the population to be a high-risk group. With only 9 observations, we can't tell much from the sample about the underlying distribution. So, the nonparametric test is in a sense a conservative choice.

Figure 10.2 ▶

```
MTB > RETRIEVE 'BPRES'

MTB > STEST sign test of median = 10 using data in C1;
SUBC> ALTERNATIVE = +1 upper tailed test.

SIGN TEST OF MEDIAN = 10.00 VERSUS  G.T.  10.00

              N  BELOW  EQUAL  ABOVE   P-VALUE    MEDIAN
BP            9      0      0      9    0.0020     14.80
MTB > SINTERVAL with 99% confidence using the 'BP' data

SIGN CONFIDENCE INTERVAL FOR MEDIAN

                          ACHIEVED
              N   MEDIAN  CONFIDENCE    CONFIDENCE INTERVAL   POSITION
BP            9    14.80    0.9609      (    13.80,    17.50)        2
                            0.9900      (    13.17,    18.06)      NLI
                            0.9961      (    12.10,    19.00)        1
```

Figure 10.2 shows commands and results for STEST and SINTERVAL. The command format for STEST and TTEST are the same. If you don't specify a null-hypothesis value for the median, it will default to zero. The ALTERNATIVE subcommand has the same format as before:

ALTERNATIVE = −1	tests a lower-tailed alternative
ALTERNATIVE = 0	tests a two-tailed alternative
ALTERNATIVE = +1	tests an upper-tailed alternative

You can specify the degree of confidence for the confidence interval with the SINTERVAL command. Each command performs a separate significance test or computes a separate confidence interval for each column specified in issuing the command.

Not surprisingly, the STEST output closely resembles that from ZTEST and TTEST. The null and alternative hypotheses appear first. Then, for each column that you have specified, Minitab prints a line bearing

- the sample size
- the number of observations below, equal to, and above the null value
- the p-value of the test
- the median of the data

All nine observations fell above the specified null value of 10, and the p-value indicates that the population median is greater than 10.

The SINTERVAL output shows some new features. One quirk of most nonparametric procedures is that the discreteness of the procedure gets in the way of computing a confidence interval at exactly the desired level of confidence. SINTERVAL responds to this problem by providing two exact confidence intervals at levels that bracket the desired level; it then approximates the level you requested by nonlinear interpolation. With 99% confidence, we can conclude that the median member of this population has a blood pressure between 13.17 and 18.06 points above normal.

Comparing the Medians of Two Populations with the Mann-Whitney-Wilcoxon Procedure (MANN-WHITNEY)

The Mann-Whitney two-sample median procedure is the nonparametric analogue of the TWOSAMPLE parametric t-procedure that you learned in Tutorial 6. We will apply it to the exam data in EXAM .MTW, which contains results of two exams given in a graduate-level statistics course. With only eight students in the class, we are uncertain about the underlying distribution; We therefore select the appropriate nonparametric procedure to compare the two medians.

Figure 10.3 ▶

```
MTB > RETRIEVE 'EXAM'

MTB > MANN-WHITNEY test alternative=0 90% confidence data in C1 C2

Mann-Whitney Confidence Interval and Test

 EXAM 1      N =    8      MEDIAN =          87.50
 EXAM 2      N =    8      MEDIAN =          84.00
 POINT ESTIMATE FOR ETA1-ETA2 IS              1.00
 91.7  PCT C.I. FOR ETA1-ETA2 IS (   -11.00,       9.00)
 W =      69.5
 TEST OF ETA1 = ETA2  VS.  ETA1 N.E. ETA2 IS SIGNIFICANT AT  0.9164

 CANNOT REJECT AT ALPHA = 0.05
```

In Figure 10.3 we illustrate the MANN-WHITNEY command. You have to specify the alternative hypothesis and the degree of confidence for the difference in the population medians on the command line itself, not in a subcommand. The data from the two samples must be stored in two columns. We choose a two-tailed alternative (ALTERNATIVE = 0, which is the default value, and therefore redundant) and a 90% degree of confidence (95% is the default).

The MANN-WHITNEY output provides:

- ▶ summary information (sample size and median) for each sample
- ▶ a point estimate of the difference of the population medians (labelled POINT ESTIMATE OF ETA1 − ETA2)
- ▶ a confidence interval (with degree of confidence as close as obtainable to the one you specified) for the difference in the medians (labelled C.I. FOR ETA1 − ETA2)
- ▶ the Mann-Whitney statistic
- ▶ the p-value

Minitab also tells you that you cannot reject the hypothesis of equal medians at the 5% level of significance. We cannot conclude that the two tests' medians are different and hence would conclude either that the students performed equally well on both exams or that our small sample of eight students didn't give us enough power to detect whatever difference was there.

Comparing the Centers of K Populations with the Kruskal-Wallis Test (KRUSKAL-WALLIS)

In Practice Problem 2 in the ANOVA Tutorial, we asked you to test whether the number of sibs (brothers and sisters) of Miami females differed for the different religions in the sample. Thinking it over, we wonder whether the discreteness and asymmetry of the data might give us reason to wonder about the appropriateness of the parametric ANOVA test. To get another perspective on the question, let's now run the parallel Kruskal-Wallis nonparametric analysis of variance on the same data.

After retrieving the MIAMI.MTW data set, we create a new variable, C25, which represents the total number of brothers and sisters for each subject in the sample. The KRUSKAL-WALLIS command operates in the same manner as the ONEWAY command, with the data stored in one column and the group identifier in another. Figure 10.4 presents the results of the nonparametric one-way ANOVA.

Figure 10.4

```
MTB > RETRIEVE 'MIAMI'

MTB > LET C25 = C8+C9
MTB > NAME C25 'SIBS'
MTB > KRUSKAL-WALLIS test of data in C25, subscripts in 'RELIGION'

LEVEL     NOBS    MEDIAN  AVE. RANK   Z VALUE
    1       23     3.000       46.0      0.94
    2       50     2.000       38.8     -1.47
    3        2     2.500       45.8      0.22
    4        8     2.500       49.2      0.89
OVERALL     83                 42.0

H = 2.259
H(ADJ. FOR TIES) = 2.423
* NOTE  * ONE OR MORE SMALL SAMPLES
MTB > LET K1=2.259
MTB > CDF K1 store in K2;
SUBC> CHISQUARE 3 df.
MTB > LET K2=1-K2
MTB > LET K3=2.423
MTB > CDF K3 store in K4;
SUBC> CHISQUARE 3 df.
MTB > LET K4=1-K4
MTB > PRINT K1 K2 K3 K4
K1        2.25900
K2        0.520421
K3        2.42300
K4        0.48936
```

The Kruskal-Wallis analysis tests the equality of the k populations' locations or medians, just as ANOVA tests the equality of their means. The results include:

- summary statistics for each sample, including:
  - the number of observations
  - the sample median
  - the average overall rank of the members of the sample
  - the sample Z value
- the Kruskal-Wallis test statistic, both unadjusted and adjusted for ties

Although Minitab does not compute the p-value for the Kruskal-Wallis test, you can look it up easily with the CDF command. The Kruskal-Wallis statistic is distributed as chi-squared, with one less degree of freedom than the number of groups.

Since the data include tied values (the response is the number of brothers and sisters, and several of the young women in the sample have families of the same size) we should use the test statistic adjusted for ties. The p value of 0.489 gives us no reason to suspect from these data that the number of children in a family bears any relationship to religion.

Sorting and Ranking Data (SORT, RANK)

Since it has to do a lot of sorting and ranking in the nonparametric results presented earlier, Minitab makes these functions available so that you can use them as such, whenever you wish. This facility makes available to you a lot of nonparametric procedures that Minitab has not "canned" in named routines — including even procedures that haven't been invented yet. You have to put the steps together "by hand," using Minitab as your very powerful hand. You might, for example, combine the RANK and the TWOWAY commands to perform a rank transformation two-way ANOVA.

The STA261.MTW data set contains some interesting data to sort and rank. On the disk, these test scores were originally sorted alphabetically by student name; we have not included the names to protect the innocent! In Figure 10.5 we create the course exam average from the three hourly exam scores and the final exam. We will sort the data and then compute everyone's class rank.

Figure 10.5 ▶

```
MTB > RETRIEVE 'STA261'

MTB > RMEAN data in C12-C15 store in C17
MTB > NAME C17 'AVERAGE'
MTB > SORT final averages C17 carry C12-C15 store in C17 and C12-C15
MTB > RANK the data in C17 store ranks in C18
MTB > NAME C18 'RANK'
MTB > PRINT C18 C17 C12-C15

 ROW   RANK   AVERAGE    T1     T2     T3  FINAL

   1    1.0     26.25    55     50      0      0
   2    2.0     53.00    62     45     67     38
   3    3.0     54.75    71     55     59     34
   4    4.0     57.75    80     52     52     47
   5    5.0     60.50    53     73     54     62
   6    6.0     61.50    60     61     72     53
   7    7.0     63.50    64     72     59     59
   .     .        .       .      .      .      .
   .     .        .       .      .      .      .
   .     .        .       .      .      .      .
  37   37.0     87.75    85     94     90     82
  38   38.5     88.25    88     90     90     85
  39   38.5     88.25    79     90     92     92
  40   40.0     88.75    88     92     85     90
  41   41.0     89.25    94     85     93     85
  42   42.0     89.50    87     93     93     85
  43   43.0     90.50    96     84     93     89
  44   44.0     91.75    87     95     94     91
  45   45.0     96.50    83    103    102     98
```

Two points about SORT:

1. The SORT command operates only on one column. That is, Minitab will sort with respect to only one variable at a time. If you want to sort with respect to several variables at a time you have to use the SORT command on each variable.
2. The SORT command rearranges only the specified column, leaving the rest of the data set unchanged and unsorted, unless you specifically request that other columns be "carried along" in the sorting process.

In Figure 10.5, we sort with respect to the exam average and carry along the four exam results. Finally, we rank the exam averages from smallest to largest, and store and name the ranks in column C18. When you run this exercise, you'll get all 45 cases; we've reproduced in the figure only the first seven and the last nine cases, to conserve space.

The lowest ranked average (rank 1.0) is 26.25 and the highest (rank 45.0) is 96.50. Notice also that two students had exactly the same exam average of 88.25; RANK assigns each of them rank 38.5, the average of ranks 38 and 39.

Three of Minitab's nonparametric procedures that we have not illustrated in this tutorial are WALSH, WDIFF, and WSLOPE. The Command Reference section provides details on these procedures.

Review

Minitab offers nonparametric procedures parallel to many of the parametric procedures we have discussed, including tests for one, two, and k samples, each yielding an appropriate point and confidence interval estimate. This tutorial has also introduced you to Minitab's sorting and ranking functions, with which you can program many other nonparametric procedures.

List of Key Commands

The commands used in this tutorial were:

RUNS	test [above and below K] using the data in C
STEST	[median = K] using the data in C . . . C
WTEST	[median = K] using the data in C . . . C

Both STEST and WTEST have the subcommand:

ALTERNATIVE	hypothesis is K

SINTERVAL	[K% confidence] using the data in C . . . C
WINTERVAL	[K% confidence] using the data in C . . . C
MANN-WHITNEY	[alternative K] [K% confidence] data in C and C
KRUSKAL-WALLIS	data in C, sample identifier in C

Practice Problems

1. Use the Wilcoxon median test to determine whether the blood pressure median in BPRES.MTW is significantly greater than 10. That is, redo the analysis in Figure 10.2, using the Wilcoxon method.
2. Obtain a 95% confidence interval for the median number of brothers a Miami female in the MIAMI.MTW data set has, using the sign and Wilcoxon procedures. Repeat the analysis for the median number of sisters.
3. Test whether the median number of brothers and sisters is equal for Miami females. Should you use a two-sample test or pair the data?
4. Apply a runs test to the percentage of mud data in COREDATA. MTW to determine whether they were collected in random sequence.
5. A doctor has claimed that the median age at first heart transplant is 55 years. Use the data in HEART.MTW to test this hypothesis.
6. Retrieve the REALEST.MTW data set.
    a. Determine whether the median selling price of homes in Oxford differs significantly for homes with different numbers of bedrooms.
    b. Is the median price of homes different for homes with different numbers of baths?
    c. Does your answer change if you use the number of cars the garage can accommodate?

d. Sort and rank the selling price of homes in Oxford. Carry along all of the data and print out your results. Is there any pattern in the ranked data and in any of the other variables?

e. Rank the selling and asking prices and save both ranks. Sort the data by the asking price and print out the two ranks. Correlate the two ranks. What do you conclude? (This correlation of the ranks is known as Spearman's rank correlation.)

11 ▶ Time-Series Analysis

Objectives

Minitab offers several powerful commands for processing and extrapolating time series. In this tutorial you will learn how to:

1. investigate the degree of autocorrelation and partial autocorrelation of a time series
2. transform a time series
3. perform a Box-Jenkins analysis of a time series
4. forecast a time series with Box-Jenkins techniques

Tutorials

A time-series analysis proceeds in four phases:

Phase I	Investigate the autocorrelation structure of the time series to determine the correct model
Phase II	Transform the data to perform the analysis
Phase III	Fit an adequate Box-Jenkins model
Phase IV	Apply the model to forecast future values

Retrieve the 47 observations stored as HOMESALE.MTW. This is a rather small data base for Box-Jenkins ARIMA time-series analysis: most authors recommend a minimum of 100 observations. For introductory purposes, though, it will suffice.

Checking for Autocorrelation in Your Data (ACF, PACF)

Figure 3.7 in Tutorial 3 used TSPLOT to plot the home-sale data series; Figure 11.1 repeats this display.

Figure 11.1 ▶

```
MTB > RETRIEVE 'HOMESALE'

MTB > TSPLOT period is 12 C1

SOLD    -
        -                   7                       7
        -
   12.00+                               78        5
        -        8                    5              8
        -
        -    5 7
        -                 5  8      3
    8.00+     6                       6        3
        -          0       6   0A          0           0
        -
        -  2            34                9 A    4    9 A
        -   34                   B   4       B
    4.00+         9           9    2               6
        -           AB1                       12
        -
        - 1            2          1
         +-----------+-----------+-----------+-----------+
         0          12          24          36          48
```

The plot indicates a seasonal trend, with the peaks tending to occur during the summer and the valleys tending to occur during the winter.

To determine an appropriate starting model, we first apply the ACF (autocorrelation function) and PACF (partial autocorrelation function) operations to the home-sale time series. Figures 11.2 and 11.3 display the resulting autocorrelation and partial autocorrelation plots.

Figure 11.2▶

```
MTB >  ACF of the data in C1

ACF of SOLD

           -1.0 -0.8 -0.6 -0.4 -0.2  0.0  0.2  0.4  0.6  0.8  1.0
             +----+----+----+----+----+----+----+----+----+----+
  1   0.243                             XXXXXXX
  2   0.258                             XXXXXXX
  3   0.047                             XX
  4  -0.232                       XXXXXXX
  5  -0.302                     XXXXXXXXX
  6  -0.615              XXXXXXXXXXXXXXXX
  7  -0.336                     XXXXXXXXX
  8  -0.164                         XXXXX
  9   0.043                             XX
 10   0.193                             XXXXXX
 11   0.256                             XXXXXXX
 12   0.606                             XXXXXXXXXXXXXXXX
 13   0.237                             XXXXXXX
 14   0.217                             XXXXXX
 15  -0.047                            XX
 16  -0.166                         XXXXX
```

In both the ACF and PACF commands you can specify the number of lags of autocorrelation to compute. If you don't, Minitab uses the default number of lags ($\sqrt{n} + 10$).

Figure 11.3

```
MTB > PACF of the data in C1

PACF of SOLD

          -1.0 -0.8 -0.6 -0.4 -0.2  0.0  0.2  0.4  0.6  0.8  1.0
            +----+----+----+----+----+----+----+----+----+----+
  1   0.243                          XXXXXXX
  2   0.211                          XXXXXX
  3  -0.060                         XX
  4  -0.318                 XXXXXXXXX
  5  -0.245                   XXXXXXX
  6  -0.513            XXXXXXXXXXXXXX
  7  -0.170                     XXXXX
  8   0.118                          XXXX
  9   0.245                          XXXXXXX
 10   0.053                          XX
 11  -0.166                     XXXXX
 12   0.250                          XXXXXXX
 13  -0.018                          X
 14   0.100                          XXXX
 15  -0.031                         XX
 16   0.030                          XX
```

In our example, the ACF plot has "spikes" at lag times 6 and 12, whereas the PACF doesn't appear to be doing anything. Since the time series appears stationary (inspecting the TSPLOT, we note that it does not "wander around"), we decide not to difference the time series. Also, the series doesn't show any major trend, either up or down. The TSPLOT shows a clear seasonal pattern, however, and we will need to adjust for this seasonality.

Based on all of this information, we decide upon a seasonal moving-average model of degree 2, with a seasonal period of 6 (two major spikes in the ACF, six months apart). Later on, we will fit this model to the home-sale data.

Transforming a Time Series for Analysis (DIFFERENCE, LAG)

Two data-manipulation tools, differencing and lagging, are important in time-series analysis. You can think of lagging as time-shifting: it shifts each element in a time series to a later point, so that it lags its previous value by the period of time that you specify. In Minitab, the LAG command shifts each element down the column by a specified number of rows. When you LAG a column in Minitab and store the lagged data, the new column is identical to the former one, except that the entries have been shifted down, or lagged, a specified number of rows. The empty rows at the beginning of the resulting column are set to the missing value symbol (*). The DIFFERENCE command is very useful in the preliminary stage of identifying the ARIMA model that you will apply.

Figure 11.4 applies the DIFFERENCE command to the home-sale data. We take differences of lag 1 (although we could have specified any desired degree of lag). The figure displays the original and differenced time series, so that you can see how the differences are formed.

Figure 11.4▶

```
MTB > DIFFERENCE of lag 1 of the time series in C1, store in C2
MTB > PRINT C1 C2

 ROW   SOLD    C2

   1      2     *
   2      6     4
   3      5    -1
   4      5     0
   5     10     5
   6      8    -2
   7     10     2
   .      .     .
   .      .     .
   .      .     .
  40      6    -2
  41     12     6
  42      4    -8
  43     14    10
  44     11    -3
  45      6    -5
  46      7     1
  47      6    -1
```

Column C2 contains the differences between adjacent values in the time series in C1. The first difference is missing, of course, since there was no earlier value to subtract from.

Box-Jenkins Analysis of a Time Series (ARIMA)

Based on the TSPLOT, ACF, and PACF output, we will initially try a seasonal moving average model of degree 2 (since there were two prominent spikes in the ACF, and the PACF died down) with a seasonality parameter of degree 6 (since the ACF spikes occurred at lags of multiples of 6). In issuing the ARIMA command you can specify both seasonal and nonseasonal parameters of the model. The nonseasonal parameters come first. If the model includes seasonal components, then you must specify all three nonseasonal components, even if they are zero. Figure 11.5 presents the basic ARIMA output for the home-sale data series, using a seasonal moving-average model.

Figure 11.5

```
MTB > ARIMA model non seasonal parameters are (p=0 d=0 q=0) &
CONT> seasonal parameters are (P=0 D=0 Q=2) S=6 using the data in C1

Estimates at each iteration
Iteration        SSE       Parameters
    0          473.708     0.100     0.100     6.909
    1          364.247     0.217    -0.050     6.876
    2          316.873     0.367    -0.129     6.844
    3          280.965     0.447    -0.279     6.848
    4          257.854     0.525    -0.429     6.838
    5          242.229     0.593    -0.579     6.799
    6          235.707     0.627    -0.671     6.750
    7          234.363     0.636    -0.706     6.730
    8          234.137     0.638    -0.719     6.724
    9          234.100     0.637    -0.724     6.721
   10          234.093     0.636    -0.726     6.720
   11          234.092     0.636    -0.727     6.720
   12          234.092     0.635    -0.727     6.720
Relative change in each estimate less than  0.0010

Final Estimates of Parameters
Type        Estimate      St. Dev.  t-ratio
SMA   6       0.6353       0.1618      3.93
SMA  12      -0.7272       0.1716     -4.24
Constant      6.7198       0.3251     20.67
Mean          6.7198       0.3251

No. of obs.:  47
Residuals:     SS = 186.544  (backforecasts excluded)
               MS =    4.240  DF = 44

Modified Box-Pierce chisquare statistic
Lag                   12            24            36             48
Chisquare    15.1(DF=10)   39.1(DF=22)   53.8(DF=34)       * (DF= *)
```

The amount of output from ARIMA can be controlled with the BRIEF command. Figure 11.5 shows the default level of output (BRIEF = 2). You can specify any level from 1 (least) to 4 (most) output. As before, the current output level remains in effect until you issue the BRIEF command again or exit Minitab.

- The first part of the output chronicles the detailed history of the iterative estimation process. The Sum of Squared Error (SSE) and the parameter estimates are printed for each iterative step until convergence is obtained (that is, until the relative change in each estimate is less than 0.001 or the SSE cannot be further reduced). If the process does not converge within 25 steps, ARIMA stops and issues a warning. With the STARTING subcommand, you can restart the iterative process where it left off.
- Next comes a detailed display of the final parameter estimates, including, for each parameter estimate:
  - an identifier. In our example, SMA 6 represents the Seasonal Moving Average degree 6 coefficient.
  - the parameter estimate
  - the estimated standard deviation
  - a t-ratio. In the example, both parameter estimates are highly significant.
- Next, the estimated variance of the white-noise or random-error component is given, with its component parts (MS = 4.240 = SSE/DF = 186.544/44).
- The last bit of output, the modified Box-Pierce chi-square statistic, measures the adequacy with which the model fits the data.

Overall, the model seems to fit adequately.

Out of curiosity, we might try other models, perhaps a seasonal autoregressive component of degree 2 in place of the moving-average component. Minitab offers you great flexibility in analyzing your data: you can try a multitude of models.

Forecasting Using ARIMA

Once we have obtained a satisfactory model, the final step is to use it to forecast future events. This was our primary goal. To forecast in Minitab we use the FORECAST subcommand in addition to the ARIMA command. After specifying the model in the ARIMA command, we issue the FORECAST subcommand, indicating

1. at what time the forecasts are to start
2. how many forecasts are to be made
3. optionally, where we want to store the forecasts and 95% forecast confidence limits. The default starting point for forecasting is the end of the time series; we accept the default in Figure 11.6. We will forecast the next year's sales and store the forecasts and confidence limits for later use.

Figure 11.6▶

```
MTB > ARIMA model (p=0 d=0 q=0) (P=0 D=0 Q=2) S=6 using the data in C1;
SUBC> FORECAST 12 months ahead store forecasts in C3, &
CONT> conf limits in C4 and C5.

Estimates at each iteration
Iteration        SSE      Parameters
    0         473.708     0.100     0.100     6.909
    1         364.247     0.217    -0.050     6.876
    2         316.873     0.367    -0.129     6.844
    3         280.965     0.447    -0.279     6.848
    4         257.854     0.525    -0.429     6.838
    5         242.229     0.593    -0.579     6.799
    6         235.707     0.627    -0.671     6.750
    7         234.363     0.636    -0.706     6.730
    8         234.137     0.638    -0.719     6.724
    9         234.100     0.637    -0.724     6.721
   10         234.093     0.636    -0.726     6.720
   11         234.092     0.636    -0.727     6.720
   12         234.092     0.635    -0.727     6.720
Relative change in each estimate less than  0.0010
```

```
Final Estimates of Parameters
Type        Estimate      St. Dev.  t-ratio
SMA  6        0.6353        0.1618     3.93
SMA 12       -0.7272        0.1716    -4.24
Constant      6.7198        0.3251    20.67
Mean          6.7198        0.3251

No. of obs.:  47
Residuals:    SS = 186.544  (backforecasts excluded)
              MS =   4.240  DF = 44

Modified Box-Pierce chisquare statistic
Lag                   12            24            36            48
Chisquare    15.1(DF=10)   39.1(DF=22)   53.8(DF=34)     * (DF= *)

Forecasts from period 47
                                 95 Percent Limits
Period         Forecast         Lower         Upper        Actual
  48             8.9455        4.9090       12.9820
  49             1.6886       -2.3480        5.7251
  50             6.0009        1.9644       10.0375
  51             8.1682        4.1317       12.2047
  52             6.1369        2.1004       10.1734
  53             8.6997        4.6632       12.7362
  54             3.8980       -0.8843        8.6804
  55            10.0669        5.2846       14.8492
  56             7.7976        3.0153       12.5799
  57             5.8012        1.0188       10.5835
  58             7.0664        2.2841       11.8488
  59             6.9446        2.1622       11.7269

MTB > SET months into C6
DATA> (1:47)
DATA> END
MTB > SET forecast months into C7
DATA> (48:59)
DATA> END
MTB > NAME C3 'FORECAST' C4 'L CL' C5 'U CL'
```

The FORECAST subcommand appends the forecasts to the ARIMA results as illustrated in Figure 11.6. As one might expect from the wiggliness of the original time series, the confidence interval around each forecast point is really quite wide, indicating that it's very hard to make a confident point prediction of such a volatile variable.

One nice way to depict the forecasts is to superimpose a plot of the original time series, the forecasts, and the interval forecasts on the same graph, as in Figure 11.7. Connect the A, B, C, and D points in different colors for a revealing display.

Figure 11.7 ▶

```
MTB > OW 80
MTB > MPLOT C1*C6 C3*C7 C4*C7 C5*C7

    -
    -                 A                   A         D
    -                                         D   D
12.0+                           AA      A       D    DDD
    -        A                A            A         D
    -     A A                                   DD  B
    -      A        A  A    A  A      A       B B BD
    -         A      A  AA        A         A        BBB
 6.0+   A         AA             A A   A   A A DBB   B
    -   AA                A  A      A         C   C C
    -        A         A    A            A      C  B C
    -  A       AAAA        A         AA         CC    CC
    -                                          B     C
 0.0+
    -                                              C
    -                                          C
    -

      +---------+---------+---------+---------+---------+------
      0        12        24        36        48        60

    A = SOLD vs. C6           C - L CL vs. C7
    B = FORECAST vs. C7       D = U CL vs. C7
```

Review

This tutorial has walked you through a time-series analysis with Box-Jenkins techniques. Autocorrelation and partial autocorrelation functions (ACF and PACF), together with lagging and differencing transformations, guided the model-building stage. The interactive character of Minitab makes it possible to try out as many preliminary models as your patience allows before you settle on a final model and begin to make forecasts. The Box-Jenkins ARIMA technique is a very powerful and flexible forecasting tool, which can fit virtually any forecasting model.

List of Key Commands

The commands used in this tutorial are:

ACF	plot [up to K lags] using the time series in C, [store in C]
PACF	plot [up to K lags] using the time series in C, [store in C]
DIFFERENCE	using lag K the data in C, store in C
LAG	using a lag of K, the data in C, store results in C
ARIMA	(p = K, d = K, q = K) (P = K, D = K, Q = K) S = K data in C [store residuals in C, [store predicteds in C, [store coefficients in C]]]

Subcommands:

CONSTANT	term in the model
NOCONSTANT	term in the model
STARTING	values for the coefficients are in C
FORECAST	[using a forecast origin of K] K forecasts ahead [store forecasts in C [store confidence limits in C and C]]

Practice Problems

1. Redo the analysis in Figure 11.5 using the BRIEF 1, BRIEF 3, and BRIEF 4 commands, and compare the levels of output that result.
2. Reset the output level to 2, and redo the analysis in Figure 11.6 under a seasonal autoregressive model of degree 2 with a seasonality parameter of 6, including the next year's forecasts. You will need to save the parameter estimates in another column, and restart the analysis using these values as starting values using the START subcommand. Compare your results with those in Figure 11.6. What do you conclude?
3. Use the electrical use data in UTILITY.MTW to answer the questions that follow.

a. Plot the electric data. Which time series should you use — the KWH data or the $ data? Over the course of several years, which variable would change due to inflation? Is the time series stationary? What kind of heat do you think is used in this house? Why?

b. Obtain the ACF and PACF for the electrical KWH usage data. What model is suggested?

c. Fit the model you suggested in part b. Is it adequate? Improve it if you need to.

d. Forecast the next year's electrical usage and save your forecasts.

e. If electricity is currently 6.14 cents per KWH in addition to a $10 monthly surcharge, how much should the family expect to spend on electricity for the next year (i.e., the next 12 months)?

4. Use the water-use data in UTILITY.MTW to answer the questions that follow.

   a. Plot water use in both gallons and dollars. Which time series should you use? How do these plots differ from the electric plots in problem 3? Does anything strike you as odd in the data? What kind of problems will it cause?

   b. Obtain the ACF and PACF for these data. What model do they suggest?

   c. Fit the suggested model. How well does it fit? Can it be improved?

   d. Forecast next year's water use, and save the forecast values. How many gallons of water does this family use per year?

5. Obtain ACF and PACF up to lag 36 for the home-sale data. After inspecting these plots, would you be inclined to raise the degree of the seasonal moving average term from 2 to 3? Fit a third-degree seasonal moving average model. Does it fit better? On what would you base your decision?

12 ▶ Distributions and Random Data

Objectives

In this tutorial, you will learn that many common statistical distributions are available in Minitab. With them, you can extract the numbers you need, and generate sets of random values that display their characteristics. Specifically, in this tutorial you will learn how to:

1. obtain p-values for most of the test statistics that you will encounter
2. obtain critical values and percentiles for most distributions
3. obtain probability distributions for both discrete and continuous random variables
4. generate data randomly from the most common statistical distributions, illustrating important statistical concepts from these data
5. sample randomly from the data in a Minitab column

Tutorials

In this tutorial, we will not introduce any new statistical tests or techniques, but we will take a systematic look at some features of Minitab that give you direct access to the most important distributions.

Looking Up Cumulative Probabilities for Various Distribution Functions (CDF)

We have already applied the CDF command to obtain p-values for tests based on the NORMAL, T (also known as STUDENT'S T), F, and CHISQUARE distributions. CDF also provides, upon command, the cumulative probability for several other important statistical distributions, both continuous and discrete: BINOMIAL, POISSON, uniform INTEGER, DISCRETE, and continuous UNIFORM.

To illustrate the CDF command once more, we use it to ask Minitab for the cumulative probability of a standard normal value of −3.49. That is, we ask: what is the probability that a member of a normal distribution lies 3.49 standard deviations or more below the mean?

Figure 12.1 displays the command and output.

Figure 12.1 ▶

```
MTB > CDF -3.49;
SUBC> NORMAL mu=0 sigma=1.
   -3.4900     0.0002
```

The output from CDF is terse and to the point. The probability that a standard normal has a value of −3.49 or lower is 0.0002.

Three points to remember about CDF:

1. You must specify a distribution and its parameters (see the Command Reference section); if you don't, then CDF defaults to the standard normal distribution (NORMAL mu = 0, sigma = 1).
2. You have to provide the parameters in the correct order; the List of Key Commands later in this tutorial lists the order of parameters for each available distribution.
3. You can save the cumulative probability in a constant or a column (K1, C3, etc.) for later manipulation.

Looking Up Critical Values and Percentiles of Distributions (INVCDF)

Similarly, the inverse CDF command, INVCDF, provides critical values or percentiles. We illustrate INVCDF for the standard normal and chi-square distributions. By this time in your statistical education, you know that the 97.5th percentile of the standard normal distribution is 1.96. Let's verify it with Minitab. Figure 12.2 requests and obtains the 97.5th percentile for a standard normal and the 99.5th percentile for a chi-square distribution with 7 degrees of freedom.

Figure 12.2▶

```
MTB > INVCDF 0.975;
SUBC> NORMAL.
    0.9750     1.9600
MTB > INVCDF 0.995;
SUBC> CHISQUARE with 7 df.
    0.9950    20.2778
```

INVCDF repeats the percentage level you specified and displays the corresponding percentile value.

- As expected, Minitab returns 1.9600 as the 97.5th percentile for the standard normal distribution.
- Likewise, the 99.5th percentile for a chi-square with 7 degrees of freedom lies at a chi-square value of 20.2778.

The CDF and INVCDF commands put at our fingertips all of the usual statistical tables contained in most introductory statistics books.

Looking Up Values of Various Probability Distribution Functions (PDF)

With the PDF command, you can obtain the probability distribution function at any specified value of each statistical distribution mentioned above. If you specify a discrete distribution without providing a value on the PDF command line, then Minitab prints out the whole probability distribution of the discrete variable.

Figure 12.3 shows how to order up

- the probability distribution of a binomial distribution with 18 trials and a probability of success of 0.38
- the value of the standard normal pdf at the value of 0.5

Figure 12.3▶

```
MTB > PDF;
SUBC> BINOMIAL n=18 p=0.38.

    BINOMIAL WITH N =  18  P = 0.380000
       K           P( X = K)
       0             0.0002
       1             0.0020
       2             0.0105
       3             0.0344
       4             0.0791
       5             0.1358
       6             0.1803
       7             0.1895
       8             0.1597
       9             0.1087
      10             0.0600
      11             0.0267
      12             0.0096
      13             0.0027
      14             0.0006
      15             0.0001
      16             0.0000
MTB > PDF at x=0.5;
SUBC> NORMAL 0 1.
    0.5000    0.3521
```

The probability distribution of the binomial random variable (n = 18, p = 0.38) is listed in Figure 12.3. It stops at 16, because the probabilities for 17 and 18 are smaller than 0.00005. We note that the standard normal density function at the value 0.5 is 0.3521. If you have a calculator that computes square roots and has an "e" function, you might want to verify Minitab's value.

The CDF command works the same way with discrete distributions: if you invoke CDF for a discrete distribution and specify no value on the command line, then you'll get the entire cumulative distribution table as output, with the tails truncated at probabilities 0.00005 and .99995.

Generating Random Data (RANDOM)

Minitab will also allow you to generate random data that display the characteristics of any of the statistical distributions mentioned above (plus Bernoulli), just as if you had sampled real populations so distributed. You can use random data of this sort to verify and explore the ramifications of the theorems and concepts crucial to statistics.

In Figure 12.4, we illustrate the RANDOM command. Note that your output will differ from ours because the RANDOM command generates a different set of values each time it is invoked.

Figure 12.4▶

```
MTB > RANDOM 100 C1;
SUBC> POISSON lambda=1.
MTB > DOTPLOT C1

Each dot represents 2 points
                      .
     .                :
     :                :
     :                :
     :                :               :
     :                :               :
     :                :               :
     :                :               :
     :                :               :
     :                :               :                :
     +---------+---------+---------+---------+---------+-------C1
  0.00      0.60      1.20      1.80      2.40      3.00
```

We generated 100 random observations from a Poisson (lambda = 1) distribution, and then used DOTPLOT to create an approximation of the Poisson (lambda = 1) probability function. In a similar fashion, we could generate data from any of the distributions available and obtain approximations of the associated probability function.

Sampling from a Column (SAMPLE)

When you are working with a large worksheet and complicated manipulations, you may wish to process only a sample of your data rather than the whole worksheet. Or, you may wish to base some sort of prediction model on part of your data and then test it on an equivalent sample, drawn independently from the same population.

The SAMPLE command selects rows of data randomly from your worksheet. To illustrate its application, we return to the STA261 data set to select 10 students at random. We will store the exam results for these 10 students in columns C16 to C19 and investigate the performance of these 10 students separately from that of their classmates.

With the SAMPLE command, you can select any desired number of rows from the worksheet and store them in new columns, carrying along data from any columns you choose. Figure 12.5 displays the commands and their results.

Figure 12.5 ▶

```
MTB > RETRIEVE 'STA261'

MTB > SAMPLE 10 rows from C12-C15, store in C16-C19
MTB > DESCRIBE C12-C19

                 N      MEAN    MEDIAN    TRMEAN     STDEV    SEMEAN
T1              45     77.73     79.00     78.05     10.65      1.59
T2              45     75.02     76.00     75.12     14.07      2.10
T3              45     73.82     72.00     74.98     16.84      2.51
FINAL           45     72.18     73.00     73.68     18.19      2.71
C16             10     81.40     84.50     81.63      7.35      2.32
C17             10     75.00     77.50     75.62     11.99      3.79
C18             10     73.10     67.50     72.62     13.06      4.13
C19             10     70.10     68.50     72.37     15.54      4.91

               MIN       MAX        Q1        Q3
T1           53.00     96.00     71.00     87.00
T2           45.00    103.00     63.50     85.00
T3            0.00    102.00     65.50     85.00
FINAL         0.00     98.00     65.50     85.00
C16          71.00     90.00     71.75     87.25
C17          55.00     90.00     66.75     83.50
C18          59.00     91.00     61.75     86.25
C19          34.00     88.00     65.25     82.00
```

SAMPLE does not produce any output; if you want to see what it has accomplished, you have to issue commands to display the parts of the worksheet that it has created. To this end, we have used DESCRIBE to display the original 45 exam results as well as the 10 randomly selected exam results. If SAMPLE does indeed take a random sample of the original 45, then our descriptive results for the 10 should be fairly close to those for the total 45.

The results are encouraging. None of the descriptive statistics are terribly different for the two data sets. The pairs of means are approximately equal, as are the standard deviations, medians, and standard errors. Again, we would not expect the results to be identical. In fact we might even be a bit suspicious if the results were too similar.

Review

This tutorial has presented the Minitab features that generate values of probability distributions, cumulative distributions, and inverse cumulative distributions that you might otherwise look up in a book of statistical tables. It has also taught you how to generate random data with various important distributional characteristics and to draw random samples from large bodies of data.

List of Key Commands

The following commands were illustrated in this tutorial:

CDF	of the values in E [store results in E]
INVCDF	of the values in E [store results in E]
PDF	of the values in E [store results in E]

RANDOM generate K observations store in C . . . C
Subcommand:

BERNOULLI trials p = K

CDF, INVCDF, PDF, and RANDOM all have the following subcommands:

BINOMIAL	n = K p = K
POISSON	mean = K
INTEGER	discrete uniform on K to K
DISCRETE	values in C, probabilities in C
NORMAL	[mu = K, [sigma = K]]
UNIFORM	[continuous on K to K]
T	degrees of freedom = K
F	numerator df = K denominator df = K
CHISQUARE	df = K

SAMPLE	K rows from C . . . C, and put in C . . . C
BASE	for random number generator K

Practice Problems

1. Obtain the probability distribution for the Poisson distribution with mean 8.5.
2. Obtain the .5, 1, 2.5, 5, 10, 90, 95, 97.5, 99, and 99.5 percentiles for a chi-square distribution with 14 degrees of freedom. Compare these values with the values in your book's chi-square table.
3. Generate 1,000 observations from an F-distribution with 13 and 21 df and obtain the DOTPLOT of the data. What might this plot lead you to conclude about the F-distribution?
4. Repeat the simulation using samples of size 10. How many of your intervals include the population mean of 38? Does the sample size affect your results? Should it?
5. Repeat the simulation using samples of size 10. How many of your intervals include the population mean of 38? Does the sample size affect your results? Should it?
6. Redo Figure 12.4, but this time use a normal distribution with mean 20 and variance 100. Does the distribution of the mean seem more normal even for the small sample size? Why should it?

13 ▶ Macros

Objectives

By now you're convinced that Minitab's interactive approach to statistics combines computing power with simplicity of operation in a wonderful way. In this last tutorial you'll learn one more way in which Minitab can make your statistical life easier: "canned" command sequences, called **macros**. Once you file away all the commands you need for an operation that you repeat often, you can issue all those commands, in the order you specified, simply by issuing a single command. In this tutorial you will learn how to:

1. store a set of Minitab commands in a file (STORE and END)
2. execute a set of commands (EXECUTE)
3. loop through a set of stored commands several times
4. use variable column numbers and constants when executing a set of commands

Tutorials

Storing a Set of Frequently Used Commands (STORE, END, EXECUTE)

In Tutorial 12, we generated 100 samples from a Poisson distribution and then calculated a confidence interval for the mean of the sample. To illustrate how to store and execute a set of Minitab commands, let's store a procedure that will generate 10 samples of size 50 from a normal distribution, and then calculate confidence intervals for the mean of each sample.

The STORE command tells Minitab to store a set of commands as a macro file. If you provide the name of a file to put them in, Minitab will comply; if not, it will put them in a file with the default file name of MINITAB.MTB. In the example in Figure 13.1, we'll store our commands in the file EXAMPLE. (Note: as we are using random data, your output will not be identical to that in Figures 13.1 and 13.2.) Unless you specify a different extension, Minitab assigns .MTB as the file name extension for macros. Once you enter the STORE command, the Minitab prompt symbol changes to STOR> until you type END. If you SET or READ within a stored set of commands, do not use the END command to signal the end of the data. If you do, Minitab will interpret it as the end of the stored set of commands. Since the END command is optional for SET and READ, simply leave it out. Minitab knows the difference between data and a Minitab command.

Figure 13.1 ▶

```
MTB > STORE the following commands in the file 'EXAMPLE'
STOR> RANDOM 50 store in C1-C10;
STOR> NORMAL mu=38 sigma=4.8.
STOR> TINTERVAL of C1-C10
STOR> END of stored commands
MTB > EXECUTE the commands in 'EXAMPLE'
MTB > RANDOM 50 store in C1-C10;
SUBC> NORMAL mu=38 sigma=4.8.
MTB > TINTERVAL of C1-C10

              N       MEAN     STDEV  SE MEAN    95.0 PERCENT C.I.
C1           50     38.611     4.888    0.691     37.222    40.001
C2           50     37.758     4.308    0.609     36.534    38.983
C3           50     38.563     4.928    0.697     37.162    39.963
C4           50     38.859     3.908    0.553     37.748    39.970
C5           50     37.258     5.141    0.727     35.796    38.719
C6           50     38.672     4.987    0.705     37.254    40.089
C7           50     38.019     5.156    0.729     36.553    39.484
C8           50     38.204     5.179    0.732     36.732    39.676
C9           50     38.280     4.765    0.674     36.925    39.634
C10          50     38.007     4.562    0.645     36.710    39.304

MTB > END of stored commands
```

Once you have saved a series of commands, you can execute them either once or several times with a single EXECUTE command. To execute the stored commands once, simply type EXECUTE with the file name in which the commands have been stored in single quotes, as we did in Figure 13.1. You will get exactly the same output as if you had typed the commands in by hand.

You can also have Minitab execute the commands several times by issuing the EXECUTE command several times. Alternatively, you can save yourself some typing by using the option on the EXECUTE command that allows you to execute the commands any number of times you wish. For example, to generate 30 confidence intervals we could either:

```
▶ MTB > EXECUTE 'EXAMPLE'
  MTB > EXECUTE 'EXAMPLE'
  MTB > EXECUTE 'EXAMPLE'
```

or, more simply:

```
▶ MTB > EXECUTE 'EXAMPLE' 3 times
```

Note: Once you start executing a Minitab macro, there is no way to stop it, so be careful.

Figure 13.2 displays the first part of the output. It's really quite easy to generate 30 confidence intervals — or 500 or 1,000, for that matter. The STORE command provides a very efficient way to execute a series of commands as many times as you may wish.

Figure 13.2 ▶

```
MTB > EXECUTE the commands in 'EXAMPLE' 3 times
MTB > RANDOM 50 store in C1-C10;
SUBC> NORMAL mu=38 sigma=4.8.
MTB > TINTERVAL of C1-C10

              N      MEAN     STDEV  SE MEAN    95.0 PERCENT C.I.
C1           50    38.355     4.338    0.613    37.122     39.588
C2           50    38.777     4.284    0.606    37.559     39.995
C3           50    38.509     4.372    0.618    37.266     39.752
C4           50    37.449     4.733    0.669    36.104     38.794
C5           50    38.173     4.711    0.666    36.834     39.512
C6           50    38.338     4.411    0.624    37.084     39.592
C7           50    38.557     4.551    0.644    37.264     39.851
C8           50    37.977     4.043    0.572    36.828     39.126
C9           50    39.105     4.524    0.640    37.819     40.391
C10          50    38.306     4.689    0.663    36.973     39.639

MTB > END of stored commands
MTB > RANDOM 50 store in C1-C10;
SUBC> NORMAL mu=38 sigma=4.8.
MTB > TINTERVAL of C1-C10

              N      MEAN     STDEV  SE MEAN    95.0 PERCENT C.I.
C1           50    37.647     4.470    0.632    36.376    38.917
C2           50    37.151     5.257    0.743    35.657    38.646
 .            .         .         .        .         .         .
 .            .         .         .        .         .         .
 .            .         .         .        .         .         .
```

A macro file doesn't have to be prepared from within Minitab, by the way. You can use any text editor or word processing program, just as long as it writes ordinary ASCII text files. Just type in the Minitab commands you wish to store, and save the file with a .MTB extension. Minitab will execute this file, just as if Minitab had stored it.

All of the examples and figures in this book were prepared from macro files created on a word processor. We also invoked the OUTFILE command to tell Minitab to store all of the commands and output in a file. Then we simply cut and pasted the Minitab commands and output into the text of this book.

Making Macros More Flexible

When you want to create a macro, you often don't know in advance how you will number or name the data columns that the macro will use. You'd like the macro to be general enough to operate on columns arranged in different ways in various worksheets.

As you know, Minitab stores single values in constants named K1, K2, and so forth. When you store a sequence of commands, you can specify stored constants in the place of the numerical parameters or column numbers that you wish to be able to vary when you execute the macro. You need only let each constant take on the value that is meaningful in the current context.

A variable column number takes the form CKn, where n is the number of the constant where you plan to store the actual column number.

For example, the Time Series Tutorial introduced the ARIMA command, which requires that you input up to seven numerical parameters of the model each time you invoke it. Since each ARIMA computation takes some time, you might find it convenient to store several different models to be run in sequence, without further intervention on your part.

Figure 13.3 illustrates this procedure. We store the basic ARIMA command in a file, assigning constants K1 through K7 to the seven parameter values, and K8 to the data column.

Figure 13.3 ▶

```
MTB > RETRIEVE 'HOMESALE'

MTB > STORE 'ARIMA'
STOR> ARIMA model (K1 K2 K3) (K4 K5 K6) K7 data in CK8
STOR> END
MTB > LET K1=0
MTB > LET K2=0
MTB > LET K3=0
MTB > LET K4=0
MTB > LET K5=0
MTB > LET K6=2
MTB > LET K7=6
MTB > LET K8=1
MTB > EXECUTE 'ARIMA'
MTB > ARIMA model (K1 K2 K3) (K4 K5 K6) K7 data in CK8

Estimates at each iteration
Iteration        SSE      Parameters
    0         473.708    0.100     0.100     6.909
    1         364.247    0.217    -0.050     6.876
    2         316.873    0.367    -0.129     6.844
    3         280.965    0.447    -0.279     6.848
    4         257.854    0.525    -0.429     6.838
    5         242.229    0.593    -0.579     6.799
    6         235.707    0.627    -0.671     6.750
    7         234.363    0.636    -0.706     6.730
    8         234.137    0.638    -0.719     6.724
    9         234.100    0.637    -0.724     6.721
   10         234.093    0.636    -0.726     6.720
   11         234.092    0.636    -0.727     6.720
   12         234.092    0.635    -0.727     6.720
Relative change in each estimate less than  0.0010

Final Estimates of Parameters
Type       Estimate     St. Dev.  t-ratio
SMA  6       0.6353      0.1618     3.93
SMA 12      -0.7272      0.1716    -4.24
Constant     6.7198      0.3251    20.67
Mean         6.7198      0.3251

No. of obs.:  47
Residuals:    SS = 186.544  (backforecasts excluded)
              MS =   4.240  DF = 44

Modified Box-Pierce chisquare statistic
Lag                  12             24             36             48
Chisquare    15.1(DF=10)   39.1(DF=22)   53.8(DF=34)      * (DF= *)
```

You want to turn off the continue prompt when executing macros. To do so use the command OH ∅.

Review

In this tutorial you have learned to store Minitab commands in a file for later execution. The file in which you put Minitab macro commands can be of any length. You can create such a file in Minitab with the STORE command, or you can create and store it with any other program, such as a word processor, and then execute it in Minitab. A word processor may make it particularly easy to correct your mistakes, either before or after you save the file. You have to be very careful when storing commands in Minitab, since STORE offers no way to make corrections other than simply starting over and retyping everything. Once you have stored a macro file, however, it is an ordinary ASCII text file which you can then edit in a word processor.

The EXECUTE command lets you execute a set of commands either once (by default) or as many times as you specify in issuing the command.

You can also generalize commands stored in Minitab macro files by associating their parameters with stored constants (e.g., K1, K2).

List of Key Commands

In this tutorial the following commands were used:

STORE	the following commands [in the file 'FILENAME']
END	of stored commands
EXECUTE	the commands [stored in 'FILENAME'] [K times]

Practice Problems

1. Using the CK capability, create a program that will
   a. compute NSCORES for a given column and store them in a given column
   b. plot the NSCORES against the raw data to create a Normal Probability Plot

2. Create a stored Minitab program that performs a separate regression analysis on a set of columns for each value of a "BY" column. Many of Minitab's descriptive commands have a BY subcommand, but REGRESS doesn't; you're now going to invent its operational equivalent. Hints: to make the program flexible, use the CK capability, and consider using the COPY command with the USE subcommand to copy the regression data to another set of columns for a given value of the BY variable.

3. Use the STORE command to write a program that will

   a. generate 50 random samples of size 25 from a normal distribution (mean = 14, stdev = 8)

   b. compute and save the mean of these 50 samples

   c. compute and save the standard deviation of these 50 samples

   d. compute and save the 90% confidence interval for each of the 50 samples

   e. create a sample identifier in the range 1–50

   f. plot the confidence intervals against the sample identifier, including the true mean value

4. Generalize the program that you wrote in problem 3 so that the number of samples and the sample size are variable and can be set at execution time.

5. Create and store a program that performs a chi-square goodness-of-fit test on columns of observed and expected frequencies already input into Minitab and displays the p-value.

Part III

Command Reference

▶ Index of Commands (in Logical Order)

The Command Reference section provides you with a complete index to all commands available in The Student Edition of Minitab. First, the Index of Commands in Logical Order lists the Minitab commands and subcommands in the same order as the Quick Reference card provided in the disk pouch at the back of this book. This logical listing provides page numbers to the actual commands and their descriptions that follow in the Command Reference section.

Next, the commands are listed alphabetically, and subcommands appear under the first command in which they can be used. Cross-references are provided throughout. All arithmetic commands are listed under "Arithmetic."

The last part of this Command Reference section, Statistical Reference Texts, contains listings of books about statistics.

1 ▶ General Information

2 ▶ Entering Numbers

2 ▶ Entering Numbers (continued)

3 ▶ Outputting Numbers

4 ▶ Editing and Manipulating Data

5 ▶ Arithmetic

5 ▶ Arithmetic (continued)

6 ▶ Column and Row Operations

Columnwise Calculations

Rowwise Calculations

7 ▶ Plots and Histograms

8 ▶ Basic Statistics

9 ▶ Regression

10 ▶ Analysis of Variance

11 ▶ Nonparametrics

12 ▶ Tables

16 ▶ Miscellaneous

17 ▶ Stored Commands and Loops (Macros)

18 ▶ Symbols

▶ Commands

*

Missing value symbol.

How to Use

Minitab uses an * to represent missing values in a column of numbers. In alpha columns—columns with letters or "strings" instead of numbers—a blank is used instead.

You can substitute an * for a missing or invalid value when entering data with READ, SET, or INSERT. For example:

```
MTB > READ C1-C3
DATA>  0  -3   *
DATA> 19   *  0.5
MTB > END
```

The * can also be used with Minitab commands. However, when it appears on the command line, it must be enclosed in single quotes, as in Figure MISSING1.REF.

MISSING1.REF ▶

```
MTB > SET C1
DATA> 5  2  -99  3  -99
DATA> END
MTB > CODE (-99) '*' C1 C2
MTB > COPY C1 C3;
SUBC>   USE C2 = '*'.
MTB > PRINT C1-C3

 ROW     C1    C2     C3

   1      5     5    -99
   2      2     2    -99
   3    -99     *
```

Minitab operations skip over missing values as necessary. For example, the PLOT command plots only those points which have both an x and a y coordinate and also tells you how many points have been excluded. REGRESS only uses cases with the dependent and all the independent variables present. When an arithmetic command (e.g., ADD, LOG, SQRT) operates on a missing value, the answer will be a missing value.

#

Comment symbol.

Syntax

\#   [any text]

How to Use

Minitab ignores everything you type between a # symbol and the end of a line. You can use this symbol to include comments on command lines, subcommand lines, data lines, or on lines by themselves. For example:

```
MTB > PRINT C1-C3      # Print sales volume for 1978-1980
```

&

Continuation symbol.

How to Use

You can type an & at the end of any line to indicate that the command or data row continues on to the next line. Minitab will return with a CONT> prompt. For example:

```
MTB > REGRESS the data in column C1 on     &
CONT> 1 independent variable in C4         &
CONT> store residuals in C10, fits in C11
```

Also see W.

ABSOLUTE

Syntax

ABSOLUTE   value of E, put into E.

See Arithmetic and Transformations.

ACF

Displays autocorrelations of time-series data in a graph.

Syntax

ACF [up to K lags] for data in C [put into C]

How to Use

This command computes the autocorrelation of the time series for time lags varying from 1 to K. (If you don't specify K, the value $\sqrt{n} + 10$ is used, where n is the number of observations in the series.) The autocorrelation values are plotted in a correlogram and optionally stored in a new column.

Figure ACF1.REF is an ACF of the number of gallons of water used each month from 1983 through June, 1986.

ACF1.REF ▶

```
MTB > RETRIEVE 'UTILITY'
MTB > ACF 'GAL'

ACF of GAL

          -1.0 -0.8 -0.6 -0.4 -0.2  0.0  0.2  0.4  0.6  0.8  1.0
            +----+----+----+----+----+----+----+----+----+----+
  1  0.819                          XXXXXXXXXXXXXXXXXXXXX
  2  0.737                          XXXXXXXXXXXXXXXXXXX
  3  0.669                          XXXXXXXXXXXXXXXXXX
  4  0.584                          XXXXXXXXXXXXXXXX
  5  0.516                          XXXXXXXXXXXXXX
  6  0.446                          XXXXXXXXXXXX
  7  0.392                          XXXXXXXXXXX
  8  0.303                          XXXXXXXXX
  9  0.269                          XXXXXXXX
 10  0.198                          XXXXXX
 11  0.159                          XXXXX
 12  0.141                          XXXXX
 13  0.070                          XXX
 14 -0.024                          XX
 15 -0.004                          X
 16 -0.097                        XXX
```

Also see PACF, CCF, and LAG.

ACOS
ADD
ANTILOG

Syntax

ACOS	(arccosine) of E, put into E
ADD	E to E . . . to E, put into E
ANTILOG	(10 to the power) of E, put into E

See Arithmetic and Transformations.

AOVONEWAY

Computes a one-way analysis of variance between two or more columns.

Syntax

AOVONEWAY   on the data in C . . . C

How to Use

This command computes a one-way analysis of variance for two or more columns of data. AOVONEWAY assumes that each column contains sample data drawn from a different population with common variance, σ^2. Sample size in each column may be different. (If only two columns are specified, AOVONEWAY is equivalent to the TWOSAMPLE command with the POOLED subcommand.)

Figure AOVO1.REF compares how car speeds were affected by: Method 1) posting a speed limit sign; Method 2) Method 1 plus a "Speed Limit Strictly Enforced" sign; Method 3) Method 1 plus a "Speed Limit Radar Controlled" sign; and Method 4) Method 1 plus a parked, empty patrol car.

AOVO1.REF ▶

```
MTB > RETRIEVE 'CARSPEED'
MTB > AOVONEWAY 'METHOD 1' 'METHOD 2' 'METHOD 3' 'METHOD 4'

ANALYSIS OF VARIANCE
SOURCE     DF        SS        MS       F        p
FACTOR      3     555.4     185.1    5.12    0.004
ERROR      40    1447.7      36.2
TOTAL      43    2003.2
                                   INDIVIDUAL 95 PCT CI'S FOR MEAN
                                   BASED ON POOLED STDEV
LEVEL       N      MEAN     STDEV  -------+---------+---------+---------
METHOD 1   12    64.417     7.103                    (------*------)
METHOD 2   10    61.700     6.961               (------*-------)
METHOD 3   11    57.727     5.081       (------*-------)
METHOD 4   11    55.364     4.456  (-------*------)
                                   -------+---------+---------+---------
POOLED STDEV =   6.016                55.0      60.0      65.0
```

Also see ONEWAY, TWOSAMPLE, and KRUSKAL-WALLIS.

ARIMA

Fits seasonal or nonseasonal models to a time series, and lets you predict future values.

Syntax

ARIMA p = K d = k Q = K [P = K D = K Q = K S = K] for data in C [put residuals into C [predicted values into C [coefficients into C]]]

CONSTANT

NOCONSTANT

STARTING

FORECAST [values in C] up to K leads [store forecasts in C [confidence limits in C C]]

How to Use

This command permits you to fit time-series data with an autoregressive integrated moving average (ARIMA) model, and optionally, to correct for seasonal trends. The input consists of a column of time-series data, plus parameters on the command line that indicate the exact model to be used. The FORECAST subcommand requests Minitab to predict future values for the same series. Results may be stored in the worksheet for future use. If desired, use the BRIEF command to decrease or increase the amount of information printed.

For nonseasonal data, the model is fully specified by the parameters p, d, and q, where p is the order of the the autoregressive (AR) component of the model, d is the number of differences used to discount trends over time, and q is the order of the moving-average (MA) component.

For example, the following command fits a moving average model of order 1 to a column of data:

```
MTB > ARIMA 0 0 1 C2
```

To describe recurring seasonal trends within the time series, the additional parameters P, D, Q, and S are required, where S is the number of units in a complete cycle. For example, for monthly data showing a one-year pattern of recurrence, you would set S = 12. The other terms are analogous to p, d, and q for the nonseasonal part: P is the order of the seasonal autoregressive component, D is the number of seasonal differences, and Q is the order of the seasonal moving-average component.

ARIMA allows you to save the residual values in the Minitab worksheet by naming an additional column on the command line. If two columns are named, the residuals as well as the predicted values are stored. Finally, a third storage column can hold the estimated model coefficients.

Figure ARIMA1.REF fits a seasonal time-series model to analyze quarterly electricity costs.

ARIMA1.REF ▶

```
MTB > RETRIEVE 'UTILITY'
MTB > ARIMA (0 0 1) (0 1 1) 4 'KWH $'

Estimates at each iteration
Iteration        SSE      Parameters
    0         177091     0.100     0.100
    1         129217    -0.034     0.250
    2          99214    -0.137     0.400
    3          79415    -0.211     0.550
    4          65288    -0.268     0.700
    5          55414    -0.321     0.850
    6          51011    -0.471     0.863
    7          48190    -0.621     0.870
    8          46619    -0.735     0.870
    9          45885    -0.807     0.866
   10          45676    -0.843     0.857
   11          45663    -0.853     0.853
   12          45662    -0.853     0.854
Relative change in each estimate less than  0.0010

Final Estimates of Parameters
Type        Estimate      St. Dev.  t-ratio
MA    1      -0.8532       0.1033     -8.26
SMA   4       0.8538       0.1743      4.90

Differencing: 0 regular, 1 seasonal of order 4
No. of obs.:  Original series 44, after differencing 40
Residuals:    SS = 44198.5  (backforecasts excluded)
              MS =   1163.1  DF = 38

Modified Box-Pierce chisquare statistic
Lag                 12           24           36          48
Chisquare   25.7(DF=10)  45.7(DF=22)  49.3(DF=34)   * (DF= *)
```

ARIMA Specifications

1. In the parameter list, at least one of the p/P or q/Q parameters must be non-zero, and none may exceed 5.
2. The maximum number of parameters to be estimated is 10.
3. There must be at least 3 data points left after differencing. That is, $S * D + d + 2$ must be less than the number of points.
4. The maximum "back order" for the model is 100. In practice, this condition is always satisfied if $S * D + d + p + P + q + Q$ is at most 100.

5. The ARIMA model normally includes a constant term only if there is no differencing (i.e., d = D = 0). See the CONSTANT and NOCONSTANT subcommands.
6. Missing observations are only allowed at the beginning or the end of a series, not in the middle.
7. The seasonal component of this model is multiplicative, and thus is appropriate when the amount of cyclical variation is proportional to the mean.

Subcommands

CONSTANT
NOCONSTANT

These subcommands explicitly instruct Minitab whether or not to include a constant term in the model. NOCONSTANT is the default condition if either d or D is positive.

STARTING values in C

You can specify starting values for the parameters in the ARIMA model. They must appear in a column in the same order as on the output: p (AR values), P (seasonal AR values), q (MA values), Q (seasonal MA values), and an optional constant. Otherwise Minitab uses the initial value 0.1 for each parameter except the constant.

FORECAST [forecast origin = K] up to K leads [store forecasts in C
[confidence intervals in C C]]

This subcommand allows you to predict the next K observations for the series. If the origin is not specified, it is assumed to be the end of the current series (i.e., the forecasts are for the future). Forecast values and confidence limits can be stored and plotted at a future time.

For more details, refer to Time Series Analysis (rev. ed.) by G. E. P. Box and G. M. Jenkins (Holden Day, 1976).

Also see ACF, PACF, LAG, and BRIEF.

Arithmetic and Transformations

Perform arithmetic and mathematical transformations on columns, stored constants, and numbers.

How to Use

Because the commands which perform mathematical operations work in a similar manner, they are grouped together here under the following headings: LET, arithmetic commands, column functions, and row functions.

LET

You can assign new values to one element in a column, to a constant, or to an entire column with the LET command. Its form is the following, with no extra text allowed (except after #):

LET E = expression

To change one element in a column—for example, to replace the third row in C1 with a 5—you can type

```
▶ MTB > LET C1(3) = 5
```

You can also use a stored constant to indicate the row number:

```
▶ MTB > LET K1 = 3
  MTB > LET C1(K1) = 5
```

An expression used in a LET command may contain the symbols + (addition), – (subtraction), * (multiplication), / (division), ** (exponentiation), and left and right parentheses. In addition, you may use SORT, RANK, LAG, and any of the arithmetic or column functions listed below in a LET expression if you include parentheses around its argument (i.e., SQRT(C1), not SQRT C1).

Within parentheses, evaluation follows the usual order of precedence: functions are always evaluated first, followed by exponentiation, then multiplication and division, and finally addition and subtraction. When two or more operations have the same precedence, they are done from left to right. For example:

```
MTB > LET C5 = C1 + C2
```

stores the sum of the numbers in columns C1 and C2 in C5.

The command

```
MTB > LET K2 = (STDEV(C5))**2
```

computes the square of the standard deviation (i.e., the variance) of C5, and stores it as the constant K2.

Arithmetic Functions

You can use the following arithmetic operations as functions within a LET command, as described above, or as stand-alone commands. As independent commands they take the forms shown below:

ADD	E to E . . . to E,	put into E
SUBTRACT	E from E,	put into E
MULTIPLY	E by E . . . by E,	put into E
DIVIDE	E by E,	put into E
RAISE	E to the power of E,	put into E
ABSOLUTE	value of E,	put into E
SIGNS	of E,	put into E
SQRT	of E,	put into E
ROUND	E to integer,	put into E
LOGE	(natural logarithms) of E,	put into E
LOGTEN	(logarithms - base 10) of E,	put into E
EXPONENTIATE	(e to the power) of E,	put into E
ANTILOG	(10 to the power) of E,	put into E
NSCORE	(normal scores) of C,	put into C
SIN	of E,	put into E
COS	of E,	put into E
TAN	of E,	put into E
ASIN	(arcsine) of E,	put into E
ACOS	(arccosine) of E,	put into E
ATAN	(arctangent) of E,	put into E
PARSUMS	(partial sums) of C,	put into C
PARPRODUCTS	(partial products) of C,	put into C

Remember that when the syntax specifies a C, the argument must be a column. When an E appears, you may use a column, stored constant, or number as an argument (see Figure ARITH1.REF).

ARITH1.REF ▶

```
MTB > READ C1-C3
DATA>  0  4   8
DATA> -1 10   0
DATA>  *  6  -1
DATA>  3  7   *
DATA> END
MTB > ADD C1 C2 3 C5
MTB > PARSUMS C1 C6
MTB > RAISE C1 2 C7
MTB > LET C8 = SQRT(C2) + SIN(C1)
MTB > SIGNS C1 C9
     1  NEGATIVE VALUES    1  ZERO VALUES    1  POSITIVE VALUES

MTB > PRINT C1 C2 C5-C9

 ROW   C1    C2    C5   C6   C7        C8   C9

   1    0     4     7    0    0   2.00000    0
   2   -1    10    12   -1    1   2.32081   -1
   3    *     6     *    *    *         *    *
   4    3     7    13    *    9   2.78687    1
```

The SIGNS command converts negative numbers, zero, and positive numbers to −1, 0, and +1 respectively, and optionally stores these new values in a column.

Column Functions

The column functions each compute one number from a column of data and can be used in LET expressions. As stand-alone commands they have the following form:

COUNT	total number of rows	in C [put in K]
N	number of nonmissing values	in C [put in K]
NMISS	number of missing values	in C [put in K]
SUM	add all values	in C [put in K]
MEAN	average all values	in C [put in K]
STDEV	standard deviation	of C [put in K]
MEDIAN	middle data value	of C [put in K]
MINIMUM	smallest number	in C [put in K]
MAXIMUM	largest number	in C [put in K]
SSQ	sum of the squared values	in C [put in K]

Figure ARITH2.REF uses the same data as Figure ARITH1.REF.

ARITH2.REF ▶

```
MTB > MEAN C1 K1
   MEAN    =       0.66667
MTB > LET C5 = COUNT(C1) - N(C1)
MTB > PRINT K1 C1 C5
K1        0.666667

 ROW   C1   C5

   1    0    1
   2   -1
   3    *
   4    3
```

Row Functions

The row functions shown below compute one number for each row in a set of columns. You can **only** use them as stand-alone commands, and the answers are always stored in a column. You can also use a stored constant or number with the row functions.

RCOUNT	total number of values per row of E . . . E, put in C
RN	number of non-missing values per row of E . . . E, put in C
RNMISS	number of missing values per row of E . . . E, put in C
RSUM	sum of all values per row of E . . . E, put in C
RMEAN	average of all values per row of E . . . E, put in C
RSTDEV	stand. dev. of all values per row of E . . . E, put in C
RMEDIAN	middle data value per row of E . . . E, put in C
RMINIMUM	smallest number per row of E . . . E, put in C
RMAXIMUM	largest number per row of E . . . E, put in C
RSSQ	sum of the squared values per row of E . . . E, put in C

Figure ARITH3.REF illustrates this using the same data used in ARITH1.REF and ARITH2.REF.

ARITH3.REF ▶

```
MTB > RMEAN C1-C3 C5
MTB > RMINIMUM C1-C3 C6
MTB > RMAXIMUM C1-C3 C7
MTB > RSUM 10 20 C1 C8
MTB > PRINT C1-C3 C5-C8

 ROW   C1    C2   C3    C5   C6    C7    C8

   1    0     4    8   4.0    0     8    30
   2   -1    10    0   3.0   -1    10    29
   3    *     6   -1   2.5   -1     6    30
   4    3     7    *   5.0    3     7    33
```

ASIN
ATAN

Syntax

ASIN (arcsine)	of E, put into E
ATAN (arctangent)	of E, put into E

See Arithmetic and Transformations.

BASE

Fixes a starting point for Minitab's random number generator.

Syntax

BASE K

How to Use

The command RANDOM allows you to generate any amount of new data having the statistical distribution you specify. Minitab normally chooses its own starting point for this process so that you don't see the same random data each session.

Sometimes, however, you may want to generate the same data more than once without having to save it in a file. In that case, your first RANDOM command should be preceded by the command BASE together with a number of your choice, telling the random number generator how to begin. You can then produce identical sample data any time you repeat the same BASE and RANDOM commands.

Also see RANDOM.

BOXPLOT

Depicts a column of data with a "box and whisker" display.

Syntax

```
BOXPLOT       for data in C
  START         at K [end at K]
  INCREMENT     = K
  NOTCH         [K% confidence] sign confidence interval
  BY            C
  LEVELS        K . . . K [for C]
  LINES         = K
```

How to Use

Boxplots, like histograms and stem-and-leaf displays, give an overview of the values in a single column and allow you to identify any extreme values. This command can also depict a confidence interval for the population median.

The display consists primarily of a rectangular box, representing the middle half of the data, and dashed lines or "whiskers" extending to either side, indicating the extent of the data. The median value is marked with a tick mark (+) inside the box, and the left and right ends of the box, each marked with an "I", are called hinges and essentially represent the first and third quartiles of the data.

The whiskers extend to the left and right to the last observation on either side within one and one-half times the box width from the box ends. Any value lying between one and one-half and three times the the box width beyond the box ends is considered a possible outlier and is plotted with an *. Any more remote value is considered an extreme outlier and is plotted with a 0.

The selling prices of homes with and without a basement are displayed in the boxplot below.

BOXPLOT1.REF ▶

```
MTB > RETRIEVE 'REALEST'
MTB > BOXPLOT 'SELL $';
SUBC>   NOTCH;
SUBC>   BY 'BASEMENT'.

BASEMENT

                    --------------
1            -----I(    +    )  I----------                               *
                    --------------

                                  --------
2         *             ---------I  (+) I---------   **
                                  --------
          --+---------+---------+---------+---------+---------+----SELL $
          20000     40000     60000     80000    100000    120000
```

Subcommands

START at K [end at K]

This subcommand specifies the first and optionally the last tick mark on the axis. Points falling outside this range will be excluded.

INCREMENT = K

This subcommand determines the distance between the tick marks (+ symbols) on the horizontal axis.

NOTCH [K percent confidence] sign confidence interval

When this subcommand is included, parentheses (notches) in each boxplot indicate the limits of a sign confidence interval for the population median, calculated as for the SINT command. Minitab finds a 90% confidence interval if no other value is given.

Minitab uses a priority system to determine what symbols will be displayed in the BOXPLOT output. If the median falls on the same space as a notch (CI parenthesis), the notch is not displayed. Similarly, if the median and an I-hinge fall on the same space, the I is not displayed.

BY C

This subcommand allows you to create separate boxplots for rows of data sorted by their values in another column C, which should contain only integers between −1000 and +1000 or the missing value symbol (*).

LEVELS K . . . K

The LEVELS option is only used in coordination with the subcommand BY when you wish to rearrange or omit the displays for some subgroups. One boxplot is drawn for each of the BY subscript values (levels) listed here in the order you indicate.

LINES = K

The option LINES = 1 horizontally condenses each boxplot from three lines to one.

Also see STEM-AND-LEAF, and SINT.

BRIEF

Controls the amount of output for the REGRESS and ARIMA commands.

Syntax

BRIEF K

How to Use

This command is used before either REGRESS or ARIMA to control the amount of information printed. The larger the value of K, the more output. BRIEF 2 is the level of detail normally provided.

The following output is available for the command REGRESS:

K = 1 The regression equation, table of coefficients, s, R-squared, R-squared adjusted, and the first portion of the analysis of variance table (regression, error and total sum of squares) are printed.

K = 2 In addition to the above output, the second portion of the analysis of variance table is printed, listing each predictor variable and its sequential sum of squares. Unusual observations (those marked with an X or an R—see the REGRESS command) are also printed.

K = 3 In addition to the above, the full table of fitted and residual values is printed.

The following output is available for the command ARIMA:

K = 1 The table of final estimates, differencing information, residual sum of squares, and the number of observations are printed.

K = 2 In addition to the above output, a table of estimates at each iteration is printed. The backforecasts are also printed if they are not dying out rapidly.

K = 3 In addition to the above, the correlation matrix of the estimated parameters is printed.

K = 4 In addition to the above, the backforecasts are always printed.

Also see ARIMA and REGRESS.

CCF

Displays the cross correlations for time-series data in a graph.

Syntax

CCF [up to K lags] between data in C and C

How to Use

This command computes and graphs the cross correlations between two time series for time lags varying from −K to K. The default value for K is $\sqrt{n} + 10$, where n is the number of rows.

Also see ACF, PACF, and LAG.

CD

Changes to a different directory or shows the current directory.

Syntax

CD [path]

How to Use

CD works in Minitab just as it does in the DOS operating system. For example, to change your current working directory to C:\STAT\WORK, you would type

```
MTB > CD \STAT\WORK
```

CD without a path displays the current directory. See the DOS manual that came with your computer for more information.

Also see DIR and TYPE.

CDF

Computes cumulative probabilities for the given values from a specified distribution.

Syntax

CDF	for values in E [put into E]
BINOMIAL	n = K, p = K
CHISQUARE	degrees of freedom = K
DISCRETE	values in C, probabilities in C
F	df numerator = K, df denominator = K
INTEGER	discrete uniform distribution on K to K
NORMAL	[mean = K [standard deviation = K]]
POISSON	mean = K
T	degrees of freedom = K
UNIFORM	continuous distribution [on K to K]

How to Use

The cumulative distribution function (CDF) for a random variable gives the probability that its value is less than or equal to x. The CDF command computes this probability for a constant or for each number in a column. For example:

```
MTB > CDF 75;
SUBC>   NORMAL 77 2.
   75.0000    0.1587
```

If no subcommand is given, Minitab assumes the distribution is normal with a mean of zero and standard deviation of one.

For discrete distributions only (BINOMIAL, POISSON, INTEGER and DISCRETE), you may omit the column or constant on the main command line to have Minitab produce a full table of cumulative probabilities.

Subcommands

See the listing under the command RANDOM for details on CDF subcommands.

Also see RANDOM, PDF, and INVCDF.

CHISQUARE

Does a chi-square test of association for the table of counts given in the input columns.

Syntax

CHISQUARE   analysis of the table in C . . . C

How to Use

This command computes a chi-square test of association (nonindependence) on a contingency table composed of two to seven columns from the worksheet. Minitab prints a table of observed values and expected values, the total chi-square statistic as the sum of its components from each cell of the table, and the number of degrees of freedom. Minitab also lists the number of cells with small expected frequencies (less than 5), if any.

Suppose we want to test if there is a relationship between where a person buys a car and brake failure. In Figure CHIS1.REF, column 1 represents cars bought from dealers, and column 2 represents cars bought privately. Row 1 refers to the number of defective brakes found, while row 2 is the number of good brakes found.

CHIS1.REF ▶

```
MTB > READ C1 C2
DATA>  931  1690
DATA> 2723  3498
DATA> END
MTB > NAME C1 'DEALER' C2 'PRIVATE'
MTB > CHISQUARE C1 C2

Expected counts are printed below observed counts

         DEALER  PRIVATE    Total
    1       931     1690     2621
        1083.14  1537.86

    2      2723     3498     6221
        2570.86  3650.14

Total      3654     5188     8842

ChiSq =  21.37 +  15.05 +
          9.00 +   6.34 = 51.77
df = 1
```

Also see TABLE with the CHISQUARE subcommand.

CODE

Copies one or more columns while recoding values.

Syntax

CODE (K . . . K) to K . . . (K . . . K) to K for data in C . . . C, put into C . . . C

How to Use

With this command, you can recode any values you choose as you copy data into a new set of columns.

CODE1.REF ▶

```
MTB > SET C1
DATA> -99  3  8  4 -99  0
MTB > END
MTB > CODE (-99)'*' (1:5)1 (6:10)2 C1 C2
MTB > PRINT C1 C2

 ROW    C1   C2

   1   -99    *
   2     3    1
   3     8    2
   4     4    1
   5   -99    *
   6     0    0
```

In figure CODE1.REF, the CODE command copies column C1 to C2, changing all occurrences of −99 to an *, numbers 1 through 5 to a 1, and numbers 6 through 10 to a 2.

Each list or range of values to be changed must be enclosed in parentheses, followed by the new code. Then the input columns, and an equal number of output columns (up to 15 of each) must be listed. If an * is used on the command line to code missing values, it must be enclosed in single quotes.

You may also use stored constants in place of numbers:

▶
```
MTB > CODE (1:K1) K2 C1 C2
```

Also see COPY.

CONCATENATE

Joins two or more alpha columns into a new, wider column.

Syntax

CONCATENATE   C . . . C, put into C

How to Use

This command pastes a set of columns together side by side, and stores them in one new column. The old columns must contain alpha data (i.e., strings of letters or other symbols); the new column will also be an alpha column, up to 80 characters wide.

Also see READ, SET, PRINT, and CONVERT.

CONSTANT

Fits a constant term in all the REGRESS and STEPWISE models that follow.

Syntax

CONSTANT

How to Use

By default, Minitab includes a constant term (the y-intercept of the regression line) in all REGRESS and STEPWISE models. The NOCONSTANT command (or subcommand) causes Minitab to exclude the constant term; CONSTANT tells Minitab to resume its usual practice.

Also see NOCONSTANT, REGRESS, and STEPWISE.

CONVERT

Converts numeric data to alpha data, or alpha data to numeric data.

Syntax

CONVERT using the conversion table in C and C, convert the values in C put into C

How to Use

This command codes a column of alpha data to a column of numbers, or the opposite. To begin with, you need two worksheet columns to serve as a conversion table, one listing alpha expressions and one listing the corresponding numbers. These are listed on the CONVERT command line in the same order as the conversion. That is, if you're converting alpha data to numeric, list the alpha column first. If you're converting numeric data to alpha, list the numeric column first.

For example, retrieve the EXAMPLE.MTW saved worksheet. Suppose we want to code the alpha expressions NO and YES in the column DIET to 0's and 1's in a new column C10. The EXAMPLE.MTW worksheet already has a conversion table in columns C6 and C7, which is shown in Figure CONVERT1.REF.

CONVERT1.REF ▶

```
MTB > RETRIEVE 'EXAMPLE'
MTB > PRINT C6 C7

 ROW     C6    C7

   1    NO      0
   2    YES     1
```

Now do the conversion as shown in Figure CONVERT2.REF.

CONVERT2.REF ▶

```
MTB > CONVERT C6 C7 'DIET' C10
MTB > PRINT 'DIET' C10

 ROW   DIET    C10

   1    NO       0
   2    YES      1
   3    YES      1
   4    YES      1
   5    NO       0
   6    NO       0
   7    YES      1
```

Also see CONCATENATE, READ, SET, PRINT, and WRITE.

COPY

Copies data to and from columns and constants.

Syntax

COPY from C . . . C into C . . . C
  USE rows K . . . K
  USE rows where C = K . . . K
  OMIT rows K . . . K
  OMIT rows where C = K . . . K

The COPY command can also take the form:

COPY from constants K . . . K into K . . . K
COPY from C into constants K . . . K
COPY from constants K . . . K into C

How to Use

This command copies all or part of the data from a set of columns or stored constants. USE says which rows to copy; OMIT says which not to copy.

COPY1.REF ▶

```
MTB > RETRIEVE 'EXAMPLE'
MTB > COPY 'HT' 'WT' C20 C21;
SUBC>   USE 'SEX'=1.
MTB > COPY 'HT' 'WT' C22 C23;
SUBC>   OMIT 'WT' = '*'.
MTB > COPY 'HT' C24;
SUBC>   USE 'HT' = 65:70.
MTB > PRINT 'SEX' 'HT' 'WT' C20-C24

 ROW   SEX    HT     WT   C20    C21    C22  C23    C24

   1     1    70    165    70    165     70  165     70
   2     2    62    110    64      *     62  110     66
   3     1    64      *    71    183     71  183     68
   4     1    71    183    68    158     68  158
   5     2    66      *                  61  106
   6     1    68    158
   7     2    61    106
```

The first COPY command in Figure COPY1.REF copies all the male ('SEX' = 1) heights and weights into C20 and C21. The second command copies all the nonmissing heights and weights into C22 and C23. The last command copies all the heights from 65 to 70 into C24.

This command can also copy a set of constants into a single column, or rows of a column into the same number of stored constants. For example:

▶

```
MTB > COPY K1-K3 C1
```

copies K1, K2, and K3 into column C1.

Subcommands

USE rows K . . . K

USE rows where C = K . . . K

This subcommand tells Minitab which rows to copy. For example, to copy rows 5, 6, 7 and 8 of C1 into C2, you could type:

```
MTB > COPY C1 C2;
SUBC >  USE 5:8.
```

OMIT rows K . . . K
OMIT rows where C = K . . . K

This subcommand works like USE, except that it tells Minitab which rows not to copy.

Also see LET, DELETE, and ERASE.

CORRELATION

Correlates pairs of columns.

Syntax

CORRELATE the data in C . . . C

How to Use

If you give two columns as input, CORRELATE calculates the (Pearson product moment) correlation coefficient for the pair. If you list more than two columns, the correlation is calculated for every possible pair of columns. The lower triangle of the correlation matrix is printed. See Figure CORR1.REF.

CORR1.REF

```
MTB > RETRIEVE 'STA261'
MTB > CORRELATE 'T1' 'T2' 'T3' 'FINAL'

             T1        T2        T3
T2        0.613
T3        0.612     0.699
FINAL     0.672     0.746     0.821
```

CORRELATE skips pairs of column values where one or both values are missing.

Spearman's rho (rank correlation) between pairs of columns of nonmissing data can be computed by ranking both columns and correlating the ranks. (Delete rows containing missing data before ranking columns.) To do this, you could use the commands:

```
MTB > RANK C1 C11
MTG > RANK C2 C12
MTB > CORRELATE C11 C12
```

Also see REGRESS and RANK.

COSINE

Syntax COSINE of E, put into E

See Arithmetic and Transformations.

COUNT

Syntax COUNT the number of values in C [put into K]

See Arithmetic and Transformations.

DELETE

Deletes rows from columns in the worksheet.

Syntax DELETE rows K . . . K in columns C . . . C

How to Use DELETE removes selected rows from columns in the current worksheet and adjusts the remaining rows to fill in any gaps. For example:

```
MTB > RETRIEVE 'EXAMPLE'
MTB > DELETE 2:4 C3-C5
```

changes the the worksheet as shown in Figure DELETE1.REF.

DELETE1.REF ▶

```
            Before                                    After

ROW     HT      WT   CHANGE             ROW    HT      WT   CHANGE

  1     70     165        5               1    70     165        5
  2     62     110       -4               2    66       *        *
  3     64       *        *     --->      3    68     158       -2
  4     71     183        0               4    61     106       -7
  5     66       *        *
  6     68     158       -2
  7     61     106       -7
```

Use a colon to abbreviate a range of rows. For example:

```
▶ MTB > DELETE 3:6 10 13 20:22 C1
```

deletes rows 3, 4, 5, 6, 10, 13, 20, 21, and 22 from column C1.

If you want to remove an entire column, you must use the command ERASE instead.

Also see COPY and ERASE.

DESCRIBE

Calculates descriptive statistics for one or more columns.

Syntax

DESCRIBE the data in C . . . C
  BY C

How to Use

This command prints a collection of summary statistics for each column listed:

N	number of nonmissing observations
N*	number of missing observations
MEAN	average value
MEDIAN	middle value
TRMEAN	a 5% trimmed mean. Minitab removes the smallest 5% and the largest 5% and computes the mean of the remaining values.

STDEV	standard deviation
SEMEAN	standard error of the mean
MIN	smallest number
MAX	largest number
Q1	first quartile (25th percentile)
Q3	third quartile (75th percentile)

These summary statistics are illustrated in Figure DESC1.REF.

DESC1.REF

▶

```
MTB > RETR 'MIAMI'
MTB > DESCRIBE 'WGT';
SUBC>   BY 'SMOKE'.

            SMOKE       N      MEAN    MEDIAN    TRMEAN     STDEV    SEMEAN
WGT             1      12    126.50    123.50    126.50     14.21      4.10
                2      71    126.66    125.00    125.98     14.90      1.77

            SMOKE     MIN       MAX        Q1        Q3
WGT             1   98.00    155.00    120.00    137.50
                2   98.00    175.00    118.00    135.00
```

You can also compute and store these summary statistics using the arithmetic commands.

Subcommand BY C

This subcommand calculates summary statistics for each distinct value in the column C, which can contain integers from −9999 to +9999 or the missing value (*).

Also see Arithmetic and Transformations.

DIFFERENCES

Computes differences between the elements of a column.

Syntax

DIFFERENCES [with lag K] for data in C, put into C

How to Use

This command calculates differences between elements in the input column, which usually contains time-series data. Minitab subtracts from each row the element K rows above, and stores the differences in a new column. The first K rows of the new column will contain asterisks. If you don't specify K, the value 1 is used. See Figure DIFF1.REF.

DIFF1.REF ▶

```
MTB > SET C1
DATA> 5  9  3  12  4
DATA> END
MTB > DIFFERENCES C1 C2
MTB > DIFFERENCES 2 C1 C3
MTB > PRINT C1-C3

 ROW    C1   C2   C3

   1     5    *    *
   2     9    4    *
   3     3   -6   -2
   4    12    9    3
   5     4   -8    1
```

Also see LAG.

DIR

Lists all file names in a directory.

Syntax

DIR [path]

How to Use

DIR works just as it does in the DOS operating system. To see a list of all the files in your current directory, type:

▶
```
MTB > DIR
```

The following three commands would list, for example: a) all files on the diskette in drive B:, b) all files in the subdirectory C:\MARY\STATWORK, and c) all files ending with .MTW in your current directory.

```
MTB > DIR B:
MTB > DIR \MARY\STATWORK
MTB > DIR *.MTW
```

Caution: make sure there is a diskette inserted in your disk drive before doing a DIR of that drive.

Also see CD and TYPE.

DIVIDE

Syntax

DIVIDE E by E, put into E

See Arithmetic and Transformations.

DOTPLOT

Draws a horizontal histogram.

Syntax

```
DOTPLOT        of the data in C . . . C
  INCREMENT      = K
  START          at K [end at K]
  BY             C
  SAME           scales for all columns
```

How to Use

DOTPLOT plots data from one or more columns as dots above a horizontal axis. Figure DOTPLOT1.REF illustrates the amount of cadmium in fish livers for two groups of fish (group 2 was exposed to cadmium; group 1 was not).

DOTPLOT1.REF ▶

```
MTB > RETR 'CD2.MTW'
MTB > DOTPLOT 'LIVER';
SUBC>   BY 'GROUP'.

 GROUP
 1
            :: .
         +---------+---------+---------+---------+---------+-------LIVER
 GROUP
 2
                     .  ..    .  . :.  .                .      :
         +---------+---------+---------+---------+---------+-------LIVER
       0.000     0.080     0.160     0.240     0.320     0.400
```

Subcommands

INCREMENT = K

This subcommand controls the distance between tick marks (+) on the horizontal axis.

START at K [end at K]

Specifies the first and (optionally) the last tick mark on the horizontal axis. Any points outside this range are omitted from the display.

BY C

BY creates a separate dotplot for each value in column C, which may contain integers between -9999 and +9999 or the missing value symbol (*).

SAME

Tells Minitab to use the same scale in drawing the dotplots for all columns listed.

Also see STEM-AND-LEAF, HISTOGRAM, and WIDTH.

ECHO

Causes macro commands to be displayed on the screen as they are executed.

Syntax

ECHO the commands that follow

How to Use

This advanced command is normally used in macros (files of stored commands). When you execute a macro, the commands are printed or echoed to the screen as they are processed. NOECHO turns the echo off, and ECHO turns it back on again.

Also see NOECHO, EXECUTE, STORE, and Tutorial 13.

END

Tells Minitab you are done typing in data (or macro commands).

Syntax

END

How to Use

When you are entering data from your keyboard with READ, SET, or INSERT, the (optional) END command should follow your last line of new data, as in Figure END1.REF. Note that the prompt at the beginning of the line changes from DATA> back to MTB> to show that Minitab is ready for your next command.

ENDF1.REF▶

```
MTB > READ C1 C2 C3
DATA> 10  -2.5  34
DATA>  5   0.5   *
DATA>  8   1.2  -6
DATA>  END
MTB >
```

END must also be used after STORE to tell Minitab when you have finished entering the commands to be stored in a macro file.

Also see READ, SET, INSERT, and STORE.

ERASE

Removes columns and constants from the current worksheet.

Syntax

ERASE E . . . E

Use ERASE to remove any combination of columns and/or constants from the current worksheet. (ERASE has no effect on columns or constants in saved worksheet files.) For example:

```
MTB > ERASE C1-C3 'COST' K2 K3
```

erases C1, C2, C3, the column named COST, and the stored constants K2 and K3.

Also see DELETE.

EXECUTE

Executes commands stored in a command file (macro).

Syntax

EXECUTE commands [in 'FILENAME'] [K times]

How to Use

Minitab is usually used interactively: you type in a command and Minitab immediately carries it out. There may be times, however, when you want to process several commands in a batch. To do this, use an editor or the Minitab STORE command to put Minitab commands in a file, often referred to as a macro. You can then use EXECUTE to carry out the commands in the macro. See Tutorial 13 for details.

Also see STORE, END, and Tutorial 13.

EXPONENTIATE

Syntax

EXPONENTIATE E, put into E

See Arithmetic and Transformations.

HEIGHT

Specifies the height of most plots.

Syntax

HEIGHT of all plots that follow is K lines

How to Use

This command controls the height of PLOT, MPLOT, LPLOT, TPLOT, and TSPLOT. It does not affect the height of HISTOGRAM, DOTPLOT, STEM-AND-LEAF or BOXPLOT. You can use any height from 5 to 400 lines; however, scales tend to be better if K is an odd number. The default height of all plots is 17 lines. For example, the command:

```
MTB > HEIGHT 25
```

will make subsequent plots 25 lines high until you issue another HEIGHT command.

Also see WIDTH.

HELP

Provides on-screen explanation of commands and subcommands, as well as general information about using Minitab.

Syntax

HELP [command [subcommand]]

How to Use

You may type HELP at any time during your Minitab session—when typing commands, subcommands, or even data. If you want information about using a specific command or subcommand, type, for example:

```
MTB > HELP HISTOGRAM BY
```

To see more about how HELP works, type:

```
MTB > HELP
```

HISTOGRAM

Draws a histogram display of a column of data.

Syntax

HISTOGRAM	of the data in C . . . C
INCREMENT	= K
START	at K [end at K]
BY	C
SAME	scales for all columns

How to Use

For each column listed, Minitab divides the data into intervals and plots points that fall within the interval or on its lower boundary with asterisks (*). The midpoint of the interval and the count of values are also printed on each line.

HIST1.REF▶

```
MTB > RETR 'UTILITY'
MTB > HIST 'KWH'

Histogram of KWH   N = 44

Midpoint   Count
     400       2  **
     800       7  *******
    1200      15  ***************
    1600       8  ********
    2000       5  *****
    2400       3  ***
    2800       3  ***
    3200       1  *
```

Subcommands

INCREMENT = K

This subcommand allows you to choose the width K of each interval (i.e., the difference between midpoints).

START at K [end at K]

START specifies the midpoint for the first and, optionally, the last interval. Any observations beyond these intervals are omitted from the display.

BY C

BY creates a separate histogram for each distinct value in C that may contain any integers from −9999 to +9999 or the missing value symbol (*).

To see electricity usage for each month, for example, you could type:

```
MTB > HISTOGRAM 'KWH';
SUBC>   BY 'MONTH'
```

SAME

This tells Minitab to use a common scale for all histograms.

Also see STEM-AND-LEAF and DOTPLOT.

INFORMATION

Summarizes the contents of the current worksheet.

Syntax

INFORMATION [on C . . . C]

How to Use

This command lists all the columns and stored constants you are currently using. The column number, column name (if there is one), number of rows, and number of missing values (if any) are printed. See Figure INFO1. REF for an example.

INFO1.REF

```
MTB > RETR 'UTILITY'
MTB > INFO

COLUMN     NAME       COUNT   MISSING
C1         MONTH         44
C2         YEAR          44
C3         KWH           44
C4         KWH $         44
C5         GAL           44         2
C6         GAL $         44         2

CONSTANTS USED: NONE
```

If you type INFO followed by a list of columns, you receive information only on those columns.

Also see DESCRIBE.

INSERT

Adds new data to columns in the worksheet.

Syntax

INSERT	data [from 'FILENAME'] [between rows K and K] in C . . . C
FORMAT	(format statement)
NOBS	= K

How to Use

With INSERT you can add new rows of data, from either the keyboard or a data file, to nonempty columns in the worksheet. INSERT does not work on empty columns or with saved worksheet files. If you don't list any row numbers, the new values will be added to the bottom of the columns. Otherwise they are inserted between the two consecutive row numbers that you specify. To insert data at the top of columns, use 0 and 1 as the row numbers.

Figure INSERT1.REF illustrates the insertion of numbers from the keyboard.

INSERT1.REF ▶

```
MTB  > RETRIEVE 'EXAMPLE'
MTB  > INSERT 2 3 C3-C4
DATA > 62 105
DATA > 63 120
MTB  > END

        Before                          After

ROW     C3      C4              ROW     C3      C4

  1     70     165                1     70     165
  2     62     110      -->       2     62     110
  3     64       *                3     62     105
  4     71     183                4     63     120
  5     66       *                5     64       *
  6     68     158                6     71     183
  7     61     106                7     66       *
                                  8     68     158
                                  9     61     106
```

To insert data from the file SAMPLE.DAT between rows four and five of columns C11 and C12, for example, you could type:

```
MTB > INSERT 'SAMPLE' 4 5  C11  C12
```

It is not necessary to type the file extension .DAT as part of the filename.

Subcommands

FORMAT (format statement)

Use this subcommand when you want to insert alpha data, or when you must give Minitab special instructions (i.e., when you want to include only part of a data file).

For example, suppose you want to append the two middle columns from a file named WIDEFILE.DAT to C11 and C12 of your current worksheet. You might type:

```
MTB > INSERT 'WIDEFILE' C11 C12;
SUBC>   FORMAT (20X,F5.2,2X,F6.0)
```

See Appendix C for more information.

NOBS K

This subcommand tells Minitab the number of rows to be inserted. NOBS is an advanced feature, which is most useful in interactive macros.

Also see READ, SET, IW, and Appendix C.

INVCDF

Computes the inverse of the cumulative distribution function (CDF).

Syntax

INVCDF	for values in E [put into E]
BINOMIAL	n = K, p = K
CHISQUARE	degrees of freedom = K
DISCRETE	values in C, probabilities in C
F	df numerator = K, df denominator = K
INTEGER	discrete uniform distribution on K to K
NORMAL	[mean = K [standard deviation = K]]
POISSON	mean = K
T	degrees of freedom = K
UNIFORM	continuous distribution [on K to K]

How to Use

The CDF command computes the probability that a random variable is less than or equal to some value E. INVCDF performs the inverse calculation. It computes the value of E that is associated with a given cumulative probability. Figure INVCDF1.REF illustrates this relationship:

INVCDF1.REF▶

```
MTB > CDF 5;
SUBC>   CHISQUARE 7.
    5.0000    0.3401

MTB > INVCDF .3401;
SUBC>   CHISQUARE 7.
    0.3401    5.0005
```

(Small differences may occur due to rounding.)

To store the INVCDF, specify an additional column or constant on the command line.

If no subcommand is used, INVCDF assumes the cumulative probabilities are from a normal distribution with a mean of 0 and a standard deviation of 1.

It is very convenient to use INVCDF to look up critical values for t, F and other distributions rather than searching through tables. For example, to find the critical, one-tailed t for an alpha of .05 and 45 degrees of freedom, type:

```
MTB > INVCDF 0.95;
SUBC>   T 45.
```

For the continuous distributions (CHISQUARE, F, NORMAL, T, and UNIFORM), the INVCDF exists for all probabilities between 0 and 1. (Whether or not INVCDF exists for 0 or 1 depends on the distribution).

For the discrete distributions (BINOMIAL, DISCRETE, INTEGER, and POISSON), there may be no value that corresponds exactly to a given probability. For example, in the command:

```
MTB > INVCDF 0.5;
SUBC>   BINOMIAL 5 0.4.
          K  P(X LESS OR = K)      K  P(X LESS OR = K)
          1            0.3370      2            0.6826
```

the INVCDF is between 1 and 2. If the result is to be stored, the larger of the two nearest values (in our example, 2) is kept.

Subcommands

See the listing under the command RANDOM for details.

Also see RANDOM, PDF, and CDF.

IW

Sets the width for input from files.

Syntax

IW   input width = K spaces

How to Use

IW tells Minitab how many characters per line to read from a data file. You may use any value between 9 and 160; the default is 160.

This command is useful if you want to read only the first part of an input line. For example, suppose the file HEALTH.DAT has 80 characters in each row. To read just the first 30 spaces into columns C1 to C5 of the worksheet, you would type:

```
MTB > IW 30
MTB > READ 'HEALTH' C1-C5
```

Also see OW and OH.

KRUSKAL-WALLIS

This is a nonparametric test for differences among several population medians.

Syntax

KRUSKAL-WALLIS test for data in C, groups in C

How to Use

This command extends the two-sample Mann-Whitney test to any number of groups, and represents a nonparametric alternative to one-way analysis of variance. It computes the test statistic H, which is used to test the null hypothesis regarding the differences among the population medians. The first column contains sample data for all the populations, which are identified by group numbers in the second column.

KRUSKAL1.REF

```
MTB > RETR 'UTILITY'
MTB > KRUSKAL-WALLIS 'GAL $' 'YEAR'

   42 CASES WERE USED
    2 CASES CONTAINED MISSING VALUES

LEVEL      NOBS      MEDIAN   AVE. RANK    Z VALUE
 1983        12       12.06        19.9      -0.54
 1984        12       12.65        20.6      -0.29
 1985        12       12.65        22.8       0.45
 1986         6       13.30        23.8       0.50
OVERALL      42                    21.5

H = 0.6304
H(ADJ. FOR TIES) = 0.6305
```

For each group or level, Minitab prints the number of observations, the median, the average rank, and the z-value (which indicates how the average rank for that group differs from the average rank for all groups).

Minitab also prints a modified H adjusted for ties in the data, calculated as:

$$H(ADJ.\ FOR\ TIES) = H/[1 - \Sigma(dj^3 - dj)/N^3 - N)]$$

where there is one dj for every distinct value in the data column, and it is equal to the number of times that value is repeated. The value of dj is 1 for values which are not repeated. N is the total number of observations. H and H(ADJ. FOR TIES) are equal if there are no ties.

Finally, Minitab prints a message if one or more groups are small (less than 5 observations).

Also see MANN-WHITNEY, AOVONEWAY, and ONEWAY.

LAG

Moves numbers in a column down a specified number of rows.

Syntax

LAG [of length K] data in C, put into C

How to Use

This time-series command moves the row elements of a column down K rows, with 1 as the default value of K, and stores the result in a new column of the same length. There will be K missing value symbols (*) at the top of the output column, while the last K values from the input column will be dropped. For an example, see Figure LAG1.REF.

LAG1.REF ▶

```
MTB > SET C1
DATA> 1 12 3 9 1
DATA> END
MTB > LAG 2 C1 C2
MTB > PRINT C1 C2

 ROW     C1     C2

   1      1      *
   2     12      *
   3      3      1
   4      9     12
   5      1      3
```

You can also copy a column with a lag of 1 using a LET expression, for example:

▶
```
MTB > LET C3 = LAG(C1)
```

Also see LET, ACF, PACF, and CCF.

LET

Syntax LET E = expression

See Arithmetic and Transformations.

LOGE

Syntax LOGE (natural logarithm) of E, put into E

See Arithmetic and Transformations.

LOGTEN

Syntax

LOGTEN (logarithm-base 10) of E, put into E

See Arithmetic and Transformations.

LPLOT

Draws a labeled plot using group codes as the plotting symbols.

Syntax

```
LPLOT            C vs C, groups in C
  YINCREMENT       = K
  YSTART           at K [end at K]
  XINCREMENT       = K
  XSTART           at K [end at K]
```

How to Use

This command plots the first column (the y-axis) against the second column (the x-axis), marking points with letters corresponding to the group numbers in the third column. All three columns must be the same length. An (x,y) pair with 1 as its group number is plotted with an A, and so on; a point with an * in the group column is plotted with an *. The complete conversion chart follows the pattern in Figure LPLOT1.REF.

LPLOT1.REF ▶

```
... -2 -1 0 1 2 3 4 5 6 7 8 9 10 11 12 13 14 15
...  X  Y Z A B C D E F G H I  J  K  L  M  N  O

16 17 18 19 20 21 22 23 24 25 26 27 28 29 ...
 P  Q  R  S  T  U  V  W  X  Y  Z  A  B  C ...
```

The group column can be coded with this chart in mind. For example, to plot data with Ms for males and Fs for females, you could use the codes 13 and 6 in the column specifying sex. (This is easy to change with the CODE command.)

In Figure LPLOT2.REF, electricity-use data for each month are plotted with a different letter. As you would expect, the highest electricity use occurs in the months January and February, which correspond to the letters A and B in the plot.

LPLOT2.REF ▶

```
MTB > RETR 'UTILITY'
MTB > LPLOT 'KWH' 'KWH $' 'MONTH'

        -
    3000+                                                     B
        -                                            A  B   B
KWH     -
        -                                         A
        -                                    B  DC
    2000+                                 A
        -                            CCC
        -                       D H2  D
        -                  A  22 2
        -                33L
    1000+             J 3 G
        -        F 3 F
        -      FJ
        -  F
        -
       0+
          +---------+---------+---------+---------+---------+------KWH $
         30        60        90       120       150       180
```

If several points fall on the same spot, a count is given as in the PLOT command.

Use the commands HEIGHT and WIDTH to control the size of the LPLOT if desired. You may override Minitab's default scaling with the subcommands listed above, which are described further under the command PLOT.

Also see PLOT, MPLOT, TPLOT, CODE, WIDTH, and HEIGHT.

MANN-WHITNEY

Performs a two-sample rank test.

Syntax

MANN-WHITNEY [alternative K] [K % confidence] for the data in C and C

How to Use

This nonparametric command performs a two-sample rank test for the difference between two population medians, and calculates corresponding point and confidence interval estimates. It is sometimes called the two- sample Wilcoxon rank test.

Minitab calculates an approximate 95% confidence interval by default, and computes the attained significance level (p-value). For a one-sided test, enter 1 as the first value of K to test the alternative hypothesis H1:(median1 > median2), or −1 for the alternative hypothesis H1:(median1 < median2). Specify a second value of K to change the default confidence level. Minitab will find a confidence interval for the difference between median 1 and median 2 that comes as close to the specified confidence as possible.

MANNI.REF ▶
```
MTB > SET C1
DATA> 90 72 61 66 81 69 59 70
DATA> END
MTB > SET C2
DATA> 62 85 78 66 80 91 69 77 84
DATA> END
MTB > MANN-WHITNEY C1 C2

Mann-Whitney Confidence Interval and Test

 C1          N =   8     MEDIAN =        69.50
 C2          N =   9     MEDIAN =        78.00
 POINT ESTIMATE FOR ETA1-ETA2 IS        -7.50
 95.1  PCT C.I. FOR ETA1-ETA2 IS (   -18.00,      4.00)
 W =      60.0
 TEST OF ETA1 = ETA2  VS.  ETA1 N.E. ETA2 IS SIGNIFICANT AT  0.2685

 CANNOT REJECT AT ALPHA = 0.05
```

Also see TWOSAMPLE and WTEST.

MAXIMUM

Syntax MAXIMUM largest number in C [put in K]

See Arithmetic and Transformations.

MEAN

Syntax MEAN average all values in C [put in K]

See Arithmetic and Transformations.

MEDIAN

Syntax

MEDIAN middle data value in C [put in K]

See Arithmetic and Transformations.

MINIMUM

Syntax

MINIMUM smallest number in C [put in K]

See Arithmetic and Transformations.

MPLOT

Plots multiple pairs of columns on the same axes.

Syntax

```
MPLOT          C vs C and C vs C and . . . C vs C
  YINCREMENT     = K
  YSTART         at K [end at K]
  XINCREMENT     = K
  XSTART         at K [end at K]
```

How to Use

This command plots several pairs of (x,y) coordinates, representing two columns each, on the same set of axes. The first pair of columns is plotted with the symbol A, the second with B, etc. If several points fall on the same spot, a count is given as in PLOT.

For example, suppose we've just completed the example under REGRESS page 266, which shows how 'BP' (number of points above normal blood pressure) varies with 'OVER WGT' (number of kilograms above normal weight), and stores the fits (y-hats) in C21. We can use MPLOT to see the original data plotted with As, and the fitted regression line, plotted with Bs, on the same plot.

MPLOT1.REF ▶

```
MTB > NAME C6 'YHAT'
MTB > MPLOT 'BP' 'OVER WGT' 'YHAT' 'OVER WGT'

          -
          -                           A
          -
          -                                                   B
     17.5+                                             B      A
          -                      A
          -                                            A
          -                           B
          -                      B
     15.0+                  2   B
          -      A   B
          -      2   A      A
          -
          -
     12.5+
          -      A
          -
           --------+---------+---------+---------+---------+--------
                  7.2       8.4       9.6      10.8      12.0

          A = OVER WGT vs. BP          B = YHAT vs. OVER WGT
```

Use the commands HEIGHT and WIDTH to control size of the MPLOT if desired. You may override Minitab's default scaling of MPLOT with the subcommands listed above, which are described further under the command PLOT.

Also see PLOT, LPLOT, TPLOT, WIDTH, and HEIGHT.

MULTIPLY

Syntax MULTIPLY E by E . . . by E, put into E

See Arithmetic and Transformations.

N

Syntax N number of non-missing values in C [put in K]

See Arithmetic and Transformations.

NAME

Names columns.

Syntax NAME for C is 'NAME' . . . for C is 'NAME'

How to Use

Use this command to assign a name, up to eight characters long, to one or more columns. You can then refer to the column by its name or number in any Minitab command. Column names must always be enclosed in single quotation marks. For example, you could type:

```
MTB > NAME C5  'Volume' C6 'Diameter'
MTB > DESCRIBE 'Volume'  'Diameter'
```

Column names must not begin or end with a space, contain the symbols # or ', or be the same as the saved-worksheet name; all other characters are valid. The command INFO shows you a list of column names already assigned. You can change the name of a column at any time with another NAME command. (The command ERASE removes both data and the column name.) To remove a column name without changing data in the column, type:

```
MTB > NAME C5 ''
```

C5 is followed by two single quotation marks, **not** a double quotation mark.

Also see INFORMATION.

NEWPAGE

Goes to the top of the next page.

Syntax

NEWPAGE

How to Use

Use this command when either the PAPER or OUTFILE command is in effect to tell Minitab that the next command you type should start at the top of a new page. (Remember that PAPER sends a copy of your Minitab session to a printer, OUTFILE sends it to a file.) The word NEWPAGE will not be printed.

Also see OUTFILE, PAPER, and OH.

NMISS

Syntax

NMISS number of missing values in C [put in K]

See Arithmetic and Transformations.

NOCONSTANT

Fits models without a constant term in all REGRESS and STEPWISE commands.

Syntax

NOCONSTANT

How to Use

Minitab normally fits a constant term (the y-intercept of the regression line) to all REGRESS and STEPWISE models. The command NOCONSTANT causes Minitab to omit the constant term from subsequent REGRESS and STEPWISE models, until you issue a CONSTANT command. When NOCONSTANT is in effect, REGRESS and STEPWISE output excludes the R-squared value since its interpretation is difficult.

Also see CONSTANT, REGRESS, and STEPWISE.

NOECHO

Suppresses the printing of commands on the screen during macro execution.

Syntax

NOECHO   the commands that follow

How to Use

This advanced command, along with ECHO, controls whether or not commands are printed or echoed on the screen as a command file (macro) is processed. See Tutorial 13 for more information.

Also see ECHO, EXECUTE, and Tutorial 13.

NOOUTFILE

Stops sending output to a file.

Syntax

NOOUTFILE

How to Use

The OUTFILE command causes everything that appears on your screen, commands and output, to be saved in a specified output file. NOOUTFILE tells Minitab to stop sending output to the file. No filename is required with the NOOUTFILE command.

Also see OUTFILE, PAPER, and NOPAPER.

NOPAPER

Stops sending output to the printer.

Syntax

NOPAPER

How to Use

The PAPER command causes everything you see on your screen, commands and output, to go directly to a printer as well. NOPAPER tells Minitab to stop printing and send output to the screen only.

Also see PAPER, OUTFILE, and NOOUTFILE.

NOTE

Precedes comments in a Minitab macro.

Syntax

NOTE [any text]

How to Use

Like the comment symbol #, NOTE is used to enter comments. For example, a line in a command file (macro) might be:

```
NOTE The table below summarizes group means.
```

Unlike #, NOTE is a command and so must be the first word on a line. Moreover, NOTE commands are printed or echoed in a special way in macros. See Tutorial 13 for details. Although NOTE is designed to work in a macro, it may be used interactively as well.

Also see #, NOECHO, ECHO, EXECUTE, and Tutorial 13.

NSCORE

Syntax

NSCORE (normal scores) of C, put into C

See Arithmetic and Transformations.

OH

Controls height of output.

Syntax

OH output height = K lines

How to Use

This command sets the output height, the maximum number of lines displayed on your terminal screen before the CONTINUE? prompt appears. The default value of OH is 24; you may specify any nonnegative integer. Setting OH to zero suppresses the CONTINUE? prompt entirely, so that output scrolls continuously.

As a subcommand to PAPER or OUTFILE, OH controls the page length of the file going to your printer or the outfile. By default, there are 66 lines per page in an output file.

Also see OW, IW, OUTFILE, and PAPER.

ONEWAY

Computes a one-way analysis of variance.

Syntax

ONEWAY on the data in C, subscripts in C [residuals in C [fitted values in C]]

How to Use

This command performs one-way analysis of variance, as does AOVONEWAY. While AOVONEWAY requires that data for each factor be in a separate column, ONEWAY expects data for all factors to be in the first column listed, with codes identifying the factor or level number in the second column. Codes may be any integers from −9999 to +9999 or the missing value symbol (*).

You can store residual values if you list a third column on the command line, fitted values if you list a fourth column. Figure ONEWAY1.REF uses ONEWAY to compare the cost of electricity over several years.

ONEWAY1.REF ▶

```
MTB > RETR 'UTILITY'
MTB > ONEWAY 'KWH $' 'YEAR' C10 C11

ANALYSIS OF VARIANCE ON KWH $
SOURCE      DF        SS        MS        F        p
YEAR         3      2530       843     0.56    0.642
ERROR       40     59737      1493
TOTAL       43     62267
                                   INDIVIDUAL 95 PCT CI'S FOR MEAN
                                   BASED ON POOLED STDEV
LEVEL        N      MEAN     STDEV   ---------+---------+---------+-------
 1983       12     85.50     23.73   (-----------*----------)
 1984       12    101.17     43.11           (-----------*----------)
 1985       12     96.24     42.92         (----------*----------)
 1986        8    106.60     42.82           (-------------*-------------)
                                     ---------+---------+---------+-------
POOLED STDEV =     38.64                     80       100       120
```

Residual values are stored in column C10, fitted values in C11.

Also see AOVONEWAY, TWOT, and KRUSKAL-WALLIS.

OUTFILE

Stores a copy of your Minitab session in a file.

Syntax

OUTFILE	'FILENAME'
OH	output height is K lines
OW	output width is K spaces
NOTERMINAL	

How to Use

After you type the OUTFILE command, all the commands and output shown on your screen are saved in the specified file until you type NOOUTFILE or end your Minitab session. (OUTFILE and PAPER cannot both be in effect simultaneously. Thus, OUTFILE can also be canceled by typing the PAPER command.) Be sure to enclose the filename in single quotation marks. For example:

```
▶ MTB > OUTFILE 'B:STATWORK'
```

tells Minitab to send a copy of the session that follows to a file on drive B: named STATWORK.LIS. (Minitab supplies the LIS file extension automatically.) After you exit from Minitab, you can view and edit this file with any word processing program or print it out. You may need to check with your instructor about where you should send your outfile (i.e., to a diskette or to a hard disk).

If you use the same filename with OUTFILE again later, new output is added to the original file. However, data typed at the DATA > prompt (after READ, SET, or INSERT) are not sent to an outfile. To include your data in the file, use the PRINT command while OUTFILE is still in effect.

While OUTFILE is in effect, typing NEWPAGE will cause the printer to skip to the top of a new page when you print the output file.

Subcommands

OH output height is K lines

The default value of OH is 66 lines per page in an outfile. Use the OH subcommand to change output height, if desired. An output height of zero suppresses all paging in the outfile.

OW output width is K spaces

Output files normally contain 79 spaces per line. To change the line width, enter any number from 30 to 132 with the OW subcommand. Note that some commands cannot produce output narrower than 70 spaces.

NOTERMINAL

This subcommand instructs Minitab to stop printing output on your terminal screen, but to continue sending results to the outfile.

Also see NOOUTFILE, PAPER, NOPAPER, OH, OW, and NEWPAGE.

OW

Sets the line width for output.

Syntax

OW   output width = K spaces

How to Use

This command sets the maximum width for each line of output on your terminal screen. The default output width is 79 spaces; you may choose any width from 30 to 132. Note that certain commands cannot produce output narrower than 70 spaces regardless of the OW setting.

OW may also be used as a subcommand with OUTFILE or PAPER to set the maximum line width for an outfile or printed output.

Also see OH, IW, OUTFILE, and PAPER.

PACF

Displays partial autocorrelations for time series data in a graph.

Syntax

PACF   [up to K lags] for data in C [put into C]

How to Use

This command computes, plots, and optionally stores partial autocorrelations for a time series, with time lags varying from 1 to K. If you don't specify K, Minitab uses the value $\sqrt{n} + 10$, where n = number of observations. In Figure PACF1.REF, partial autocorrelations are computed and stored in column C10.

PACF1.REF ▶

```
MTB > RETR 'UTILITY'
MTB > PACF 3 'KWH $' C10

PACF of KWH $

       -1.0 -0.8 -0.6 -0.4 -0.2  0.0  0.2  0.4  0.6  0.8  1.0
         +----+----+----+----+----+----+----+----+----+----+
 1   0.530                           XXXXXXXXXXXXXX
 2  -0.238                     XXXXXXX
 3  -0.182                      XXXXXX
```

Also see ACF, CCF, and LAG.

PAPER

Sends a copy of your Minitab session to the printer.

Syntax

PAPER

OH	output height is K lines
OW	output width is K spaces
NOTERMINAL	

How to Use

After you type this command, all the commands and output on your screen are also sent to the printer until you type NOPAPER or end your Minitab session. PAPER and OUTFILE cannot both be in effect simultaneously. Thus, PAPER can also be cancelled by typing the OUTFILE command.

In order for PAPER to work, you must have a printer cabled to your computer. **Caution:** if you are working on a network, do **not** use the PAPER command without your instructor's or lab director's explicit permission. If you're not sure you have the proper setup, use OUTFILE to save a copy of your session in a file which you can print out after you exit Minitab.

While PAPER is in effect, typing NEWPAGE will cause the printer to skip to the top of a new page.

Subcommands

OH   output height is K lines

There are normally 66 lines of output per page. Use the OH subcommand to change output height if desired. An output height of zero suppresses all paging.

OW   output width is K spaces

Printed output is normally 79 spaces wide. To change the output width, enter any number from 30 to 132 with the OW subcommand. Some commands cannot produce output less than 70 spaces wide regardless of the OW setting.

NOTERMINAL

This subcommand tells Minitab to stop displaying output on the screen, but to continue sending it to the printer.

Also see NOPAPER, OUTFILE, OH, OW, and NEWPAGE.

PARPRODUCTS

Syntax

PARPRODUCTS   (partial products) of C, put into C

See Arithmetic and Transformations.

PARSUMS

Syntax

PARSUMS   (partial sums) of C, put into C

See Arithmetic and Transformations.

PDF

Computes probabilities, or the probability density function, for the given values from a specified distribution.

Syntax

PDF	for values in E [put into E]
BINOMIAL	n = K, p = K
CHISQUARE	degrees of freedom = K
DISCRETE	values in C probabilities in C
F	df numerator = K, df denominator = K
INTEGER	discrete uniform distribution on K to K
NORMAL	[mean = K [standard deviation = K]]
POISSON	mean = K
T	degrees of freedom = K
UNIFORM	continuous distribution [on K to K]

How to Use

This command computes the probability or the probability density function associated with a constant or column of numbers. The distribution can be specified with any of the subcommands listed above; otherwise Minitab assumes a normal distribution with a mean of 0 and standard deviation of 1.

For continuous distributions (CHISQUARE, F, NORMAL, T, and UNIFORM), PDF calculates the continuous probability density function, the height of the curve for each number specified. For example, you could compute the PDF for the numbers 28 through 32 from a normal distribution with a mean of 35 and a standard deviation of 2 as shown in Figure PDF1.REF.

PDF1.REF ▶

```
MTB > SET C4
DATA> 28:32
DATA> END
MTB > PDF C4 C5;
SUBC>   NORMAL 35 2.
MTB > PRINT C4 C5

 ROW    C4          C5

   1    28   0.0004363
   2    29   0.0022159
   3    30   0.0087642
   4    31   0.0269955
   5    32   0.0647588
```

Since a storage location (column C5) was given for the PDF values, they were not displayed on the screen. They are displayed automatically if no storage is specified.

For discrete distributions (BINOMIAL, POISSON, INTEGER and DISCRETE), PDF calculates the probability of occurrence of the values indicated on the command line. You may also omit this argument to have Minitab produce a full table of probabilities for the discrete distribution chosen.

Subcommands See the listing under the command CDF for details.

Also see RANDOM, CDF, and INVCDF.

PLOT

Plots one column against another.

Syntax

PLOT	C versus C
YINCREMENT	= K
YSTART	at K [end at K]
XINCREMENT	= K
XSTART	at K [end at K]
SYMBOL	'symbol'

How to Use

This command plots the data in the first column on the (vertical) y-axis versus the data in the second column on the (horizontal) x-axis. In Figure PLOT1.REF, we plot some data.

PLOT1.REF

```
MTB > RETRIEVE 'UTILITY'
MTB > PLOT 'KWH' 'KWH $'

        -
    3000+                                                        *
        -                                             *  *   *
KWH     -
        -                                          *
        -                                    *  **
    2000+                                 *
        -                              ***
        -                       * *2  *
        -                  *  22 2
        -                33*
    1000+             * 3 *
        -        * 3 *
        -      **
        -  *
        -
       0+
          +---------+---------+---------+---------+---------+------KWH $
         30        60        90       120       150       180
```

Individual points are plotted with an *. When two or more points coincide, Minitab prints a count instead. If more than 9 points fall on the same spot, the symbol + is printed.

Use the commands HEIGHT and WIDTH to control size of the PLOT if desired. You may override Minitab's default scaling with the subcommands described below.

Subcommands

YINCREMENT = K

YINCREMENT controls the vertical scale: K is the distance between the tick marks (+) on the y-axis of the plot.

YSTART at K [end at K]

This subcommand specifies the first and, optionally, the last value to be represented on the vertical axis. Data points outside this range are excluded.

XINCREMENT = K

XINCREMENT controls the horizontal scale: K is the distance between the tick marks (+) on the x-axis.

XSTART at K [end at K]

This subcommand specifies the first and, optionally, the last value to be represented on the horizontal axis. Data points outside this range are omitted.

SYMBOL 'symbol'

By default, Minitab plots points with an *. To plot points with the symbol of your choosing, specify one character, enclosed in single quotes, with this subcommand. For example:

```
MTB > PLOT C1 C2;
SUBC>   SYMBOL '.'.
```

would plot individual points as periods.

Also see LPLOT, MPLOT, WIDTH, and HEIGHT.

PRINT

Displays the data in the current worksheet on the screen.

Syntax

PRINT view the data in E . . . E
  FORMAT (format statement)

How to Use

PRINT displays data from the worksheet on your screen. You may list any combination of columns or constants in any order with PRINT. See Figure PRINT1.REF.

PRINT1.REF ▶

```
MTB > RETRIEVE 'EXAMPLE'
MTB > PRINT K1-K3 C1-C4
K1       10.0000
K2       25.0000
K3       *

 ROW   SEX   DIET    HT     WT

   1     1   NO      70    165
   2     2   YES     62    110
   3     1   YES     64      *
   4     1   YES     71    183
   5     2   NO      66      *
   6     1   NO      68    158
   7     2   YES     61    106
```

If only one column is listed, it appears across the screen. Multiple columns are printed vertically. Minitab chooses the number of decimal digits for each number unless you give it specific instructions with the FORMAT subcommand. You can also change the width of the display with the OW command.

PRINT does not send data to your printer. One way to get a paper copy of data in your worksheet is to use PRINT while an OUTFILE command is in effect. After you exit from Minitab you can edit the file, if you wish, and then print it.

Subcommand FORMAT

This subcommand tells Minitab exactly how and where to print column data on your screen. You may not use a format to print stored constants. See Appendix C for more details on format statements.

Also see WRITE, READ, OUTFILE, and Appendix C.

RAISE

Syntax

RAISE E to the power of E, put into E

See Arithmetic and Transformations.

RANDOM

Generates random samples of numbers.

Syntax

RANDOM	K observations into each column C . . . C
BERNOULLI	p = K
BINOMIAL	n = K, p = K
CHISQUARE	degrees of freedom = K
DISCRETE	values in C probabilities in C
F	df numerator = K, df denominator = K
INTEGER	discrete uniform distribution on K to K
NORMAL	[mean = K [standard deviation = K]]
POISSON	mean = K
T	degrees of freedom = K
UNIFORM	continuous distribution [on K to K]

How to Use

With this command, you can generate a random sample of K values from a given distribution in each column listed. If no subcommand is given, Minitab assumes a normal distribution with a mean of zero and a standard deviation of one. Unless you use the BASE command, RANDOM will generate different numbers each time you use it.

The example in RANDOM1.REF generates five values into columns C1 and C2 from a normal distribution with a mean of 100 and a standard deviation of 15. It also generates six integers between 5 and 25 into columns C3 to C5.

RANDOM1.REF ▶

```
MTB > RANDOM 5 C1 C2;
SUBC>   NORMAL 100 15.
MTB > RANDOM 6 C3-C5;
SUBC>   INTEGER 5 25.
MTB > PRINT C1-C5

 ROW        C1         C2   C3   C4   C5

   1   107.474   107.149   23   10   17
   2   120.808    96.970    7   10   16
   3   109.788   108.490   12    6   18
   4   116.441   113.872   18    7   23
   5    86.064    93.908   23   11   24
   6                       25    9   15
```

Subcommands

BERNOULLI p = K

Each Bernoulli trial results in success (1) or failure (0), with p as the probability of success.

BINOMIAL n = K, p = K

The binomial is the distribution of the number of successes after n Bernoulli trials, with p as the probability of success on each trial.

CHISQUARE degrees of freedom = K

You need to specify the degrees of freedom for the chi-square distribution.

DISCRETE values in C, probabilities in C

You can describe your own discrete distribution. First, enter the list of discrete values and their associated probabilities into two worksheet columns. Then use the DISCRETE subcommand, specifying those two columns.

For example, five random values can be generated into C7 based on the discrete distribution in C5 and C6 as shown in Figure RANDOM2.REF.

RANDOM2.REF ▶

```
MTB > READ C5 C6
DATA> -1   0.25
DATA>  0   0.50
DATA>  1   0.75
DATA> END
MTB > RANDOM 5 C7;
SUBC>   DISCRETE C5 C6.
MTB > PRINT C7

C7
   1    0    -1    1    1
```

F   df numerator = K, df denominator = K

For the F-distribution, you must specify the associated degrees of freedom for the numerator and denominator.

INTEGER   discrete uniform distribution on K to K

In this distribution, each integer value in the interval from K to K occurs with equal probability. K may be any integer from −32767 to +32767.

NORMAL   [mean = K [standard deviation = K]]

The normal distribution is determined by its mean and its standard deviation. If the Ks are omitted, the mean is assumed to be 0 and the standard deviation is assumed to be 1.

POISSON   mean = K

The specified mean must be greater than 0 and less than or equal to 50.

T   degrees of freedom = K

This subcommand specifies the Student's t-distribution with K degrees of freedom.

UNIFORM   continuous distribution [on K to K]

This distribution covers the interval from K to K. If the Ks are omitted, then the interval from 0 to 1 is used.

Also see PDF, CDF, INVCDF, BASE, and SAMPLE.

RANK

Assigns rank scores to values in a column.

Syntax

RANK the data in C, put ranks in C

How to Use

RANK assigns the number 1 to the smallest value in the first column, 2 to the next smallest value, and so on. Ties are assigned the average of their ranks. For an example, see Figure RANK1.REF.

RANK1.REF ▶

```
MTB > SET C1
DATA> 8 3 1 3 7
DATA> END
MTB > RANK C1 C2
MTB > PRINT C1 C2

 ROW   C1     C2

   1    8    5.0
   2    3    2.5
   3    1    1.0
   4    3    2.5
   5    7    4.0
```

Also see SORT, Arithmetic and Transformations.

RCOUNT

Syntax

RCOUNT total number of values per row of E . . . E, put in C

See Arithmetic and Transformations.

READ

Enters data row by row into worksheet columns.

Syntax

```
READ        data [from 'FILENAME'] into C . . . C
  FORMAT      (format statement)
  NOBS        = K
```

How to Use

READ enters data one row at a time into one or more worksheet column, either from the keyboard or from a data file. Any existing values in the columns will be erased. (Compare INSERT, which adds data to existing columns, or SET, which enters a single column of data.)

Each row of data must start on a new line and contain one value per column. At least one space or comma should separate the numbers (unless the FORMAT subcommand is used). Letters or words on the data line are normally ignored. (To read in alpha data, use the FORMAT subcommand.) The missing value code (*) and data in exponential (scientific) notation such as 1.23E-2 are valid entries. Type END when you are finished, as in Figure READ1.REF.

READ1.REF ▶

```
MTB > READ C1 C2
DATA> 1   -3
DATA>  0      *
DATA> 1.5  -50
DATA> END
      3 ROWS READ
MTB > PRINT C1 C2

 ROW     C1    C2

   1    1.0    -3
   2    0.0     *
   3    1.5   -50
```

In the figure, C1 now contains 1, 0, and 1.5, while C2 contains −3, *, and −50.

The command:

```
MTB > READ 'A:HOMEWORK' C1-C10
```

enters 10 columns of data from the file HOMEWORK.DAT on a disk in drive A:. Use READ with data (ASCII) files such as those created with WRITE (with the extension .DAT); RETRIEVE is for saved worksheet files (with the extension .MTW).

Subcommands

FORMAT (format statement)

Use this subcommand when you want to enter alpha data, or when you must give Minitab special instructions.

READ2.REF

```
MTB > READ C1 C2;
SUBC>   FORMAT (A3,1X,F2.0).
DATA> LOW 25
DATA> MED 30
DATA> HI  20
DATA> END
      3 ROWS READ
MTB >
```

The example in Figure READ2.REF tells Minitab to read alpha data from the first three spaces into C1, skip a space, read a number from the next two spaces into C2, then continue until there are no more data rows. See Appendix C for more explanation.

You may enter up to 4 characters (A4 format) into an alpha column with READ, up to 80 characters (A80 format) with SET and INSERT. Two or more alpha columns can be pasted together into a new column, up to 80 characters wide, with the command CONCATENATE.

NOBS

You may use this subcommand to indicate how many rows will be entered. The END command is not necessary when NOBS is used.

Also see SET, INSERT, WRITE, CONCATENATE, and Appendix C.

REGRESS

Fits a linear regression model to the data.

Syntax

REGRESS	y in C on K, predictors in C . . . C [standardized residuals in C [fitted values in C]]
NOCONSTANT	
COEFFICIENTS	put in C
PREDICT	for E . . . E
RESIDUALS	put into C
DW	(Durbin-Watson statistic)

How to Use

REGRESS fits a linear equation to your data by the least squares method. List the dependent or y variable, the number of predictors, and the columns containing the predictor variables. You may list an additional column to store the standardized residuals, and another to store the fitted values. Figure REGRESS1.REF shows a simple regression example, in which blood pressure (number of points above normal) is examined as a function of weight (number of kilograms over normal weight).

REGRESS1.REF ▶

```
MTB > RETRIEVE 'BP'
MTB > REGRESS 'BP' 1 'OVER WGT' C20 C21;
SUBC>   COEFFICIENTS C22;
SUBC>   RESIDUALS C23.

The regression equation is
BP = 9.29 + 0.704 OVER WGT

Predictor        Coef        Stdev     t-ratio        p
Constant        9.291        2.737        3.40    0.012
OVER WGT       0.7041       0.3027        2.33    0.053

s = 1.755        R-sq = 43.6%     R-sq(adj) = 35.5%

Analysis of Variance

SOURCE        DF          SS          MS         F        p
Regression     1      16.678      16.678      5.41    0.053
Error          7      21.571       3.082
Total          8      38.249
```

In the figure, the REGRESS command stores standardized residuals in C20, fitted values (y-hats) in C21, regression coefficients in C22, and residuals (observed minus fitted values) in C23. To view the contents of C20 to C23, PRINT the columns.

Minitab prints the regression equation followed by a table listing the coefficient, standard deviation, t-ratio, and p-value for each variable in the model. The output also includes s, the estimated standard deviation about the regression line (equal to the square root of MS Error), R-squared (the coefficient of determination), and R-squared adjusted for degrees of freedom, followed by the analysis of variance table.

Finally, Minitab lists unusual observations (if there are any), noted with an X if the predictors are unusual (leverage value is large) or with an R if the response is unusual (standardized residual is greater than 2). Leverage values greater than 3p/n, where p is the number of predictors and n is the number of observations, are considered large.

The BRIEF command can be issued before REGRESS to increase or decrease the amount of output displayed.

Subcommands

NOCONSTANT

This subcommand tells Minitab not to fit the intercept (where the line crosses the y-axis) term in the regression model. NOCONSTANT can also be used as a main command.

COEFFICIENTS   put into C

Stores coefficients of the regression model in the specified column.

PREDICT   for E . . . E

The PREDICT subcommand computes fitted values based on the regression equation. To use it, specify one argument (column or constant) for each predictor on the main command line. Several PREDICT subcommands may be used with the same REGRESS command. REGRESS output will include associated fitted values plus their 95% confidence intervals and 95% prediction intervals.

For example, using the same BP.MTW data set used in Figure REGRESS1.REF, you could predict blood pressure values for two sets of predictor values by typing:

```
MTB > REGRESS 'BP' 3 'OVER WGT' 'FATS' 'EXERCISE';
SUBC>    PREDICT 14.3  4.5  9.6;
SUBC>    PREDICT  8.6  6.2 10.3.
```

If you specify an unusual case (leverage value greater than 3p/n, where p is the number of predictors and n the number of observations), Minitab prints an X at the end of the output line. Extreme cases (leverage value greater than 5p/n) are marked with XX.

RESIDUALS put into C

Differences between observed y-values and fitted y-values are stored in the specified column.

DW (Durbin-Watson statistic)

Prints the Durbin-Watson statistic for autocorrelation in the data.

Also see BRIEF, NOCONSTANT, and STEPWISE.

RESTART

Begins a new Minitab session without exiting the program.

Syntax

RESTART

How to Use

RESTART is a quick way to erase all the data in the worksheet and reset all parameters (e.g., BRIEF, OH, WIDTH) to their default values without leaving Minitab. RESTART also closes all open files. Be sure to save any important data before using this command.

Also see ERASE and SAVE.

RETRIEVE

Enters a saved worksheet file into the current worksheet.

Syntax

RETRIEVE ['FILENAME']
  PORTABLE

How to Use

RETRIEVE erases all the data in the current worksheet and replaces it with data from a saved worksheet file. Be sure to save any important data before using this command. RETRIEVE can only enter a file created with the Minitab command SAVE. All the columns, column names, and stored constants contained in the worksheet when it was saved will be present when it is retrieved.

The filename must be enclosed in single quotes and should include path information (drive letter and/or directory name) if appropriate. For example:

```
MTB > RETRIEVE 'STA261'
WORKSHEET SAVED 11/11/1987

Worksheet retrieved from file: STA261.MTW
```

Alternatively, typing:

```
MTB > RETRIEVE 'B:STA261'
```

would enter the contents of the file STA261.MTW on a disk in drive B: into the current worksheet. The default file extension for a saved Minitab worksheet is .MTW. If the RETRIEVE command is issued without a filename, Minitab searches for MINITAB.MTW.

The lines of information Minitab prints when you RETRIEVE a file have been omitted from other examples in this chapter to save space. Also, the date your copy of the worksheet was saved will probably differ from the date shown in the example above.

Subcommand

PORTABLE

This subcommand retrieves a saved worksheet created by Minitab on a different computer type using SAVE with the PORTABLE subcommand. This retrieval takes a few seconds longer than the retrieval of a regular saved Minitab worksheet.

Also see SAVE and Appendix A.

RMAXIMUM

Syntax RMAXIMUM largest number per row of E . . . E, put in C

See Arithmetic and Transformations.

RMEAN

Syntax RMEAN average of all values per row of E . . . E, put in C

See Arithmetic and Transformations.

RMEDIAN

Syntax RMEDIAN middle data value per row of E . . . E, put in C

See Arithmetic and Transformations.

RMINIMUM

Syntax RMINIMUM smallest number per row of E . . . E, put in C

See Arithmetic and Transformations.

RN

Syntax RN number of nonmissing values per row of E . . . E, put in C

See Arithmetic and Transformations.

RNMISS

Syntax RNMISS number of missing values per row of E . . . E, put in C

See Arithmetic and Transformations.

ROUND

Syntax ROUND E to integer, put into E

See Arithmetic and Transformations.

RSSQ

Syntax RSSQ sum of the squared values per row of E . . . E, put in C

See Arithmetic and Transformations.

RSTDEV

Syntax RSTDEV standard deviation of all values per row of E . . . E, put in C

See Arithmetic and Transformations.

RSUM

Syntax RSUM sum of all values per row of E . . . E, put in C

See Arithmetic and Transformations.

RUNS

Performs a two-sided runs test.

Syntax

RUNS test [above and below K] for data in C

How to Use

This nonparametric procedure does a two-sided runs test to check if the data are in random order. A run is a series of one or more observations in a row that are greater than K, or one or more observations in a row that are less than or equal to K. If K is not specified, the mean of the column is used.

RUNS1.REF ▶

```
MTB > RETRIEVE 'MIAMI'
MTB > RUNS 'GPA'

    GPA

    K =      3.2651


    THE OBSERVED NO. OF RUNS =  43
    THE EXPECTED NO. OF RUNS =  42.4458
    40 OBSERVATIONS ABOVE K   43 BELOW
              THE TEST IS SIGNIFICANT AT  0.9025
              CANNOT REJECT AT ALPHA = 0.05
```

In Figure RUNS1.REF, we check the randomness of student GPAs. Minitab calculates the expected number of runs, and then it computes the probability that the observed number of runs will vary by this amount from the expected value.

SAMPLE

Randomly samples rows from one or more columns.

Syntax

SAMPLE K rows from columns C . . . C, put in C . . . C

How to Use

With this command, you can sample K rows at random, without replacement, from a block of columns. In Figure SAMPLE1.REF, rows 1, 5, and 4 were chosen from 'HT', 'WT' and 'CHANGE'.

SAMPLE1.REF ▶

```
MTB > RETRIEVE 'EXAMPLE'
MTB > SAMPLE 3 'HT' 'WT' 'CHANGE' C12-C14
MTB > PRINT 'HT' 'WT' 'CHANGE' C12-C14

 ROW    HT     WT  CHANGE   C12    C13    C14

   1    70    165       5    70    165      5
   2    62    110      -4    66      *      *
   3    64      *       *    71    183      0
   4    71    183       0
   5    66      *       *
   6    68    158      -2
   7    61    106      -7
```

Also see RANDOM.

SAVE

Copies the current worksheet into a saved worksheet file.

Syntax

SAVE ['FILENAME']
  PORTABLE

How to Use

SAVE copies all the columns, data, column names, and constants from the current worksheet into a file with the default extension .MTW. For example, the command:

```
MTB > SAVE 'B:STATDATA'

Worksheet saved into file: B:STATDATA.MTW
```

creates a saved worksheet file STATDATA.MTW on the disk in drive B:. You can then use the command RETRIEVE to enter this file into the current worksheet of a Minitab session on any DOS microcomputer. (For use on other computers, see the subcommand PORTABLE below.) The file cannot be sent to a printer or used by another software package.

Filenames may be any combination of letters and numbers up to eight characters long; blanks are not allowed. If you don't enter a filename, Minitab saves your worksheet as MINITAB.MTW.

Subcommand PORTABLE

This subcommand saves the worksheet in a file with the default extension .MTP that can be used by Minitab on any type of computer (e.g., a mainframe); just use RETRIEVE with the PORTABLE subcommand.

Also see RETRIEVE and WRITE.

SET

Enters data into one column.

Syntax

SET data [from 'FILENAME'] into C
  FORMAT (format statement)
  NOBS = K

With SET you can enter data into a column from the keyboard or from a data file. Use at least one space or a comma between data values.

SET1.REF▶

```
MTB > SET C1
DATA> 6   1 *
DATA> 0 -2
DATA> END
MTB >
```

In Figure SET1.REF, the SET command puts the values 6, 1, *, 0, and −2 into column C1. The END command tells Minitab you are finished entering data. As with READ (used for entering multiple columns), SET automatically erases the existing contents of the column listed. (To add numbers to existing columns, use INSERT.) A stored constant such as K1 may also be used as part of the data.

SET2.REF▶

```
MTB > LET K1 = 2
MTB > SET C1
DATA> 5(1) 5(2) *
DATA> 2(1:3) (-2:0)2
DATA> 3(8:10)K1
DATA> 4:2/0.5
DATA> END
MTB >
```

By using the symbols ( ), :, and / it is very easy to enter patterned data with SET. In Figure SET2.REF, these commands store 46 elements in C1. The first DATA> line enters 11 values: five 1's, five 2's and the missing value symbol (*). The second DATA> line produces 12 more rows: 2(1:3) expands as 1, 2, 3, 1, 2, 3 (two sets of the numbers 1 through 3), and (−2:0)2 expands as −2, −2, −1, −1, 0, 0 (each integer from -2 to 0 is entered twice). The third DATA> line stores another 18 values: the series 8, 8, 9, 9, 10, 10, entered three times. The last DATA> line enters five more numbers: 4, 3.5, 3, 2.5, 2. The symbol / tells Minitab to keep increasing or decreasing the numbers by the value that follows.

If you make a mistake while typing in data, and your cursor is on the same line as the mistake, backspace to correct it. If not, use the LET command to make the correction.

Subcommands

FORMAT (format statement)

Use this subcommand when you want to enter alpha data or need to give Minitab special instructions. For example, to copy data into column C10 from a file TEST.DAT on the disk in drive B:, you could type:

```
MTB > SET 'B:TEST' C10;
SUBC>    FORMAT (5F2.0)
```

Each line of the file contains five whole numbers, with two spaces per number. See Appendix A for more information on formatted input and output.

NOBS = K

The NOBS subcommand tells Minitab how many rows you will enter. The END command is not necessary if you use NOBS.

Also see READ, INSERT, and LET.

SIGNS

Syntax SIGNS of E, [put into E]

See Arithmetic and Transformations.

SIN

Syntax SIN of E, put into E

See Arithmetic and Transformations.

SINTERVAL

Computes confidence intervals for the median.

Syntax SINTERVAL [confidence = K] on data in C . . . C

How to Use This command calculates three confidence intervals around the median for each column listed: one with confidence just above K, one with confidence just below K, and a middle interval which approximates K. The middle interval in SINTERVAL, denoted by NLI, and the confidence interval displayed by BOXPLOT;NOTCH are calculated using a nonlinear interpolation procedure described in Hettmansperger and Sheather, 1986 (see Appendix F). If K is not specified, Minitab uses 95%.

SINT1.REF▶

```
MTB > RETRIEVE 'STA261'
MTB > SINTERVAL 95 'FINAL'

SIGN CONFIDENCE INTERVAL FOR MEDIAN

                              ACHIEVED
             N    MEDIAN    CONFIDENCE    CONFIDENCE INTERVAL    POSITION
FINAL       45     73.00      0.9275      (   69.00,   81.00)          17
                              0.9500      (   68.54,   81.00)         NLI
                              0.9643      (   68.00,   81.00)          16
```

In Figure SINT1.REF, the 17 under POSITION means that the first confidence interval goes from the 17th smallest value to the 17th largest one.

Also see STEST and BOXPLOT.

SORT

Sorts data in ascending order.

Syntax

SORT data in C [carry along corresp. rows of C . . . C], put into C [corresp. rows into C . . . C]

How to Use

This command sorts data in a series of columns by rows, according to the values in the first column you list, then stores the rearranged data in the second series of columns.

SORT1.REF ▶

```
MTB > RETRIEVE 'EXAMPLE'
MTB > SORT 'WT' 'HT' 'CHANGE' C12-C14
MTB > PRINT 'WT' 'HT' 'CHANGE' C12-C14

 ROW     WT     HT   CHANGE     C12     C13     C14

   1    165     70        5     106      61      -7
   2    110     62       -4     110      62      -4
   3      *     64        *     158      68      -2
   4    183     71        0     165      70       5
   5      *     66        *     183      71       0
   6    158     68       -2       *      64       *
   7    106     61       -7       *      66       *
```

For example, the SORT command in Figure SORT1.REF, sorts the rows in 'WT', 'HT' and 'CHANGE' by the values in 'WT' and stores them in columns C12 to C14. Note that * symbols are placed last.

Also see RANK.

SQRT

SQRT   of E, put into E

See Arithmetic and Transformations.

SSQ

Syntax

SSQ   Sum of the squared values in C [put in K]

See Arithmetic and Transformations.

STACK

Stacks blocks of columns and/or constants on top of each other.

Syntax

STACK   (E . . . E) . . . on top of (E . . . E) put in (C . . . C)
  SUBSCRIPTS   into C

How to Use

The first block is always placed on top of the second block, and so on, with results stored in the last block listed. In Figure STACK1.REF, the numbers in C16 show which block the values originally came from.

STACK1.REF▶

```
MTB > RETRIEVE 'EXAMPLE'
MTB > STACK (C8 C11) (C7 C9) (14 8) (C14 C15);
SUBC>   SUBSCRIPTS C16.
MTB > PRINT C8 C11 C7 C9 C14-C16

 ROW    C8   C11    C7    C9   C14    C15    C16

   1     1     5     0     5     1      5      1
   2     2     6     1     6     2      6      1
   3     3     7                 3      7      1
   4     4     8                 4      8      1
   5                             0      5      2
   6                             1      6      2
   7                            14      8      3
```

Columns within each block must be of the same length. You may omit the parentheses around each block if your blocks are only one column (or constant) wide.

Subcommand SUBSCRIPTS into C

This subcommand stores an extra column of numbers to show which block each row came from. Rows from the first block are assigned the value of 1, the second block a value of 2, and so on, as in Figure STACK1.REF.

Also see UNSTACK.

STDEV

Syntax STDEV standard deviation of C [put in K]

See Arithmetic and Transformations.

STEM-AND-LEAF

Constructs a histogram with digits from the actual data values.

Syntax

```
STEM-AND-LEAF    of the data in C . . . C
  TRIM             outliers
  INCREMENT        = K
  BY               C
```

How to Use

The STEM-AND-LEAF display has three columns. The column on the left is a cumulative count of values from the top of the figure down and the bottom of the figure up to the middle. The number in parentheses is the count of values in the row containing the median. Each number in the second column is called a stem, while the numbers to its right are the leaves, each of which is a single digit to place after the stem digits, representing one data value. The leaf unit tells you where to put the decimal place in each number.

STEM1.REF ▶

```
MTB > RETRIEVE 'STA261'
MTB > STEM-AND-LEAF 'FINAL'

Stem-and-leaf of FINAL     N  = 45
Leaf Unit = 1.0

    1    0 0
    1    1
    1    2
    3    3 48
    4    4 7
    7    5 359
   18    6 12356666899
  (7)    7 0011378
   20    8 11111225555899
    6    9 001258
```

In the stem-and-leaf display in Figure STEM1.REF, each leaf digit is in the ones position. Thus the lowest grade was a 0, followed by 34, 38, 47, and so on. The median, 73, is the fifth value in the row, the count of which is enclosed by parentheses. The highest grade was a 98.

Parentheses around the median row are omitted if the median falls between two lines of the display.

Subcommands

TRIM outliers

This subcommand omits outliers (see BOXPLOT for a definition) from the stem-and-leaf display, and shows them on lines labeled LO and HI. TRIM and BY cannot be used together.

INCREMENT = K

This controls vertical scaling. The value of K will be the difference between the smallest possible values on adjacent lines.

BY C

BY produces a stem-and-leaf display for each distinct value in C, which may contain whole numbers from −9999 to +9999 or the missing value symbol (*). This is useful if the column C contains codes for subgroup membership (e.g., 1's and 2's for males and females). BY cannot be used with TRIM.

Also see HISTOGRAM and BOXPLOT.

STEPWISE

Performs a stepwise regression to find the best subset of predictors with respect to the F-statistic.

Syntax

STEPWISE regression of y in C on the predictors C . . . C
- FENTER = K
- FREMOVE = K
- FORCE C . . . C
- ENTER C . . . C
- REMOVE C . . . C
- BEST K alternative predictors
- STEPS = K

How to Use

This command does a linear regression step by step in a search for a good subset of the possible predictors. You can vary the basic procedure to allow for forward selection or for backwards elimination. Unless you are running STEPWISE from a command file, you can also intervene at any pause to modify the procedure with new subcommands. Models are fit with a constant term unless the NOCONSTANT command is in effect.

Default Procedure

The basic method alternates between stages of adding and removing variables until no more predictors can enter or leave the model. In step one, Minitab calculates an F-statistic for each predictor already in the model. If that value is less than FREMOVE (4, unless otherwise specified) for any predictor, the predictor with the lowest F-statistic is removed, and output from the resulting model is printed. In step two, Minitab calculates an F-statistic for each predictor not in the current model. If that value is greater than FENTER (4, unless otherwise specified) for any predictor, the predictor with the highest F-statistic is entered, and output from the resulting model is printed.

Forward Selection

This method adds predictors to the model as in the default procedure, but never removes any. To do forward selection, set FREMOVE to zero.

Backwards Elimination

This method starts with a model containing all possible predictors, then removes them one at a time without ever reentering any. To do backwards elimination, set FENTER = 100000 and list all predictors on the ENTER subcommand.

User Intervention

After each screenful of STEPWISE output, Minitab displays the prompt MORE?. You may respond YES to continue the procedure, NO to terminate it, or you may alter the model with one or more of the subcommands described below. (The STEPS subcommand let you control the amount of output in one screenful.)

Output

Minitab prints the constant term (if applicable), the coefficient and t-ratio for each predictor, and the s and R-squared values for each step.

STEP1.REF▶

```
MTB > RETRIEVE 'STA261'
MTB > STEPWISE 'FINAL' C1-C14

STEPWISE REGRESSION OF  FINAL  ON 14 PREDICTORS, WITH N =  45

    STEP        1        2        3        4
CONSTANT    6.747   -7.132  -15.094  -15.487

T3          0.886    0.632    0.589    0.642
T-RATIO      9.41     5.24     5.19     6.00

T2                    0.43     0.38     0.39
T-RATIO               3.01     2.80     3.12

Q2                             1.23     1.36
T-RATIO                        2.76     3.28

Q6                                     -0.67
T-RATIO                                -2.75

S            10.5     9.65     8.97     8.33
R-SQ        67.33    73.13    77.34    80.93
 MORE? (YES, NO, SUBCOMMAND, OR HELP)
SUBC> NO
MTB >
```

In Figure STEP1.REF, the response to the MORE? prompt was NO. Alternatively, the responses shown in STEP2.REF

STEP2.REF ▶

```
 MORE? (YES, NO, SUBCOMMAND, OR HELP)
SUBC> FENTER = 1;
SUBC> FREMOVE = 1.
```

would cause Minitab to compute and display five more steps, while lowering the required F-values.

Subcommands

FENTER = K

With this subcommand, you can change the minimum F-value required to enter a predictor variable into a model from the default value of 4. The value for FENTER must be greater than or equal to FREMOVE.

FREMOVE = K

This allows you to set the F-value below which a predictor variable will be removed from a model. The default value is 4.

FORCE C . . . C

Here you list predictor variables that you want included in all subsequent models, until you change their status with a REMOVE or an ENTER subcommand.

ENTER C . . . C

These variables are to be entered in the current model. Any of them may be removed in the next step if its F-value falls below FREMOVE.

REMOVE C . . . C

These variables are to be removed from the current model. Any of them may reenter the model at the next step if its F-value rises above FENTER.

BEST K alternative variables

For each step in which a variable is added to the model, the next K best alternatives (in terms of the F-statistic) are printed, along with their associated t-statistics. Each t-value shown is obtained by replacing the variable actually chosen by the alternative variable. The default value of K is 0.

STEPS = K

You can set the number of steps of output printed before the MORE? prompt allows you to intervene again. K can be any number from 1 up to the maximum allowed by the width of your screen (or by the OW command).

Also see REGRESS, CONSTANT, NOCONSTANT, and OW.

STEST

Computes a sign test for one or more columns.

Syntax

STEST [median = K] on data in C . . . C
  ALTERNATIVE = K

How to Use

Does a nonparametric, two-sided sign test of whether or not the median for each column listed is equal to the value K (unless you use the ALTERNATIVE subcommand).

STTEST1.REF▶

```
MTB > RETRIEVE 'STA261'
MTB > STEST 13.5 'Q1' 'Q2'

SIGN TEST OF MEDIAN = 13.50 VERSUS  N.E.  13.50

                  N  BELOW  EQUAL  ABOVE   P-VALUE    MEDIAN
Q1               45     12      0     33    0.0025     14.00
Q2               45     23      0     22    1.0000     13.00
```

The example in Figure STEST1.REF tests whether the median score on quizzes 1 and 2 is equal to 13.5. Minitab prints the median, the number of observations below, equal to, and above the median, and the p-value or probability based on the binomial distribution.

The default value of K is 0. Any values equal to K are omitted from the sign test.

Subcommand

ALTERNATIVE = K

Does a one-sided test of the alternative hypothesis H1:(median < K) for ALTERNATIVE = −1, or H1:(median > K) for ALTERNATIVE = 1. The null hypothesis in both cases is H0:(median = K). ALTERNATIVE = 0 performs the same two-sided test as STEST with no subcommand.

Also see SINTERVAL.

STOP

Exits from the Minitab program.

Syntax

STOP

How to Use

STOP ends your Minitab session and erases the current worksheet. Be sure to SAVE any data you may want to reuse before typing STOP.

Also see SAVE.

STORE

Stores subsequent commands in a command file.

Syntax

STORE [in 'FILENAME'] the following Minitab commands

How to Use

A command file, or macro, contains Minitab commands which can be processed with the EXECUTE command. STORE tells Minitab to enter all subsequent commands into the specified file (its default name is MINITAB.MTB) until it encounters the command END. Macros are given the default file extension .MTB; they are standard (ASCII) files that may be edited or sent to a printer. See Tutorial 13 for more information and examples.

Also see EXECUTE and END.

SUBTRACT

Syntax SUBTRACT E from E, put into E

See Arithmetic and Transformations.

SUM

SUM add all values in C [put in K]

See Arithmetic and Transformations.

SYSTEM

Temporarily exits from your Minitab session to DOS.

Syntax SYSTEM

How to Use

SYSTEM allows you to leave Minitab temporarily in order to execute DOS commands (e.g., MKDIR, FORMAT, PRINT) and then return to your Minitab session by typing EXIT.

Caution: It is safest to SAVE your worksheet before using the SYSTEM command. Also, never change your DOS path if you wish to return to a suspended Minitab session.

Also see DIR, TYPE, and CD.

TABLE

Produces one-way or multi-way tables.

Syntax

```
TABLE          the classification variables in C . . . C
  MEANS          for C . . . C
  MEDIANS        for C . . . C
  SUMS           for C . . . C
  MINIMUMS       for C . . . C
  MAXIMUMS       for C . . . C
  STDEV          for C . . . C
  STATS          for C . . . C
```

DATA	for C . . . C
N	for C . . . C
NMISS	for C . . . C
PROPORTION	of cases = K [thru K] in C . . . C
COUNTS	
ROWPERCENTS	
COLPERCENTS	
TOTPERCENTS	
CHISQUARE	analysis [output code = K]
MISSING	level for the classification variable C . . . C
NOALL	in margins
ALL	for the classification variables C . . . C
FREQUENCIES	are in C

How to Use

To display Minitab data in table form, enter the TABLE command, followed by up to ten classification variables (e.g., sex, year, group number). The values in the first column listed determine the row headings of the table, and the values in the second column determine the column headings. A separate table is produced for every possible combination of values from the remaining columns listed. They may contain whole numbers between −9999 to +9999 or the missing value symbol (*). Variables listed in subcommands (except for MISSING and ALL) may be of any type (discrete or continuous). If no subcommands are used, Minitab prints the number of observations in each cell of the table.

The example in Figure TABLE1.REF tabulates the number of observations and the average GPA for students who do and do not watch soap operas, and for those who do and do not have a boyfriend.

TABLE1.REF ▶

```
MTB > RETRIEVE 'MIAMI'
MTB > TABLE 'SOAPS' 'BOYFRND';
SUBC>   COUNTS;
SUBC>   MEAN 'GPA'.


ROWS: SOAPS     COLUMNS: BOYFRND

             1         2       ALL

1           11        12        23
        3.0909    3.0417    3.0652

2           37        23        60
        3.3514    3.3261    3.3417

ALL         48        35        83
        3.2917    3.2286    3.2651

   CELL CONTENTS --
                   COUNT
                GPA:MEAN
```

Minitab prints subtotals (marginal values) across rows in a row labeled ALL and down columns in a column labeled ALL.

To list actual GPA values instead of an average for each cell, you could change the subcommands given above as follows:

▶

```
MTB > TABLE 'SOAPS' 'BOYFRND';
SUBC>   DATA 'GPA'.
```

Subcommands

MEANS   for C . . . C

Prints the mean for each cell and the overall marginal means for each row and column.

MEDIANS   for C . . . C

Prints the median for each cell; marginal medians are not printed.

SUMS   for C . . . C

Prints the sum of the data for each cell.

MINIMUMS for C . . . C

Prints the minimum value for each cell.

MAXIMUMS for C . . . C

Prints the maximum value for each cell.

STDEV for C . . . C

Prints the standard deviation for each cell.

STATS for C . . . C

Prints the number of nonmissing values, the mean, and the standard deviation for each cell.

DATA for C . . . C

Prints all the data values for each cell.

N for C . . . C

Prints the number of nonmissing data values for each cell.

NMISS for C . . . C

Prints the number of missing values for each cell.

PROPORTION of cases = K [thru K] in C . . . C

Prints the proportion of observations equal to K or in the range from K to K for each cell. There should not be any missing value symbols (*) in columns listed with this subcommand.

COUNTS

Prints the total number of values (missing and nonmissing) for each cell.

ROWPERCENTS

Calculates what percentage each cell represents of the total observations in the row.

COLPERCENTS

Calculates what percentage each cell represents of the total observations in the column.

TOTPERCENTS

Calculates what percentage each cell represents of all the observations in the table.

CHISQUARE   analysis [output code = K]

Prints the chi-square statistic, used to test the independence of the rows and columns in a two-way table, together with its associated degrees of freedom. The following data are printed in each cell depending on the value of the output code K (its default value is 1):

K = 1	Observed counts for each cell.
K = 2	Observed and expected counts for each cell.
K = 3	Observed and expected counts and the standardized residuals for each cell, which are computed as (observed count − expected count) divided by the square root of the expected count.

MISSING   level for the classification variables C . . . C

Adds an additional row or column labeled MISSING to the display, containing counts of the missing observations in each cell for any variables (from the TABLE command line) that are listed after this subcommand and have missing values.

NOALL   in margins

This subcommand cancels the printing of marginal values in rows and columns labeled ALL.

ALL   for the classification variables C . . . C

Prints marginal values only for the classification variables from the TABLE command line that are listed with this subcommand.

FREQUENCIES   are in C

The TABLE command normally assumes that each row in the input columns refers to one case. Sometimes you may find it necessary to combine the raw-data values into partial or full-frequency counts. This subcommand tells Minitab where to find the frequencies (or weights) for each row.

Also see CHISQUARE and TALLY.

TALLY

Tallies information for each value in the columns listed.

Syntax

TALLY	the data in C . . . C
COUNTS	
PERCENTS	
CUMCOUNTS	cumulative counts
CUMPERCENTS	cumulative percentages
ALL	four statistics above

How to Use

The columns listed with TALLY must represent classification variables (e.g., sex, group number, year) and contain only whole numbers between −9999 and +9999 or missing value symbols (*). If no subcommands are used, TALLY prints only the counts for each value in the columns listed.

In Figure TALLY1.REF, the values 1, 2, and 3 represent short, medium-length, and long hair respectively. TALLY shows that 34 individuals (about 41% of the total) have short hair, 39 (about 47%) have medium-length hair, and 10 (about 12%) have long hair. Cumulative counts and percentages are also displayed.

TALLY1.REF▶

```
MTB > RETRIEVE 'MIAMI'
MTB > TALLY  'HAIR LNG';
SUBC>   ALL.

HAIR LNG  COUNT CUMCNT PERCENT  CUMPCT
       1     34     34   40.96   40.96
       2     39     73   46.99   87.95
       3     10     83   12.05  100.00
      N=     83
```

Subcommands

COUNTS

Prints the number of times each distinct value occurs in the columns listed. This information is printed by default if you don't list any subcommands.

PERCENTS

Prints the relative frequency of each nonmissing value in the columns listed.

CUMCOUNTS

Prints cumulative counts of the nonmissing values in each column listed.

CUMPERCENTS

Prints cumulative relative frequencies of the nonmissing values in each column listed.

ALL

Prints counts, cumulative counts, percentages, and cumulative percentages for the distinct value in each column listed.

Also see TABLE.

TAN

Syntax TAN of E, put into E

See Arithmetic and Transformations.

TINTERVAL

Calculates a confidence interval for the mean of each column.

Syntax TINTERVAL [K% confidence] for data in C . . . C

How to Use With this command you can calculate a confidence interval for the mean of one or more variables (assumed to be normal) without knowing their standard deviations. The procedure uses values from the Student's t-distribution, and it assumes K = 95% as the default confidence level. Note that K may be expressed either as a percentage or as a decimal such as .95. Figure TINT1.REF is an example of a TINTERVAL test on one column of data.

TINT1.REF ▶

```
MTB > RETRIEVE 'EXAMPLE'
MTB > TINTERVAL 90 'HT'

             N      MEAN     STDEV  SE MEAN    90.0 PERCENT C.I.
HT           7     66.00      3.87     1.46  (    63.15,    68.85)
```

Also see TTEST, ZINTERVAL, ZTEST, SINTERVAL, and WINTERVAL.

TPLOT

Constructs a pseudo-three-dimensional plot.

Syntax

```
TPLOT           y in C vs x in C vs z in C
  YINCREMENT      = K
  YSTART          at K [end at K]
  XINCREMENT      = K
  XSTART          at K [end at K]
```

How to Use

This command plots the data from three columns. The first column is represented on the y-axis of the plot, the second column is represented on the x-axis of the plot, and the third, or z, column is represented with a set of special plotting symbols.

The plotting symbol used for z is "0" if z is more than one standard deviation below its mean, "." if z is within one standard deviation below the mean, "/" if z is within one standard deviation above the mean, or "X" if z is more than one standard deviation above the mean. This is illustrated in Figure TPLOT1.REF.

TPLOT1.REF ▶

```
MTB > RETR 'UTILITY'
MTB > TPLOT 'KWH $' 'KWH' 'GAL'

        -
        -                                                        0
     180+                                                    .
        -                                                 /  /
KWH $   -                                         0
        -                                        /0
        -                                       /
     120+                                   //0
        -                               // 0 0
        -                           03 3 X
        -                      3 //
        -                  20X/
      60+          0/2 /
        -       /X/
        -  0
        -
        -
          ----+---------+---------+---------+---------+---------+--KWH
            500      1000      1500      2000      2500      3000

     N* = 2

     '0' <    501.27 < '.' <  2390.86 < '/' <  4280.45 < 'X'
```

If several points fall on the same spot, a count is printed instead. Use the commands HEIGHT and WIDTH to control the size of the TPLOT if desired. You may override Minitab's default scaling with the sub commands listed above, which are described further under the command PLOT.

Also see PLOT, LPLOT, MPLOT, HEIGHT, and WIDTH.

TSPLOT

Plots time-series data.

Syntax

TSPLOT	[with period K] time series data in C
INCREMENT	= K
START	at K [end at K]
ORIGIN	= K
TSTART	at K [end at K]

How to Use

This command plots the data on the vertical axis against time on the horizontal axis, with the numbers 1 through K (period length) as plotting symbols. For example, if you specify a period length of 5, each group of five observations will be plotted with the numbers 1, 2, 3, 4 and 5. For a period length greater than 9, data are plotted with a 0 for 10, A for 11, . . . , Z for 36. The period sets the distance between tick marks (+) on the horizontal axis. It may be any positive integer up to 36; the default is 10. See Figure TSPLOT1.REF.

TSPLOT1.REF ▶

```
MTB > RETRIEVE 'UTILITY'
MTB > TSPLOT 12 'KWH'

            -
        3000+                          2
            -             12                        2
   KWH      -
            -                                     1
            -  2             4          3
        2000+                         1
            -   3           3                       3
            -    4   8            9  B               4
            - 1       9       5          45      AB
            -     5 7    B      7            8        5  8
        1000+          0         8            90        7
            -      6    A           A       7          6
            -                  6   0
            -                              6
            -
          0+
            +-----------+-----------+-----------+-----------+
             0          12          24          36          48
```

Use the commands HEIGHT and OW (not WIDTH) to control the size of the TSPLOT if you wish. You may override Minitab's default scaling of TSPLOT with the subcommands described below.

Subcommands

INCREMENT = K

This subcommand controls vertical scaling: K is the distance between the tick marks (+) on the y-axis.

START at K [end at K]

This subcommand specifies the first and, optionally, the last value to print on the vertical scale of the TSPLOT. Data outside this range are excluded.

ORIGIN = K

This subcommand tells Minitab the scale of numbers to use when labeling the horizontal axis. The first point will be plotted directly above K. For example, if your series consisted of annual figures starting in the year 1950, you might enter ORIGIN = 1950.

TSTART K [end at K]

This subcommand allows you to graph a subset of your time series by specifying the first and, optionally, the last observation to plot. For example, TSTART = 4 begins the TSPLOT with the fourth observation. If you specify a scale with the ORIGIN subcommand, any values of K with TSTART must be on the same scale.

Also see PLOT, LPLOT, MPLOT, TPLOT, OW, and HEIGHT.

TTEST

Performs a t-test for the mean of each column listed.

Syntax

```
TTEST                [mu = K] on C . . . C
  ALTERNATIVE          = K
```

How to Use

This command does a two-sided t-test of the null hypothesis H0:(mu = K) versus H1:(mu≠K) on each column of data, where the standard deviation is not known. The default value of K is 0. TTEST also computes the probability (p) of getting a value as extreme as, or more extreme than, the computed t-value from a t-distribution with (n − 1) degrees of freedom. You can use the ALTERNATIVE subcommand to do a one-sided test.

Subcommand

ALTERNATIVE = K

Does a one-sided test of the alternative hypothesis H1:(mu < K) for ALTERNATIVE = −1, or H1:(mu > K) for ALTERNATIVE = 1. The null hypothesis is H0:(mu = K) for both cases. (ALTERNATIVE = 0 does the same test as TTEST without a subcommand.) For an example, see Figure TTEST1.REF.

TTEST1.REF▶

```
MTB > RETRIEVE 'STA261'
MTB > TTEST 75 'FINAL';
SUBC>   ALTERNATIVE 1.

TEST OF MU = 75.000 VS MU G.T. 75.000

           N      MEAN     STDEV   SE MEAN        T    P VALUE
FINAL     45    72.178    18.189     2.711    -1.04       0.85
```

Also see TINTERVAL, ZTEST, ZINTERVAL, and SINTERVAL.

TWOSAMPLE

Compares the means of two populations with a t-test, and computes a confidence interval for the difference.

Syntax

TWOSAMPLE [K% confidence] for data in C and C
  ALTERNATIVE = K
  POOLED

How to Use

This command does a two-sided t-test of the null hypothesis H0:(mu_1 = mu_2) versus H1:($mu_1 \neq mu_2$) on two columns of data of any length, and finds a confidence interval for ($mu_1 - mu_2$). It computes the probability

(p) of getting a value as extreme as, or more extreme than, the computed t-value from a t-distribution with (n − 1) degrees of freedom. TWOSAMPLE is illustrated in Figure TWOS1.REF.

TWOS1.REF ▶

```
MTB > RETRIEVE 'CARSPEED'
MTB > TWOSAMPLE 'METHOD 1' 'METHOD 4'

TWOSAMPLE T FOR METHOD 1 VS METHOD 4
            N      MEAN     STDEV   SE MEAN
METHOD 1   12     64.42      7.10       2.1
METHOD 4   11     55.36      4.46       1.3

95 PCT CI FOR MU METHOD 1 - MU METHOD 4: (3.9, 14.2)

TTEST MU METHOD 1 = MU METHOD 4 (VS NE): T= 3.69  P=0.0017  DF=  18
```

TWOSAMPLE differs from the usual two-sample test in that it does not calculate a t-statistic based on an assumption that the two populations have equal variances. It is based on the statistic:

$$T = (\bar{x}_1 - \bar{x}_2)/s$$

where:

$$s = \sqrt{(s_1^2/n_1) + (s_2^2/n_2)}$$

where s_1 and n_1 are the standard deviation and number of observations in the first column, and s_2 and n_2 are the corresponding values from the second column. The T statistic has approximately a t-distribution with degrees of freedom given by the integer part of:

$$df = \frac{(s_1^2 + s_2^2)^2}{[(s_1^2)^2/n_1 - 1] + [(s_2^2)^2/n_2 - 1]}$$

To do the usual pooled t-test, which assumes the populations have equal variances, use the POOLED subcommand.

You may specify a confidence K either as a percentage or as a decimal such as 0.90; the default is 95%. You can use the ALTERNATIVE subcommand to do a one-sided test.

Subcommands

ALTERNATIVE = K

Does a one-sided test of the alternative hypothesis H1:($mu_1 < mu_2$) for ALTERNATIVE = −1, or H1:($mu_1 > mu_2$) for ALTERNATIVE = 1. The null hypothesis is H0:($mu_1 = mu_2$) in both cases. ALTERNATIVE = 0 does the same test as TWOSAMPLE without a subcommand.

POOLED

Tells Minitab to assume the two populations have a common variance.

Also see TTEST, TWOT, AOVONEWAY, and MANN-WHITNEY.

TWOT

Compares the means of two populations with a t-test, and computes a confidence interval for their difference.

Syntax

```
TWOT              [K% confidence] for data in C, subscripts in C
  ALTERNATIVE       = K
  POOLED
```

How to Use

TWOT does exactly the same tests and confidence-interval computation as the TWOSAMPLE command. The only difference is in where Minitab looks for the data. With TWOSAMPLE, sample data from two populations are in two separate columns. With TWOT, all sample data are in the first column listed. The corresponding row in the second column tells Minitab which of the two populations each value belongs to. Subscripts may be any integers from −9999 to +9999 or the missing value symbol (*). For an example, see Figure TWOT1.REF.

TWOT1.REF ▶

```
MTB > RETRIEVE 'MIAMI'
MTB > TWOT 'CREDITS' 'JOB'

TWOSAMPLE T FOR CREDITS
JOB    N       MEAN      STDEV    SE MEAN
1     41      16.78       1.84       0.29
2     42      17.05       1.87       0.29

95 PCT CI FOR MU 1 - MU 2: (-1.08, 0.54)

TTEST MU 1 = MU 2 (VS NE): T= -0.66  P=0.51  DF=  80
```

See TWOSAMPLE for further explanation of this test and of the subcommands. (You can use STACK or UNSTACK to combine or separate sample data sets easily.)

Also see TTEST, TWOSAMPLE, and ONEWAY.

TWOWAY

Performs a two-way analysis of variance for balanced data.

Syntax

TWOWAY for the data in C, subscripts in C and C [store residual values in C [fits in C]]

  ADDITIVE

  MEANS for the subscripts in C [C]

How to Use

In a two-way analysis of variance, data are classified by two sets of factors representing treatments or blocks, each having more than one level. The number of levels in factor one times the number of levels in factor two equals the number of cells, which represents the number of different factor-level combinations. Each of these cells must contain an equal number of observations (i.e., the data must be balanced).

The first column listed with TWOWAY should contain the sample data. The corresponding row in the second (factor one) and third (factor two) columns listed tells Minitab which cell each data value belongs to. Specify additional columns with TWOWAY if you want to store residuals and fitted values. See Figure TWOWAY1.REF.

TWOWAY1.REF▶

```
MTB > READ C1-C3
DATA>    47     2     1
DATA>    43     2     1
DATA>    46     2     2
DATA>    40     2     2
DATA>    62     3     1
DATA>    68     3     1
DATA>    67     3     2
DATA>    71     3     2
DATA>    41     4     1
DATA>    39     4     1
DATA>    42     4     2
DATA>    46     4     2
DATA> END
MTB > TWOWAY C1 C2 C3;
SUBC>    MEAN C2 C3.

ANALYSIS OF VARIANCE   C1

SOURCE          DF         SS          MS
C2               2     1544.0       772.0
C3               1       12.0        12.0
INTERACTION      2       24.0        12.0
ERROR            6       62.0        10.3
TOTAL           11     1642.0

                        Individual 95% CI
    C2       Mean       ---+---------+---------+---------+--------
     2       44.0          (----*----)
     3       67.0                                      (----*----)
     4       42.0        (---*----)
                        ---+---------+---------+---------+--------
                         40.0      48.0      56.0      64.0

                        Individual 95% CI
    C3       Mean       ---+---------+---------+---------+--------
     1       50.0       (------------*------------)
     2       52.0              (------------*------------)
                        ---+---------+---------+---------+--------
                        47.5      50.0      52.5      55.0
```

Hint: After you compute the appropriate F-statistics (which depend on whether the factors are fixed or random), you can use Minitab to find the corresponding critical F-value with the INVCDF command. Type

INVCDF with the desired p-value ($1 - \alpha$), entering the appropriate degrees of freedom for the numerator and denominator of F. For example, to find the critical F for group C2 with $\alpha = 0.05$, type:

```
MTB > INVCDF 0.95;
SUBC>   F 2 6.
    0.9500     5.1431
```

Factor columns may contain any integers from −9999 to +9999 or missing values (*). An interaction term will automatically be included in the model if there is more than one observation per cell. To produce cell means and standard deviations use the TABLE command.

For a quick test to see whether or not your data are balanced, use the TABLE command with your two factor columns. The number of observations per cell will be displayed.

Subcommands

ADDITIVE

This subcommand tells Minitab to fit a model without an interaction term. In this case, the fitted value for cell (i,j) is (mean of observations in row i) + (mean of observations in row j) − (mean of all observations).

MEANS for the factors C [C]

This subcommand calculates marginal means and 95% confidence intervals for each level of either or both factor columns. Each confidence interval is calculated from the Student's t-distribution, using MS ERROR degrees of freedom and a pooled standard deviation equal to $\sqrt{\text{MS ERROR}}$.

Also see ONEWAY, TABLE, INVCDF, and CDF.

TYPE

Lists the contents of an ASCII file.

Syntax

TYPE file name

How to Use

You can use the TYPE command in Minitab just as in DOS to display the contents of a file on your screen. The file name should contain path information (disk drive and directory name) if necessary, and should

not be enclosed in single quotes. Any standard format (ASCII) file can be displayed. For example:

```
MTB > TYPE B:MYMACRO.MTB
```

tells Minitab to display the contents of a file named MYMACRO.MTB located on a diskette in drive B:.

Also see CD, DIR, and OH.

UNSTACK

Separates one block of columns into several shorter blocks of columns or constants.

Syntax

UNSTACK (C . . . C) into (E . . . E) . . . (E . . . E)
  SUBCRIPTS are in C

How to Use

UNSTACK separates the first block of columns by rows into several blocks of new columns or constants according to the values in the SUBSCRIPTS column. Rows with the smallest subscript are stored in the first block, rows with the next smallest subscript are stored in the second block, and so on. All blocks must be enclosed in parentheses unless they are only one column wide. Using the EXAMPLE.MTW saved worksheet, for example, we can use UNSTACK to store male ('SEX' = 1) heights and weights in columns C11 and C12, and female ('SEX' = 2) heights and weights in columns C13 and C14, as shown in Figure UNSTACK1.REF.

UNSTACK1.REF

```
MTB > RETRIEVE 'EXAMPLE'
MTB > UNSTACK ('HT' 'WT') (C11 C12) (C13 C14);
SUBC>   SUBSCRIPTS 'SEX'.
MTB > PRINT 'SEX' 'HT' 'WT' C11-C14

 ROW   SEX    HT     WT   C11    C12   C13    C14

   1     1    70    165    70    165    62    110
   2     2    62    110    64      *    66      *
   3     1    64      *    71    183    61    106
   4     1    71    183    68    158
   5     2    66      *
   6     1    68    158
   7     2    61    106
```

As another example, suppose you want to create a column containing every second row of the column 'HT', which has seven rows. With SET you can make a column of distinguishing subscripts for UNSTACK to use.

UNSTACK2.REF ▶

```
MTB > SET C12
DATA> 1  2  1  2  1  2  1
MTB > END
MTB > UNSTACK 'HT' C13 C14;
SUBC>   SUBSCRIPTS C12.
MTB > PRINT 'HT' C12 C13 C14

 ROW     HT    C12    C13    C14

   1     70      1     70     62
   2     62      2     64     71
   3     64      1     66     68
   4     71      2     61
   5     66      1
   6     68      2
   7     61      1
```

The example shown in Figure UNSTACK2.REF puts alternating 1's and 2's into column C6, and then uses these subscripts to store every second row of 'HT' in column C14.

If the SUBSCRIPTS command is not used, Minitab assumes that each row from the first column should be put in a separate block. For example:

```
MTB > UNSTACK C11 K1 K2 K3
```

stores the three elements of C11 in constants K1 through K3.

Subcommand

SUBSCRIPTS   are in C

The values in column C tell Minitab which block of columns or constants to store unstacked data in. The subscripts must be integers from −9999 to +9999 or missing values (*).

Also see STACK and SET.

WALSH

Calculates the averages of all pairs of values from one column.

Syntax

WALSH averages for C, put into C [put indices into C and C]

How to Use

This command, useful for nonparametric tests, calculates the average for each possible pair of values from the column, including the average of each value with itself. For n data values, there will be n(n + 1)/2 Walsh averages stored. If you list two extra output columns, the indices i and j for each average $(X_i + X_j)/2$ will also be stored.

WALSH1.REF▶

```
MTB > SET C1
DATA> 77 88 85
DATA> END
MTB > WALSH C1 C2 C3 C4
MTB > PRINT C1-C4

 ROW    C1     C2   C3    C4

   1    77   77.0    1     1
   2    88   82.5    1     2
   3    85   88.0    2     2
   4         81.0    1     3
   5         86.5    2     3
   6         85.0    3     3
```

Also see WDIFF, WSLOPE, WINTERVAL, and WTEST.

WDIFF

Computes all possible differences between pairs of row elements from two columns.

Syntax

WDIFF for C and C, put into C [put indices in C and C]

How to Use

This command, useful for nonparametric tests and confidence intervals, calculates all differences of the form $X_i - Y_j$ for X values from the first column and Y values from the second. Differences are stored in the third column listed. If two additional columns are specified, they will contain the row numbers i and j used for each difference. See Figure WDIFF1.REF.

WDIFF1.REF ▶

```
MTB > RETRIEVE 'EXAMPLE'
MTB > WDIFF C8 C9 C10 C11 C12
MTB > PRINT C8-C12

 ROW   C8   C9   C10    C11    C12
   1    1    5    -4      1      1
   2    2    6    -5      1      2
   3    3         -3      2      1
   4    4         -4      2      2
   5              -2      3      1
   6              -3      3      2
   7              -1      4      1
   8              -2      4      2
```

Also see WALSH and MANN-WHITNEY.

WIDTH

Controls the width of plots.

Syntax

WIDTH   of all plots that follow is K spaces

How to Use

You can set the width of all subsequent BOXPLOT, DOTPLOT, LPLOT, MPLOT, PLOT, and TPLOT (but not TSPLOT) displays with this command. WIDTH may be any number from 10 to 150; its default value is 57 spaces.

Also see HEIGHT, OW, and OH.

WINTERVAL

Calculates a one-sample Wilcoxon rank estimate and confidence interval for the center of a symmetric population.

Syntax

WINTERVAL   [K% confidence] for data in C . . . C

How to Use

This command is a nonparametric alternative to TINTERVAL. It assumes only that each column of data is a random sample from a continuous, symmetric population. Minitab calculates an approximate 95% confidence interval if you do not enter a value for K (which may be expressed as a percentage or as a decimal such as 0.95).

WINT1.REF▶

```
MTB > RETRIEVE 'STA261'
MTB > WINTERVAL 'FINAL'

                      ESTIMATED    ACHIEVED
                N        MEDIAN  CONFIDENCE   CONFIDENCE INTERVAL
FINAL          45         74.50        95.0  (    69.00,    78.50)
```

The estimated median shown in Figure WINT1.REF is the median of the Walsh averages for the column. The confidence interval for the population median is based on the Wilcoxon test (WTEST). It is displayed together with its achieved confidence level, which is as close to the value of K as possible.

Also see WALSH and WTEST.

WRITE

Writes data in the current worksheet to a file or to the screen.

Syntax

WRITE [to 'FILENAME'] the data in columns C . . . C
  FORMAT (format statement)

How to Use

The WRITE command saves data from your current worksheet in a standard format (ASCII) file which can be edited, printed out or read by packages other than Minitab. Only data from columns are written to the specified file; column names and constants are not. The default file extension for a file created by the WRITE command is .DAT. For example:

```
▶ MTB > WRITE 'B:MYDATA' C1-C6
```

stores the data from columns C1-C6 of your current worksheet in a file MYDATA.DAT on a disk in drive B:. If no filename is specified, WRITE displays data on your screen.

Files created with WRITE may be input with the READ, SET, or INSERT commands. If you WRITE to a file and all the columns do not fit on one line, Minitab puts the continuation symbol (&) at the end of the line and continues onto the next. If you WRITE columns of unequal length to a file, Minitab adds missing value symbols (*) to the bottom of the shorter columns.

Subcommand

FORMAT (format statement)

The FORMAT subcommand tells Minitab exactly where and how the data should appear on the output line. The format statement is always enclosed by parentheses. See Appendix C for more explanation and examples.

Also see SAVE, PRINT, READ, SET, INSERT, and Appendix C.

WSLOPE

Computes slopes for all pairs of rows from two columns.

Syntax

WSLOPE y in C, x in C, put slopes in C [put indices in C,C]

How to Use

This nonparametric command is useful in finding robust estimates of the slope of a line through the data from two columns, with y-coordinates in column one and x-coordinates in column two. WSLOPE calculates the slopes of all lines through pairs of points (X_i, Y_i) and (X_j, Y_j) from rows i and j of the input columns and stores these slopes in the third column listed. You can also allocate two columns for the indices i and j.

WSLOPE1.REF ▶

```
MTB > RETRIEVE 'EXAMPLE'
MTB > WSLOPE C8 C10 C11 C12 C13
MTB > PRINT C8 C10-C13

 ROW   C8   C10        C11    C12    C13

   1    1   1.1    1.11111      2      1
   2    2   2.0    0.58824      3      1
   3    3   4.5    0.40000      3      2
   4    4   2.0    3.33333      4      1
   5                     *      4      2
   6              -0.40000      4      3
```

As shown in Figure WSLOPE1.REF, if there are missing values, if the two input columns are of unequal length, or if a slope is undefined (e.g., the slope of a vertical line), the slope is stored as a missing value (*).

WTEST

Does a one-sample Wilcoxon signed-rank test for one or more columns.

Syntax

WTEST [of center K] on the data C . . . C
  ALTERNATIVE = K

How to Use

WTEST is a nonparametric alternative to TTEST, assuming only that each column of data is a random sample from a symmetric population. It performs a two-sided test of whether the center (median) is equal to the number K. You can also use the ALTERNATIVE subcommand to do a one-sided test. The default value of K is 0.

WTEST1 ▶

```
MTB > RETRIEVE 'STA261'
MTB > WTEST 'FINAL'

TEST OF MEDIAN = 0.000000000 VERSUS MEDIAN N.E. 0.000000000

                  N FOR  WILCOXON            ESTIMATED
             N    TEST  STATISTIC  P-VALUE      MEDIAN
FINAL       45      44      990.0    0.000       74.50
```

In the output in Figure WTEST1.REF, N FOR TEST is the number of observations not equal to K. Walsh averages are calculated for these values. The Wilcoxon statistic is the number of Walsh averages greater than K, plus one-half the number of Walsh averages equal to K. (The Wilcoxon statistic can also be computed in terms of signed ranks.)

The p-value is the probability, assuming the null hypothesis is true, of a Wilcoxon statistic being as extreme as, or more extreme than, the one observed. The estimated median shown is the median of the Walsh averages.

Subcommand ALTERNATIVE = K

Performs a one-sided test of the alternative hypothesis H1: (center < K) for ALTERNATIVE = −1, or H1:(center > K) for ALTERNATIVE = 1. The null hypothesis is H0:(center = K) for both cases. (ALTERNATIVE = 0 does the same test as WTEST without a subcommand.)

Also see WALSH and WINTERVAL.

ZINTERVAL

Calculates a confidence interval for the mean of each column.

Syntax

ZINTERVAL [K% confidence] assumed sigma = K, for data in C . . . C

How to Use

With this command you can calculate a confidence interval for the mean of one or more variables with standard deviation sigma = K. The default confidence level is 95%, as shown in Figure ZINT1.REF.

ZINT1.REF▶

```
MTB > RETRIEVE 'STA261'
MTB > ZINTERVAL 15 'FINAL'

THE ASSUMED SIGMA =15.0

              N      MEAN     STDEV   SE MEAN    95.0 PERCENT C.I.
FINAL        45     72.18     18.19      2.24 (   67.79,    76.57)
```

If you specify a fractional value for K, say 0.80, Minitab automatically multiplies it by 100 to give 80% confidence.

Also see ZTEST, TINTERVAL, TTEST, WINTERVAL, and SINTERVAL.

ZTEST

Performs a z-test on one or more columns.

Syntax

ZTEST [of mu = K] assumed sigma = K on C . . . C
  ALTERNATIVE = K

How to Use

This command does a two-sided test on each column of data, computing the appropriate p-value. You can also use the ALTERNATIVE subcommand to do a one-sided test. The default value for mu is 0. For an example, see Figure ZTEST1.REF.

ZTEST1.REF ▶

```
MTB > SET C1
DATA> 40.1  30.2  39.4  39.8  39.0
DATA> END
MTB > ZTEST 40 0.4 C1

TEST OF MU = 40.000 VS MU N.E. 40.000
THE ASSUMED SIGMA = 0.400

            N     MEAN    STDEV   SE MEAN        Z    P VALUE
C1          5   37.700    4.213     0.179   -12.86     0.0000
```

Subcommand

ALTERNATIVE = K

Performs a one-sided test of the alternative hypothesis H1:(mu < K) for ALTERNATIVE = −1, or H1:(mu > K) for ALTERNATIVE = 1. The null hypothesis is H0:(mu = K) for both cases. (ALTERNATIVE = 0 does the same test as ZTEST without a subcommand.)

Also see ZINTERVAL, TTEST, TINTERVAL, STEST, and WTEST.

▶ Statistical Reference Texts

The following references provide statistical background related to the Minitab commands.

Belsley, D. A., E. Kuh, and R. E. Welsch. *Regression Diagnostics*. New York: John Wiley & Sons, Inc., 1980.

Box, G. E. P., and G. M. Jenkins. *Time Series Analysis*. Revised ed. San Francisco: Holden Day, 1976.

Cook, R. D., and S. Weisberg. *Residuals and Influence in Regression*. Chapman and Hall, 1982.

Cryer, J. D. *Time Series Analysis*. Boston, MA: Duxbury Press, 1986.

Dongarra, J. J., J. R. Bunch, C. B. Moler, and G. W. Stewart. *Linpack User's Guide*. Philadelphia: Society for Industrial and Applied Mathematics, 1979.

Draper, N. R., and H. Smith. *Applied Regression Analysis*. 2d ed. New York: John Wiley & Sons, Inc., 1981.

Goodnight, James H. "A Tutorial on the Sweep Operator." *The American Statistician*, 33 (1979), pp. 149–158.

Hettmansperger, T. P., and S. J. Sheather. *Statistics and Probability Letters*. Volume 4, No. 2 (1986), pp. 75–79.

Hoaglin, D. C., and R. E. Welsch. "The Hat Matrix in Regression and ANOVA." *American Statistician*, 32 (1978), pp. 17–22, and Corrigenda, p. 146.

Hollander, Myles, and Douglas A. Wolfe. *Nonparametric Statistical Methods*. New York: John Wiley & Sons, 1973.

Johnson, R., and D. Wichern. *Applied Multivariate Statistical Methods*. Englewood Cliffs, NJ: Prentice Hall, 1982.

Lehmann, E. L. *Nonparametrics: Statistical Methods Based on Ranks*. San Francisco: Holden Day, 1975.

Miller, R. B., and D. W. Wichern. *Intermediate Business Statistics*. New York: Holt, Rinehart and Winston, 1977.

Miller, W. "Performing Armchair Roundoff Analysis of Statistical Algorithms." *Communications in Statistics* (1978), pp. 243–255.

Morrison, D. *Multivariate Statistical Methods*. New York: McGraw Hill, 1976.

Nelson, C. R. *Applied Time Series Analysis*. San Francisco: Holden Day, Inc., 1973.

Neter, J., W. Wasserman, M. H. Kutner. *Applied Linear Statistical Models*. 2d ed. Homewood, Illinois: Irwin, Inc., 1985.

Noether, G. *Statistics — A Non-Parametric Approach*. Boston: Houghton-Mifflin, 1971.

Ryan, Jr., T. A., B. L. Joiner, and B. F. Ryan. *Minitab Student Handbook*. Duxbury Press, 1976.

Searle, S. R. *Linear Models*. New York: John Wiley & Sons, 1971.

Stewart, G. W. *Introduction to Matrix Computations*. New York: Academic Press, 1973.

Winer, B. J. *Statistical Principles in Experimental Design*. 2d ed. New York: McGraw-Hill, 1971.

Part IV

Appendixes

A. ▶ Files

The files that Minitab can create fall into three general categories (see Introduction to Minitab, page 24):

1. files that store data from the worksheet
2. files that store commands and output from a Minitab session, and
3. files that store Minitab commands only

We will discuss files that store data here. Refer to the Files section of the Introduction to Minitab for more information on other types of Minitab files.

There are two types of files that store data from the worksheet:

1. Saved worksheet (binary) files, identified by an .MTW extension, work with the commands SAVE and RETRIEVE. These commands operate on the worksheet as a whole.
2. Data (ASCII) files, identified by a .DAT extension, work with the commands READ, WRITE, SET and INSERT. These commands operate on individual columns.

Combining Files

There are several ways to combine worksheet files in Minitab. First, in Figure A.1, we create two small saved worksheet files.

Figure A.1 ▶

```
MTB > READ C1-C3
DATA> 1 2 3
DATA> 1 2 3
DATA> END
      2 ROWS READ
MTB > SAVE 'FILE1'

Worksheet saved into file: FILE1.MTW
MTB > ERASE C1-C3
MTB > READ C1-C3
DATA> 4 5 6
DATA> 4 5 6
DATA> END
      2 ROWS READ
MTB > SAVE 'FILE2'

Worksheet saved into file: FILE2.MTW
```

Example 1. Side-by-Side

Combine FILE1.MTW side-by-side with FILE2.MTW, and save as a six-column worksheet, WIDEFILE.MTW as shown in Figure A.2.

Figure A.2 ▶

```
MTB > RETRIEVE 'FILE2'
MTB > PRINT C1-C3
  ROW   C1   C2   C3

    1    4    5    6
    2    4    5    6

MTB > WRITE 'FILE2' C1-C3     # store as data (ASCII) file
MTB > RETRIEVE 'FILE1'
MTB > PRINT C1-C3
  ROW   C1   C2   C3
    1    1    2    3
    2    1    2    3

MTB > READ 'FILE2' C4-C6
      2 ROWS READ

 ROW   C4   C5   C6

   1    4    5    6
   2    4    5    6

MTB > PRINT C1-C6
 ROW   C1   C2   C3   C4   C5   C6

   1    1    2    3    4    5    6
   2    1    2    3    4    5    6

MTB > SAVE 'WIDEFILE'

Worksheet saved into file: WIDEFILE.MTW
```

Example 2. Stack Top to Bottom

Stack FILE1.MTW on top of FILE2.MTW, and save as a three-column worksheet TALLFILE.MTW. (Note, all of the steps in this process are outlined in Figure A.3 even though there is some repetition with the side-by-side example.)

Figure A.3 ▶

```
MTB > RETRIEVE 'FILE2'
MTB > PRINT C1-C3
  ROW   C1   C2   C3

    1    4    5    6
    2    4    5    6

MTB>  WRITE 'FILE2' C1-C3     # store as data (ASCII) file
MTB > RETRIEVE 'FILE1'
MTB > INSERT 'FILE2' C1-C3
MTB > PRINT C1-C3

  ROW   C1   C2   C3

    1    1    2    3
    2    1    2    3
    3    4    5    6
    4    4    5    6

MTB > SAVE 'TALLFILE'

Worksheet saved into file: TALLFILE.MTW
```

Transferring Files

There are three common situations in which you might need to transfer data files:

1. from Minitab to other software
2. from other software to Minitab
3. between Minitab on your microcomputer and Minitab on another type of computer (e.g., a mainframe).

From Minitab to Other Software

Most software can input data from a file in standard ASCII format. Use the WRITE command to store data from columns in your current worksheet into a standard ASCII file. (See examples above and the

Command Reference Section for more information on WRITE.) You can view a file created with WRITE using the DOS TYPE command; it should contain columns and rows of data with space between each column.

From Other Software to Minitab

Minitab can input files in standard ASCII format with the commands READ, SET or INSERT. The easiest file to input contains numbers only (no alpha data), arranged in columns and rows, with a comma or at least one space between each column, and each row of data fits on one line. For example, to READ in the file FILE2.DAT created above, you could type:

```
MTB > READ 'FILE2' C1-C3
```

If a data file contains alpha data (letters or "character strings") or columns that are not separated by a space or a comma, use the FORMAT subcommand with READ, SET or INSERT. This subcommand tells Minitab exactly how to enter data from a file (see Appendix 3, Formatted Input and Output).

There are several ways to read in a data file with rows longer than one line (more than 80 spaces long):

If a data file contains numbers only (no alpha data), has rows no longer than 160 characters, and has at least one space or comma between each column of numbers, a simple READ command will enter that file into the current worksheet. For example:

```
MTB > READ 'FILENAME' C1-C30
```

If a data file has rows no longer than 256 characters, you can enter it into the current worksheet using READ with a FORMAT subcommand, even if it contains alpha data and/or columns are not separated by a space or comma. (See Appendix 3 for more information.)

If a data file contains numbers only (no alpha data) and has at least a space or comma between each column, but has rows longer than 160 characters, you can still use a simple READ command to enter it into the worksheet. First, however, you must edit the file with word-processing software (e.g., WordStar, EDLIN, Microsoft Word), and place the continuation symbol (&) at the end of each line of data, except the last. For example, suppose a file named WIDE.DAT contained one row, which looked like:

```
1111 2222 3333 4444 5555 6666 7777 8888 9999 &
0000 1111 2222 3333 4444 5555 6666 7777 8888 &
9999 0000
```

You could enter this row into the current worksheet with the command:

```
MTB > READ 'WIDE' C1-C20
```

Between Minitab on Your Micro and Minitab on a Mini or Mainframe

Saved worksheet files are stored differently on different types of computers. Thus, if you SAVE a worksheet on a DOS microcomputer, you could RETRIEVE it on another DOS microcomputer, but not on a mini or mainframe (e.g., a VAX or an IBM mainframe). There are two ways to transfer this data: as ASCII data files, or as PORTABLE saved worksheet files.

ASCII Data Files

Use the WRITE command to store your worksheet columns in an ASCII data file, which can then be transported to another computer. From Minitab, use READ, SET or INSERT to input the data file.

PORTABLE Saved Worksheet Files

This method can be used if the mini or mainframe computer has Release 6 or higher of Minitab. From the first machine, SAVE your worksheet using the PORTABLE subcommand, for example:

```
MTB > SAVE 'MYFILE';
SUBC>   PORTABLE.
```

This creates a file named MYFILE.MTP, which can then be transported to another computer. To enter this file into Minitab on the second computer, you could type,

```
MTB > RETRIEVE 'MYFILE';
SUBC>    PORTABLE.
```

B. ▶ Alpha Data

Alpha data, sometimes called alphabetic or character data, refers to data values such as names, social security numbers, or labels, such as male or female (i.e., data values that are not treated as numbers). Although Minitab is best suited to handle numeric data, it can handle alpha data in a limited fashion.

Two general limitations are:

1. No alpha data value may exceed 80 characters.
2. A single column cannot contain both alpha and numeric data.

In addition, only certain commands can handle alpha data; these are listed below:

CONCATENATE	Pastes alpha columns together into a new, wider column. Used to work around the small width (A4) allowed with READ.
CONVERT	Used to convert numeric data to alpha data, or alpha data to numeric data.
ERASE	Removes all data from columns listed.
INSERT	Works the way SET does with one column, or READ does with more than one column.
PRINT, WRITE	When used to output alpha data, a FORMAT subcommand may be used, but is not necessary.
READ	Input with the FORMAT subcommand. Maximum width for any data point is 4 (i.e., up to A4 format is allowed).

SAVE, RETRIEVE	Handle alpha columns just as they do numeric columns.
SET	Input with the FORMAT subcommand. Maximum width for any data point is 80 (i.e., up to A80 format is allowed).

See Command Reference Section for a full description of these commands.

C. ▶ Formatted Input and Output

General Description

Formatted input and output allows you to tell Minitab precisely how to read in or write out data. It is normally not needed, but is useful if you want to:

- ▶ read in alpha data
- ▶ read in columns of numbers not separated by a comma or space
- ▶ specify the number of decimal digits in numbers to be read in
- ▶ output data in a format other than Minitab's default

You can give Minitab these special instructions with the FORMAT subcommand, which may be used with the commands: READ, SET, INSERT, PRINT and WRITE. FORMAT is used to input or output columns, not constants. The format must always be enclosed by parentheses. In Figure C.1, the FORMAT subcommand tells Minitab to read a number with no decimal digits from the first 2 spaces of each data line into C1, skip 1 space, then read an alpha character from the next space into C2. END tells Minitab you are finished entering data.

Figure C.1 ▶

```
MTB > READ C1 C2;
SUBC>   FORMAT (F2.0, 1X, A1).
DATA> 85 M
DATA> 87 F
DATA> END
```

You may specify up to 256 characters in any given format. If the FORMAT subcommand is used, data to be input or output must match the format exactly.

Allowable formats include:

Fw.d	to specify a number with or without decimal digits
Aw	to specify alpha data
Ew.d	to specify exponential format (scientific notation)
nX	to skip n spaces
n	repeat an operation n times
,	comma, used to separate format items
/	slash, to tell Minitab to skip a line

In these formats, w is width, and d is the number of decimal digits. Fw.d tells Minitab to read a number from the next w spaces and to insert a decimal point d spaces from the right of that number if it doesn't already have a decimal point. If there is a decimal point, it overrides the d.

If a data point is less than width w, it should normally be typed "right justified"; otherwise, Minitab will add zero's to the end of the number. If a data point entered from your keyboard is greater than width w, Minitab will ignore everything past width w; if it is entered from a file, Minitab will convert that data to a missing value *.

FORMAT with READ

Suppose you only want to read certain values from a file named SAMPLE.DAT. The example:

```
MTB > READ 'SAMPLE' C1-C10;
SUBC>   FORMAT (F3.0, 4(1X,F6.2), /, 3X, 5F8.1).
```

reads each row of data from 2 lines. From the first line, it reads a number with no decimal digits from the first 3 spaces into C1. Then it repeats the following pattern 4 times, reading data into columns C2, C3, C4 and C5: skip 1 space, read a number with 2 decimal digits from the next 6 spaces. The / tells Minitab to skip to the second line. From the second line, it skips 3 spaces, then reads numbers into the next 5 columns (C6 to C10), each of which is no more than 8 spaces and contains 1 decimal digit.

FORMAT with PRINT

You can override Minitab's default for printing columns with the FORMAT subcommand. If you do a formatted PRINT, you should always skip at least one space (with the X format) before printing the first value. (On many computers, the data in the first space is used for line-spacing or carriage-control instructions.) For example:

```
MTB > PRINT C11-C15;
SUBC>   FORMAT (1X, 5F10).
```

skips 1 space, then displays the numbers in columns C11 to C15, right-justified, in fields that are 10 spaces wide.

FORMAT with WRITE

You can override Minitab's default for writing columns with the FORMAT subcommand. The example:

```
MTB > WRITE 'MYFILE' C1-C4;
SUBC>   FORMAT (2F10, 5X, F6.2, /, 4X, F5.2).
```

would write a file with two lines for each row of data. In the first line of the row, C1 would be in spaces 1 to 10 (Minitab would pick the number of places after the decimal point), and C2 would be in spaces 11 to 20. The X format says to skip 5 spaces, and C3 would be in the next 6 spaces with 2 decimal digits. The / says to move to the second line, 4X says to skip 4 spaces, and F5.2 says to put C4, with 2 decimal digits, in the next 5 spaces.

D. ▶ Advanced Options

The advanced options discussed in this appendix are designed for customizing your version of Minitab, and are not required to run Minitab. We will discuss the following options:

- ▶ customizing Minitab screen colors
- ▶ starting Minitab with a BATCH file
- ▶ using the initializing file called STARTUP.MTB
- ▶ using a RAM disk
- ▶ running Minitab on a network
- ▶ taking advantage of special keys.

Customizing Minitab Screen Colors

Minitab gives you the option of selecting the foreground and background colors for monochrome and color monitors. If you have a monochrome monitor, changing colors will result in achieving the desired contrast between foreground and background.

You can select or change these colors three different ways.

First, you can use the MINSTALL program to define foreground and background screen colors. A color grid will be displayed after you select the Select Screen Colors menu option. The colors you select will be written to the MINITAB.BAT file, which resides on the backup DISK A or in the Minitab directory on the hard disk, if you have one. The program will prompt you for the location of this file.

Second, you can write your choices on the "MTB61_A" line of a .BAT file. See the next section, Starting Minitab from a BATCH File, on page xxs for further details.

Third, you can temporarily change the screen colors by using command-line modifiers to the Minitab startup command. The colors selected by this method will only be displayed during the current Minitab session.

The following example shows how to do this. Suppose you would like to see black letters on a cyan background (cyan is a shade of light blue), then type:

```
A> MINITAB -f BLACK -b CYAN
```

The "-f" means foreground and the "-b" means background. Please note that you must use lower case letters for "-f" and "-b", but the color names can be upper or lower case.

You will now see the initial Minitab screen displayed with black letters on a cyan background. If you STOP Minitab and start it again without these command-line modifiers, then you will see the colors selected during MINSTALL.

The possible color choices you have are:

Foreground Colors	black
	blue
	green
	cyan
	red
	magenta
	yellow
	white
	lightblack (grey)
	lightblue
	lightgreen
	lightcyan
	lightred
	lightmagenta
	lightyellow
	lightwhite (brighter than white)

Background Colors	black
	blue
	green
	cyan
	red
	magenta
	yellow
	white

Starting Minitab with a BATCH File

If you have installed Minitab on a hard disk, the best way to start Minitab is to execute a DOS "batch" file. A batch file contains a set of DOS commands that are executed when you type the name of the batch file. You can create or edit a file called MTB.BAT and keep it in your root directory.

To create this file, follow the sequence in Figure D.1, making sure to type the underscore between the MTB61 and the "A."

Figure D.1 ▶

```
C> COPY CON MTB.BAT
PROMPT $P$G
PATH = C:\;C:\MINITAB
CD \MINITAB\DATA
MTB61_A %1 %2 %3 %4 %5
CD \
AUTOEXEC
<CTRL>-Z    Press the <CTRL> and the Z keys simultaneously.
<ENTER>
```

The last two commands ("CD\" and "AUTOEXEC") are optional. They simply help to reconfigure your system to its original state.

Then, any time you want to run Minitab, simply boot your computer and type:

▶
```
C> MTB
```

The six commands in Figure D.1 will then be executed, and you will be presented with the initial Minitab screen. When you STOP Minitab, you will be returned to the root directory, and the system will be reconfigured back to its original state.

The %1 %2 %3 %4 %5 parameters on the MTB61_A line will allow you to use the "-f" and "-b" command line modifiers when typing MTB. You may also specify screen colors right on this line by inserting -f "foreground color" and -b "background color" between MTB61_A and %1.

The STARTUP.MTB Initializing File

STARTUP.MTB is a special Minitab command file (macro) which is automatically executed when Minitab is started or restarted. It is a handy tool for users who wish to avoid typing in the same commands each session or for network administrators who want a common initialization file for all users.

The startup file is created using an editor or the Minitab STORE command, just like any other Minitab macro. The file must be named STARTUP.MTB. On a hard disk, Minitab will look for this file in the user's default directory. When running from diskettes, STARTUP .MTB must be on DISK 1. If found, STARTUP.MTB is executed. If the file is not found, nothing happens and Minitab is ready for interactive use.

Some applications of the STARTUP.MTB file are:

1. set up an OUTFILE
2. set up output height or width (OH or OW)
3. automatically RETRIEVE a data set
4. send users messages via the NOTE command

Installing/Running Minitab on a RAM Disk

RAM Disk Basics

A RAM disk speeds up Minitab's running time and can reduce or eliminate disk swapping if you are running Minitab from diskettes. Setting up a RAM disk requires special software and sufficient memory on your computer.

A RAM disk is a portion of your computer's random access memory that has been reconfigured to look like another disk drive to DOS. For example, suppose your machine has 640 kilobytes of memory. You can partition some of this memory, 270 kilobytes for example, to look like a new disk drive. Your new "pseudo-disk drive" will take the next available drive letter. If you have a system with two diskette drives and no hard disk, then your RAM disk will become drive C:. If you have a hard disk, then your RAM disk will usually become drive D:. After you install this RAM disk, DOS will think that your machine has an extra disk drive, but only 370K of memory, since 270K of your memory will be tied up in the RAM disk. Minitab will still run since it only requires 320K of memory.

You take advantage of the RAM disk by copying the Minitab program files to it. Then, when you run Minitab from diskettes, DOS will be able to find these Minitab files without having to ask you to swap diskettes. Reading files from a RAM disk is also very fast, since it is an "electronic" disk and has no moving parts. If you have Minitab installed to a hard disk and copy some of the program files to the RAM disk, then Minitab will run even faster.

The only disadvantage of a RAM disk is that all its files are lost when the machine is turned off. This is not a problem since only those files which are permanently stored on your diskettes will be copied to the RAM disk.

The two following sections will provide the details for implementing the RAM disk option. The first section describes how to install Minitab to a RAM disk. The second section describes how to start and run Minitab from the newly created RAM disk.

Installing Minitab to a RAM Disk

Minitab needs 320K to run. Any memory you have in excess of 320K can be used as a RAM disk, and the more the better. On most PC or XT and PS/2 Model 30-type machines, the most total memory you can have is 640K. This provides you with enough excess memory to set up a 320K RAM disk. On AT and PS/2 Model 50 through 80 type machines, you can have 2M (2 megabytes) of memory or more. This would allow you to set up a very large RAM disk, 1.6M for example.

Where can you get RAM-disk software? If you have MS-DOS 3.0 or later, you already have the software in the form of RAMDRIVE.SYS. The RAM-disk software packaged with IBM's PC-DOS is called VDISK .SYS. If you bought a memory board that gives you extra memory, chances are there is RAM-disk software packaged with the board. If not, the manufacturers of the board should send you the software if you ask for it. There are also a lot of public domain (free and legal) RAM-disk programs that you can get from local user's groups, friends, and even computer stores.

Installing the RAM disk is a matter of following the directions that come with the software. To use Minitab, you need to copy one or both of the .OVL files to the RAM disk.

Suppose you have the following system: an IBM-PC or a PS/2 Model 30 with 640K of memory, two diskette drives, A: and B: (no hard disk) and MS-DOS 3.0 or later. If your machine is running IBM PC-DOS, then use VDISK.SYS everywhere RAMDRIVE.SYS is used in the following example. The first thing you need to do is create or edit a configuration file called CONFIG.SYS. This is a file in the root directory of your DOS disk that is read during the boot up process and configures your system. In this file, there should be a line that states:

```
DEVICE = RAMDRIVE.SYS 270
```

If you don't have a CONFIG.SYS file on your DOS boot disk, you can create one without an editor as follows:

Insert DOS Disk into Drive A:, and type, A:

then type,

```
A> COPY CON CONFIG.SYS
DEVICE = RAMDRIVE.SYS 270
<Crtl>-Z    Press the <CTRL> and Z keys simultaneously.
<Enter>
```

You may have other parameters and devices in CONFIG.SYS, but we are only concerned with the RAM disk here. To activate the RAM disk, you need to reboot the system. The RAM disk will be installed every time you reboot until you change the CONFIG.SYS file. After rebooting, try typing:

```
A> C:
```

and you should see

```
C>
```

which indicates that the RAM disk was indeed installed and it is called drive C:. Now you can copy M61 2 A1.OVL from DISK 2 (or DISK 1/2) to the RAM disk drive by inserting DISK 2 into drive A: and typing:

```
C> A:
A> COPY M61_2_A1.OVL C:
```

Be sure to include the underscore between M61 and 2, and between 2 and A1 - M61_2_A1.) If you have an IBM-AT or PS/2 Model 80 type machine with 1 megabyte of memory or more, then set up a RAM disk of 600K and copy M61_1_A1.OVL and M61_2_A1.OVL onto it. After initial startup, the only disk I/O that occurs will be for data files or HELP. Minitab will be very fast.

Running Minitab from a RAM Disk

To run Minitab from your newly created RAM disk, insert DISK A in drive A:, and make A: the default drive by typing A:,

then type:

```
A> PATH C:\;A:\
A> MINITAB
```

Note that there is a semicolon, ";", between the first "\" and the "A" in the path command.

You will soon see the initial Minitab screen. Strike any key to get the Minitab prompt:

```
MTB >
```

You are now ready to execute Minitab commands.

Disk swapping will be greatly reduced or even eliminated, and Minitab will run very fast. Remember to keep your Work Disk in drive B: and perform any required Minitab disk swapping in Drive A:.

Running Minitab on a Network

Installing and running Minitab on a network is very easy. Simply personalize and install Minitab to the server as you would to any computer with a hard disk.

The Minitab command PAPER may cause difficulties in a network environment. On single-user machines, PAPER prints an ongoing record of the Minitab session. When this command is used on a network, a temporary file (MINITAB.LIS) is created that is queued when the Minitab session ends. Some networks cannot handle the multiple PAPER files that are generated by many users. Use the OUTFILE 'FILENAME' command instead to create an ASCII file of the Minitab session. This file can then be printed when a user terminates his or her session. This avoids the problem of trying to queue multiple PAPER files that will all have the same name.

Special Keys

Certain key sequences perform convenient and useful functions. (In the following examples, press the second key while holding the first key down.)

To control the scrolling of output to your screen:

`<Ctrl>-S`	"freezes" screen (i.e., scrolling stops)
`<Ctrl>-Q`	"unfreezes" screen (i.e., scrolling continues)

To interrupt a process:

`<Ctrl>-C`	exit to DOS
`<Ctrl>-<Alt>-<Delete>`	restarts (reboots) the entire machine

To send output to a printer:

`<PrtSc>`	entire screen display is printed all at once
`<Ctrl>-P`	output is printed as it appears on the screen

To get a printed copy of a file during a Minitab session, press <Ctrl>-P, then issue the command TYPE pathname\filename.

E. ▶ Troubleshooting

Error detection and messages are safeguards used by Minitab to help users avoid mistakes that could produce incorrect answers or destroy valuable data. This section explains common error conditions and provides proper corrective actions.

Another resource that may be valuable to you in troubleshooting problems is the ASCII file entitled PROBLEMS.DOC. It is located on DISK 2. This file contains a listing of known Minitab problems and includes strategies for working around them. To view this file, insert DISK 2 in Drive A: and type,

▶ `TYPE A:PROBLEMS.DOC`

To get a printed copy, type

▶ `PRINT A:PROBLEMS.DOC`

Error Messages and What to Do

In this section we present common error messages or error conditions, an explanation of the error, and the corrective action. The exact text is used so that you will see exactly the same message that appears on the screen.

1. `Not ready error reading drive A`
   `Abort, Retry, Ignore`

   This message indicates that the diskette drive specified by a Minitab command is empty.
   ACTION: Insert the proper diskette in Drive A:. Type I, for Ignore, to return to Minitab. If necessary, retype the Minitab command.

We suggest that you use caution with the RETRY or ABORT options. Under certain conditions, RETRY can destroy the files on the diskette by overwriting the directory. ABORT will exit Minitab without giving you the chance to SAVE your worksheet.

2. `Write protect error writing drive A`
   `Abort, Retry, Ignore`

   The diskette in Drive A: contains a write protect tab.
   ACTION: Remove the write protected diskette from Drive A:. Remove the write protect tab. Make sure this is the diskette on which you want to write. Insert the proper diskette into Drive A:. Type I, for Ignore, to ignore the WRITE command and return to Minitab. We suggest that you use caution with the RETRY or ABORT options. Under certain conditions, RETRY can destroy the files on the diskette by overwriting the directory. ABORT will exit Minitab without giving you the chance to SAVE your worksheet.

3. `* ERROR * REQUESTED FILE DOES NOT EXIST`

   Minitab cannot locate the file requested by a RETRIEVE, READ, SET, INSERT, or EXECUTE command. Either the file is not in the directory you have specified, or the file extension differs from what the Minitab command expects.
   ACTION: Check to see if the requested file exists in your default directory by typing:

```
MTB > DIR
```

If you do not see the file, then examine other possible directory locations by typing:

```
MTB > DIR directory
```

where "directory" is another possible location of the file. When you locate the file, retype your Minitab command with the proper pathname \ filename enclosed in single quotes. This will tell Minitab exactly where to find your file.

If you get the same error message, then pay attention to the extension of the desired file. The extension of a file named DATA.MTW is the .MTW part. Minitab commands SAVE and RETRIEVE work with files with .MTW and .MTP extensions. READ, WRITE, SET, and INSERT expect .DAT extensions. EXECUTE and STORE use

the .MTB extension by default. These file types are important. You cannot READ a .MTW file; you must use RETRIEVE. Retype your Minitab command making sure that the command you use is compatible with the file type.
For more information regarding the different file types used by Minitab, type:

```
MTB > HELP OVERVIEW 7
```

4. `* ERROR * No worksheet has been saved`

   This message is given when you forget to enclose the name of the worksheet file in single quotes.
   ACTION: Type,

```
MTB > RETRIEVE 'FILENAME'
```

   making sure to enclose the name of your worksheet in single quotes. For more information regarding this command, type:

```
MTB > HELP RETRIEVE
```

5. `Bad command or file name`

   You will get this message in response to typing Minitab, when DOS cannot locate MINITAB.BAT, the command file required to start Minitab.
   ACTION: If you are starting Minitab from diskettes, this is an indication that you have the wrong diskette in your default drive. Insert DISK A into Drive A: and type:

```
A:\> A: MINITAB
```

   On a hard disk this indicates that the MINITAB directory is not in your path. Specify the path using the DOS PATH command, or add this command to your AUTOEXEC.BAT file and reboot.
   Refer to Running Minitab from Diskettes on page 13 or Running Minitab from a Hard Disk on page 14, whichever is appropriate. Additional information about specifying a path is in the section entitled Starting Minitab from a BATCH File on page 330.

6. !'@+#)$*%&(^"#.... and other unintelligible characters.

You are trying to view a saved Minitab worksheet using the TYPE command. This is a binary file and can only be retrieved in Minitab. ACTION: Type,

```
▶ C:\> MINITAB
```

to start Minitab, and then type:

```
▶ MTB > RETRIEVE 'FILENAME'
```

to bring data into the worksheet.

To obtain a brief description of the data file, type:

```
▶ MTB > INFORMATION
```

7. `Minitab file not found: COMMAND.COM`
   `Please insert your DOS disk; then RETURN to continue`

   The file COMMAND.COM is a DOS file required by Minitab to perform the SYSTEM command. When running Minitab on a dual diskette drive system, this file cannot be found, since the DOS boot disk has been removed from Drive A:.
   ACTION: Simply insert your DOS disk in drive A: and press <Enter>.

8. `* NOTE * Please insert MINITAB DISK 1.`
   `Press <Enter> to continue or '.' to quit Minitab ==>`

   Minitab is expecting DISK 1 in the default drive and cannot find it there.
   ACTION: Insert DISK 1 in the default drive and press <Enter>

   or

   Type X:, where X is the letter of the drive containing DISK 1.

9. `[2;75H`

   All users without ANSI.SYS in their CONFIG.SYS file will momentarily see "[2;75H" on their screens when starting Minitab. This code sequence appears when Minitab queries DOS for its screen configuration.
   ACTION: No action is required; Minitab is functioning normally.

F ▶ Companion Textbooks to Minitab Statistical Software

The following is a list of textbooks and textbook supplements that integrate Minitab into their presentation of statistical concepts and methods.

Books About Minitab

Miller, Robert B. *Minitab Handbook for Business and Economics.* Boston: PWS Kent Publishing Co., 1988.

Minitab, Inc. *Minitab Reference Manual: Release 6.1.* State College, PA: Minitab, Inc., 1988.

Ryan, Barbara F., Brian L. Joiner, and Thomas A. Ryan, Jr. *Minitab Handbook.* 2d ed. Boston: Duxbury Press, 1985.

General Statistics Textbooks

Anderson, T. W., and Barrett P. Eynon. *Minitab Guide to the Statistical Analysis of Data.* Redwood City, CA: The Scientific Press, 1986.

Byrkit, Donald R. *Statistics Today: A Comprehensive Introduction.* Menlo Park, CA: Benjamin/Cummings, 1987.

Chase, Warren, and Fred Bown. *General Statistics.* New York: John Wiley and Sons, 1986.

Devore, Jay, and Roxy Peck. *Statistics: The Exploration and Analysis of Data.* St. Paul, MN: West Publishing Co., 1986.

Goldman, Robert N., and Joel S. Weinberg. *Statistics: An Introduction.* Englewood Cliffs, NJ: Prentice-Hall, 1985.

Johnson, Robert. *Elementary Statistics.* 5th ed. Boston, MA: Duxbury Press, in press.

Kitchens, Larry J. *Exploring Statistics: A Modern Introduction.* St. Paul, MN: West Publishing Co., 1987.

Mansfield, Edwin. *Basic Statistics with Applications.* 3rd ed. New York: W. W. Norton and Co., 1986.

McGhee, John W. *Introductory Statistics.* St. Paul, MN: West Publishing Co., 1985.

Mendenhall, William *Introduction to Probability and Statistics.* Boston, MA: Duxbury Press, 1987.

Ott, Lyman *Introduction to Statistical Methods and Data Analysis.* 3d ed. Boston, MA: Duxbury Press, in press.

Ott, Lyman, and William Mendenhall. *Understanding Statistics.* 4th ed. Boston, MA: Duxbury Press, 1985.

Scott, James P., and Kenneth M. Bond. *Minitab Student Supplement to Accompany Johnson's Elementary Statistics, 5th Edition.* Boston, MA: Duxbury Press, in press.

Sevin, Anne. *Minitab Supplement to Accompany Chase/Bown General Statistics.* New York: John Wiley and Sons, Inc., 1987.

Sincich, Terry. *Statistics by Example.* 3rd ed. San Francisco: Dellen Publishing Co., 1987.

Sincich, Terry. *Computer Supplement for Statistics by Example, 3rd Edition.* San Francisco: Dellen Publishing Co., 1987.

Soskin, Mark, and Behravesh, Nariman. *Using Minitab with Mansfield's Basic Statistics: 3rd Edition.* New York: W. W. Norton and Co., 1987.

Weiss, Neil A. *Minitab Supplement to Accompany Weiss/Hassett Introductory Statistics, 2nd Edition.* Reading, MA: Addison-Wesley Publishing Co., 1987.

Weiss, Neil A., and Matthew J. Hassett. *Introductory Statistics.* 2nd ed. Reading, MA: Addison-Wesley Publishing Co., 1987.

Business Statistics Textbooks

Bell, P. C., and E. F. P. Newson. *Statistics for Business with Minitab.* Redwood City, CA: Scientific Press, 1985.

Bell, P. C., and E. F. P. Newson. *Statistics for Business with Minitab: Text & Cases.* Redwood City, CA: Scientific Press, 1987.

Berenson, Mark L., and David M. Levine. *Basic Business Statistics: Concepts and Applications.* 3rd ed. Englewood Cliffs, NJ: Prentice-Hall, 1986.

Bond, Kenneth M., and James P. Scott. *Minitab Student Supplement to Accompany Johnson/Siskin Elementary Statistics for Business, 2nd Edition.* Boston, MA: Duxbury Press, 1985.

Kvanli, Alan H., Stephen C. Guynes, and Robert J. Pavur. *Introduction to Business Statistics: A Computer Integrated Approach.* St. Paul, MN: West Publishing Co., 1986.

Mendenhall, William, James E. Reinmuth, Robert Beaver, and Dale Duhan. *Statistics for Management and Economics.* 5th ed. Boston, MA: Duxbury Press, 1986.

Pfaffenberger, Roger C., and James H. Patterson. *Statistical Methods for Business and Economics.* 3rd ed. Homewood, IL: Richard D. Irwin, Inc., 1987.

Roberts, Harry V. *Data Analysis for Managers Using Minitab.* Redwood City, CA: The Scientific Press, in press.

Sincich, Terry. *Business Statistics by Example.* 3rd ed. San Francisco: Dellen Publishing Co., 1987.

Soskin, Mark, and Behravesh, Nariman. *Using Minitab with Mansfield's Basic Statistics: 3rd Edition.* New York: W. W. Norton and Co., 1987.

Van Matre, Joseph G., and Glenn H. Gilbreath. *Statistics for Business and Economics.* 3rd ed. Plano, TX: Business Publications, Inc., 1987.

Wells, Jane. *Using Minitab with Olson/Picconi's Statistics for Business Decision Making.* Glenview, IL: Scott, Foresman and Co., 1984.

Special Topics

Cryer, Jonathan D. *Time Series Analysis.* Boston, MA: Duxbury Press, 1986.

Fox, William P., Frank R. Giordano, Stephen L. Maddox, and Maurice D. Weir. *Mathematical Modeling with Minitab.* Monterey, CA: Brooks/Cole, 1987.

Hildebrand, David K. *Statistical Thinking for Behavioral Scientists.* Boston, MA: Duxbury Press, 1986.

Howell, David C. *Fundamental Statistics for the Behavioral Sciences.* Boston, MA: Duxbury Press, 1985.

Mendenhall, William, and Terry Sincich. *A Second Course in Business Statistics: Regression Analysis.* 2nd ed. Boston, MA: Duxbury Press, 1986.

Velleman, Paul F., and David C. Hoaglin. *Applications, Basics and Computing of Exploratory Data Analysis.* Boston, MA: Duxbury Press, 1981.

Younger, Mary Sue. *A First Course in Linear Regression.* 2nd ed. Boston, MA: Duxbury Press, 1985.

G ▶ Description of Data Sets Used in the Student Edition of Minitab

AGGRESS.MTW

This is another aspect of the cadmium investigation. In this part of the study, the aggressive behavior of 10 fish (5 controls and 5 exposed to cadmium) was recorded, both before and after exposure. The number of aggressive encounters, averaged over a week, was recorded.

COLUMN	NAME	COUNT	DESCRIPTION
C1	CONT BFR	5	Encounters for control fish before exposure to tap water
C2	CONT AFT	5	Encounters for control fish after a week of exposure to tap water
C3	CD BFR	5	Encounters for cadmium fish before exposure to cadmium
C4	CD AFT	5	Encounters for cadmium fish after a week exposure to cadmium

BPRES.MTW

This data is the result of a study investigating the relationship between blood pressure, diet, and fitness. Nine subjects were interviewed and several measurements recorded.

COLUMN	NAME	COUNT	DESCRIPTION
C1	BP	9	Number of points above normal diastolic blood pressure
C2	OVER WGT	9	Number of kilograms overweight
C3	FATS	9	Average number of grams saturated fatty foods consumed per day
C4	EXERCISE	9	Average number of minutes of exercise per day

CARSPEED.MTW

(Used with permission, from *Statistics Today,* Byrkit, page 634.) Speed along a certain highway was monitored using four different speed control methods consisting of various speed limit signs and a parked state highway patrol car. Speeds of out-of-state cars were obtained for each speed control method.

COLUMN	NAME	COUNT	DESCRIPTION
C1	METHOD 1	12	Speeds of cars using method 1
C2	METHOD 2	10	Speeds of cars using method 2
C3	METHOD 3	11	Speeds of cars using method 3
C4	METHOD 4	11	Speeds of cars using method 4

CDI.MTW

In a study of cadmium twelve fish were exposed to cadmium and after exposure, the cadmium concentration was measured in the gill, liver, and kidney. Five control fish were also studied and after a similar time in ordinary water, their gill, liver, and kidney concentrations were measured.

COLUMN	NAME	COUNT	MISSING	DESCRIPTION
C1	CTL FISH	5		Control fish number
C2	CTL LIV	5		Control fish liver cadmium concentration
C3	CTL KIDN	5		Control fish kidney cadmium concentration
C4	CTL GILL	5	1	Control fish gill cadmium concentration
C5	CD FISH	12		Cadmium fish liver cadmium concentration
C6	CD LIV	12		Cadmium fish kidney cadmium concentration
C7	CD KIDN	12		Cadmium fish gill cadmium concentration
C8	CD GILL	12	1	Control fish liver cadmium concentration

CD2.MTW

The same data as CD1.MTW, but the data has been stacked into 5 columns.

COLUMN	NAME	COUNT	MISSING	DESCRIPTION
C1	FISH	17		Fish number
C2	LIVER	17		Liver concentrations
C3	KIDNEY	17		Kidney concentrations
C4	GILL	17	2	Gill concentrations
C5	GROUP	17		Group number (1=control, 2=cadmium)

COREDATA.MTW

A geology graduate student obtained core samples from several locations. (These data are taken from one of those core samples.) The student measured the percent mud in the sample core, approximately every 10 feet.

COLUMN	NAME	COUNT	DESCRIPTION
C1	DEPTH	21	Depth measured in feet
C2	% MUD	21	Percent mud at the depth

EXAM.MTW

These data are the results of two hourly exams given in an small graduate statistics class.

COLUMN	NAME	COUNT	DESCRIPTION
C1	EXAM 1	8	Exam 1 results
C2	EXAM 2	8	Exam 2 results

FALCON.MTW

A study was done to investigate the residual effect of the pesticide DDT in falcons. Falcons from three nesting areas (US, Canada, and the Arctic region) and three different ages (young, middle-aged, and old) were captured and the DDT measured.

COLUMN	NAME	COUNT	DESCRIPTION
C1	DDT	27	The DDT measurement
C2	SITE	27	The nesting site of the bird
C3	AGE	27	The age of the bird

GUARD.MTW

A study was done investigating the effect of water acidity/alkalinity (pH) on the parental care behavior of fish. Forty pairs of fish were used in the study. Each pair of fish was housed in individual aquaria and exposed to one of four levels of pH, 7.0, 6.5, 6.0, and 5.5 (10 pairs per level). The fish were monitored daily for ten days. The data represent the average time spent guarding the nest for each sex on each day for each of the 4 pH groups. In each column the first 10 observation are the averages of the male fish for days 1–10 for that exposure group and the second 10 observations are the average for the female fish for days 1–10 for that exposure group.

COLUMN	NAME	COUNT	DESCRIPTION
C1	PH 7.0	20	Data for pH 7.0
C2	PH 6.5	20	Data for pH 6.5
C3	PH 6.0	20	Data for pH 6.0
C4	PH 5.5	20	Data for pH 5.5

HEART.MTW

Twenty male heart transplant patients were randomly selected and the age at the time of their first heart transplant obtained.

COLUMN	NAME	COUNT	DESCRIPTION
C1	AGE	20	Age at first heart transplant

HOMESALE.MTW

The number of homes sold by a local realtor over the past four years is recorded for each month.

COLUMN	NAME	COUNT	DESCRIPTION
C1	SOLD	47	Number of homes sold per month

MIAMI.MTW

These data are the result of a questionnaire given to all females in an introductory statistics course at Miami University. The questionnaire was designed to provide demographic information about Miami females. 197 females participated in the study; however, only 83 responses have been provided (all that will fit into the 2000 element worksheet). This same data for the 83 females has also been saved in ASCII format in the file MIAMI.DAT.

COLUMN	NAME	COUNT	DESCRIPTION
C1	HAIR	83	Hair color
C2	EYE	83	Eye color
C3	SCHOOL	83	School of major
C4	SORORITY	83	Belong to sorority?
C5	OH RES	83	Ohio resident?
C6	BIRTH	83	Birth month
C7	RELIGION	83	Religion
C8	BROTHERS	83	Number of brothers
C9	SISTERS	83	Number of sisters
C10	GLASSES	83	Wear glasses?
C11	HAIR LNG	83	Length of hair
C12	CREDITS	83	Number of credits currently enrolled for
C13	LIVING	83	Living arrangements
C14	BOYFRND	83	Boyfriend?
C15	ALCOHOL	83	Drink alcohol?
C16	P EARS	83	Number of pierced ears
C17	SLEEP	83	Average number of hours of sleep per night
C18	SOAPS	83	Watch soap operas regularly?
C19	SMOKE	83	Smoke regularly?
C20	DIET	83	Currently dieting?
C21	JOB	83	Currently working?
C22	HGT	83	Height (in inches)
C23	WGT	83	Weight (in pounds)
C24	GPA	83	Grade point average

REALEST.MTW

Information on each home sold in Oxford, Ohio, during 1987 was collected and summarized. Information on the asking and selling price as well as information on the characteristics of the home were obtained.

COLUMN	NAME	COUNT	MISSING	DESCRIPTION
C1	SELL $	51		Asking price of home
C2	ASK $	51		Selling price of home
C3	BATHS	51		Number of baths
C4	BEDROOMS	51		Number of bedrooms
C5	AGE	51	8	Age of home
C6	BASEMENT	51	1	Basement?
C7	CARS	51		Size of garage

SPEED2.MTW

This is the CARSPEED data but simply stacked in one column with a method identifier.

COLUMN	NAME	COUNT	DESCRIPTION
C1	SPEED	44	Car speeds
C2	METHOD	44	Method of speed control

STA261.MTW

This is the complete grade information for an introductory class in statistics of the 45 students. The results of the 11 quizzes, the three hourly exams, and the final exam are given. The quiz scores are all out of 11 possible and the four exams out of 100 possible points.

COLUMN	NAME	COUNT	DESCRIPTION
C1	Q1	45	Quiz 1 results
C2	Q2	45	Quiz 2 results
C3	Q3	45	Quiz 3 results
C4	Q4	45	Quiz 4 results
C5	Q5	45	Quiz 5 results
C6	Q6	45	Quiz 6 results
C7	Q7	45	Quiz 7 results
C8	Q8	45	Quiz 8 results
C9	Q9	45	Quiz 9 results
C10	Q10	45	Quiz 10 results
C11	Q11	45	Quiz 11 results
C12	T1	45	Exam 1 results
C13	T2	45	Exam 2 results
C14	T3	45	Exam 3 results
C15	FINAL	45	Final exam results

STA368.MTW

This data represents the results of the first quiz in another introductory statistics course.

COLUMN	NAME	COUNT	DESCRIPTION
C1	QUIZ	25	Quiz 1 results

UTILITY.MTW

The utility usage of a family was monitored for approximately four years. Electricity and water usage, as well as costs, were obtained on a monthly basis.

COLUMN	NAME	COUNT	MISSING	DESCRIPTION
C1	MONTH	44		Month
C2	YEAR	44		Year
C3	KWH	44		Kilowatts of electricity used
C4	KWH $	44		Cost of electricity
C5	GAL	44	2	Gallons of water used
C6	GAL $	44	2	Cost of water

VOICE.MTW

A professor in a theater department was interested in determining if a particular voice training class improved a performer's voice quality. Twenty subjects were used; ten took the class and ten did not. The data below are for the ten subjects who took the class. The subjects' voice quality was rated by six judges on a scale of 1–6 (6=best). Two ratings were made: one before the class and the other after.

COLUMN	NAME	COUNT	DESCRIPTION
C1	1 BEFORE	6	Subject 1's before scores
C2	1 AFTER	6	Subject 1's after scores
C3	2 BEFORE	6	Subject 2's before scores
C4	2 AFTER	6	Subject 2's after scores
C5	3 BEFORE	6	Subject 3's before scores
C6	3 AFTER	6	Subject 3's after scores
C7	4 BEFORE	6	Subject 4's before scores
C8	4 AFTER	6	Subject 4's after scores
C9	5 BEFORE	6	Subject 5's before scores
C10	5 AFTER	6	Subject 5's after scores
C11	6 BEFORE	6	Subject 6's before scores
C12	6 AFTER	6	Subject 6's after scores
C13	7 BEFORE	6	Subject 7's before scores
C14	7 AFTER	6	Subject 7's after scores
C15	8 BEFORE	6	Subject 8's before scores
C16	8 AFTER	6	Subject 8's after scores
C17	9 BEFORE	6	Subject 9's before scores
C18	9 AFTER	6	Subject 9's after scores
C19	10 BEFORE	6	Subject 10's before scores
C20	10 AFTER	6	Subject 10's after scores

1STGRADE.MTW

As part of a class exercise, a first grade teacher recorded the heights and weights of each of her 73 students. The exercise was to determine how height and weights were related and also to see if the class was normal with respect to U.S. government standards on height and weight.

COLUMN	NAME	COUNT	DESCRIPTION
C1	HGT	73	Heights of students in inches
C2	WGT	73	Weights of students in pounds

▶ Index

The Student Edition of MINITAB is published by Addison-Wesley Publishing Company, Inc. and Benjamin/Cummings Publishing Company, Inc. Contributors include:

Alan Jacobs	Product Line Manager
Dana Degenhardt	Product Development Manager
Mary Coffey	Software Production Supervisor
Karen Wernholm	Software Production Editor
Lu Anne Piskadlo	Media Manufacturing Supervisor
Marshall Henrichs	Art Director
Jean Hammond	Text Designer
Editorial Services of New England, Inc.	Production Coordination
CPC Type and Graphics	Compositor

The Student Edition of MINITAB was developed and programmed by Minitab, Inc. Contributors include Gwen Stimely, Technical Support Specialist.